MASSACHUSETTS REAL ESTATE SALES EXAM

LEARNINGEXPRESS®

NEW YORK

Library of Congress Cataloging-in-Publication Data:
Massachusetts real estate sales exam.
    p. cm.
  ISBN 1-57685-538-4
  1. Real estate agents—Licenses—Massachusetts—Examinations, questions, etc.
2. Real estate business—Licenses—Massachusetts—Examinations, questions, etc.
I. LearningExpress (Organization). II. Title.
HD278.M36 2006
333.3309744—dc22

                          2006000431

Printed in the United States of America

9 8 7 6 5 4 3 2 1

ISBN 1-57685-538-4

For more information or to place an order, contact LearningExpress at:
  55 Broadway
  8th Floor
  New York, NY 10006

Or visit us at:
  www.learnatest.com

About the Contributors

Debra Agliano has been selling real estate since 1991. She is a licensed Massachusetts real estate educator and a GRI instructor. Debra teaches both live in-person classes and live-distance (Internet) classes about real estate, marketing, and integrating technology into a real estate career.

John M. Anjos is president of Anjos Realty Institute and has been a licensed broker and real estate educator for thirty years. He is a graduate of the University of Massachusetts–Dartmouth, where he now teaches as an adjunct instructor, as well as at Bristol Community College. He is the former president of Kinyon-Campbell Business School.

Robert Hahigian, FRICS, SIOR, CRE, is principal of Auburndale Realty Co., a commercial real estate firm in Newton, Massachusetts. He is a senior real estate instructor with Boston University, SIOR, MAR, and a Massachusetts CE instructor.

Contents

CHAPTER

Massachusetts Real Estate Sales Exam

CHAPTER SUMMARY

A career in real estate sales can be challenging, rewarding, and profitable. Massachusetts has a broad range of properties. You can sell anything from brownstones in Back Bay to horse properties in the Berkshires. Licensed, knowledgeable, and qualified salespeople are in demand. This is great news for you, since you have already decided that you want to get your real estate sales license.

OW YOU NEED to pass the exam. But becoming a licensed salesperson in Massachusetts requires more than simply passing the exam. There are many other steps you must complete (either before and/or after the exam) in order to arrive at your ultimate goal—receiving your real estate sales license. This chapter will guide you through these steps, including the requirements; the exam application process; the exam content and format; and the sales license application process.

This chapter also serves as a guide for using this book effectively. LearningExpress wants you to succeed, so use this book to maximize your preparation for your upcoming exam.

The State of Massachusetts does have reciprocity or an expedited license process with all states except for Vermont. The rules vary per state. To receive a copy of the current rules, contact the Board of Registration of Real Estate Brokers and Salespersons at 617-727-2373 or go online to www.mass.gov/dpl/boards/re/forms/recinf01.pdf.

▶ Who Needs to Take the Massachusetts Real Estate Sales Exam?

Anyone wishing to make official, licensed real estate transactions in Massachusetts must have a valid Massachusetts Real Estate Sales License and be employed by a broker licensed by the Commonwealth of Massachusetts. In order to receive your license, you must first pass the exam.

Note: You may not legally perform licensed transactions before associating with a licensed real estate broker.

▶ Eligibility Requirements

The Board of Registration of Real Estate Brokers and Salespersons (the Board) requires that all licensees meet the following minimum requirements:

- **Age**—You must be at least 18 years old.
- **Moral Character**—Your license application must include a recommendation that you have a reputation for honesty signed by three people (not related to you) who either live or work in Massachusetts. Conviction of a criminal offense or failure to file all state tax returns and pay all state taxes required by law may be cause for denial.
- **Education**—You must take 24 hours of classroom instruction and pass a test on the material covered.

Requirements

All applicants must complete a Board-approved pre-licensing course for sales associates consisting of 24 classroom hours and covering topics required by the Board (facilities can be found on the Board's website). The Board requires that you provide evidence of successful completion of the real estate course when submitting your license application for licensure processing.

All required courses must be completed through Board-approved course sponsors. Fortunately, the approved course is offered at many community colleges, local real estate boards, and proprietary schools.

Attorney Exemption

If you are a Massachusetts attorney in good standing, you shall not be required to take the exam. Consult the Board's website for more information regarding how to obtain an education waiver from the Board.

If you have Internet access, consult The Board of Registration of Real Estate Brokers and Salespersons' website for more information:

www.mass.gov/dpl/boards/re/index.htm

If you do not have Internet access, or if you are unable to get your question(s) answered on the website, please contact the Board for all examination and licensing questions at:

The Board of Registration of Real Estate Brokers and Salespersons
239 Causeway Street, Suite 500
Boston, MA 02114
Voice: 617-727-2373
E-mail: neal.fenochietti@state.ma.us

▶ Applying for the Exam

Once you complete your education requirements, you will have two years to pass the license exam. You will receive the Education Certification form from the school where you attended the approved course. Your school will provide you with an application form. Fill it out completely and honestly, otherwise you may experience long delays, or worse—rejection. It is recommended that you consult the Commonwealth of Massachusetts Real Estate Candidate Handbook for more information: www.asisvcs.com/publications/pdf/090200.pdf.

Exams are given in the following cities:

- Worcester
- Boston
- Woburn
- Springfield
- North Dartmouth

To make an examination reservation, call Promissor Customer Care at 1-800-274-0501. Telephone reservations must be made at least three business days before the desired examination date. You can also send a Fax Reservation Form (located in the Commonwealth of Massachusetts Real Estate Candidate Handbook). Fax reservations must be made at least four business days before the desired examination date. Candidates will receive a confirmation number when they make their reservation. You must make a reservation. Walk-in examinations are not available.

Exam Fee: $107.00

The fee for honorably discharged veterans is $80. You must have a copy of your discharge papers (DD-214) with you on exam day to qualify for the reduced fee.

Note: The examination fee must be paid by certified check, cashier's check or money order made payable to "Promissor." **No personal checks or cash will be accepted.** Contact Promissor (www.promissor.com or call 1-800-274-0501) for more information.

What to Bring

- two forms of signature identification, one of which must be a picture ID (candidates will not be admitted without proper identification)
- correct exam fees
- completed (front and back) Education Certification form
- the Massachusetts licensing fee of between $93 and $124 (The fee is prorated from month to month. When you call for your exam reservation, you will be told the amount of your licensing fee.) **Note: You must be prepared to pay for your license at the exam center once you pass the exam.**
- confirmation number provided to you at the time of the reservation
- a noiseless, tapeless, non-alphanumeric handheld calculator (No PDAs or cell phones will be permitted.)

There are two parts to the exam: the general portion and the state portion. If you pass one portion of the exam but fail the other, you need to retake only the failed portion. However, you must wait 24 hours to schedule a reexamination. An exam fee of $65 applies each time you retake the exam.

▶ Exam Content

You will have four hours to complete your Massachusetts Real Estate Sales examination.

The law requires that examinees demonstrate adequate reading and writing skills in the English language and the ability to perform basic real estate math computations. Furthermore, examinees must have proficient knowledge of real estate principles and practices, real estate law, and real estate mathematics.

The following are the major sections that will be tested on the exam. This list of items covered in the Massachusetts Real Estate Sales exam is from the Board of Registration of Real Estate Brokers and Salespersons and can be found online at www.mass.gov/dpl/boards/re/contedu/sal00.htm.

CPA license
real estate
appraisers license
12/12/12

Property/Property Rights/Ownership
Real versus Personal Property
Property Rights
Limits to Property Rights
Estates
Forms of Ownership
Transfer of Rights
Encumbrances and Liens
Water Rights

Condominiums/Cooperatives/Time Sharing Leases and Options
Condominiums
Cooperatives
Time Sharing
Leases
Types of Tenancy
Common Leases
Obligation of Parties
Options
Property Management

Contracts/Deeds
Real Estate Contracts
Essential Elements of Contracts
Termination of an Offer
Valid/Void/Voidable Contracts
Purchase and Sale Agreement
Breach of Contract
Deeds
Elements of a Deed
Torrens System
Massachusetts Tax Stamps
Title Search

Financing/Mortgages
Real Estate Cycle
Financing Procedure
Types of Lending Institutions
Money as a Commodity

Types of Mortgages
Secondary Mortgage Market
Truth-in-Lending Law (Regulation Z)
Mortgage Note and Mortgage Deed
Real Estate Settlement and Procedures Act (RESPA)

Brokerage
Brokerage Definition
Law of Agency
Creation of Agency
Types of Listings
Duties of an Agent
Termination of Agency
Commissions
Broker versus Salesman
Commission Splits

Appraisal
Appraisal and Value
Establish Appraisal Purpose
Elements of Value
Forces Affecting Value
Economic Principles
Market Data Approach
Income Approach
Cost Approach

Fair Housing/Consumer Protection
Basic Concepts
Federal Civil Rights Act of 1866
Federal Fair Housing 1968 (Title VIII)
Massachusetts General Laws

Massachusetts License Law
Duties and Powers of the Real Estate Board of Registration
Licensing Requirements
Statutory Requirements Governing Activities of Licensees

Passing the Exam

You will have four hours to complete the exam, and you must receive a score of 70 to pass.

The 80 questions on the general portion of the exam will be broken down as follows:

- real property characteristics, definitions, ownership, restrictions, and transfer—20%
- assessing and explaining property valuation and the appraisal process—15%
- contracts, agency relationships with buyers and sellers, and federal requirements—25%
- financing the transaction and settlement—25%
- leases, rents, and property management—15%

The state-specific portion of the exam has 30 questions and is broken down as follows:

- duties and powers of the Board of Registration of Real Estate Brokers and Salespersons—5%
- licensing requirements—10%
- requirements governing licensees—45%
- additional topics (i.e., excise stamps, Massachusetts Fair Housing Law, property taxes, landlord/tenant relationships, zoning and land use regulations, forms of ownership, Massachusetts Consumer Protection Act, Massachusetts Consumer Protection Law, hazardous materials, and environmental issues)—40%

Real Estate Math

If you are worried about the math that will be covered on the exam—relax. The math problems on the exam will not be terribly complex, and they will all relate to real estate, so you may have already tackled problems like these in your real estate courses. Plus, LearningExpress understands that math can intimidate many people, especially on exams, so there is an entire chapter in this book devoted to reviewing real estate math to help you brush up on those skills.

Also, you will not be expected to figure out these problems entirely in your head. You will be provided with scratch paper at the exam, and you are allowed to bring a calculator with you. Remember to take the problem step by step, reading it carefully and using your scratch paper to set up the problem before you start punching in numbers.

Exam Day

Try to get a good night's sleep the night before the exam, and allow plenty of time in the morning to get to your exam location, especially if you are unfamiliar with the area. You must report to the exam center 30 minutes or more before your exam in order to sign in, present your identification, and get yourself settled.

Receiving Your Massachusetts Salesperson License

All examinees must score 70 or above to pass the exam. If you meet all the licensing requirements, pass the exam, and pay the licensing fee, you will receive your license immediately at the exam center. The license application fee

The calculator you bring to the exam must be a pocket-sized, silent, battery-operated, electronic calculator with no printing capability or alphabetic keyboard. It is a good idea to bring a calculator that you are already familiar with using and make sure you have extra batteries. Calculators in PDAs or cell phones are not permitted to be used at the exam site.

(which is different from the exam fee) may be paid by personal check, cashier's check or money order payable to "Promissor" and must be for the exact amount told to you when you made your reservation. Cash is not accepted.

License Application Fees

Your license application fee is between $93 and $124. (The fee is prorated from month to month. When you call for your exam reservation, you will be told the amount of your licensing fee.)

How to Prepare for the Exam

You have made it this far—you have completed the required real estate course and have made the decision to read this book—so you have already shown that you have the commitment it will take to prepare for the exam. This book is designed to be a valuable tool in preparing you for the big day.

▶ Test-Taking Techniques

Chapter 2, The LearningExpress Test Preparation System, does exactly as the title suggests—it teaches you how to prepare for the test effectively. In this chapter, you will learn to:

- set up a realistic study plan
- use your study time and exam time efficiently
- overcome test anxiety

The best approach for effective studying is to be disciplined, to stay on your study schedule, and not to procrastinate.

Study Materials

Utilize all of your study materials. By reviewing information from a variety of sources, you are more likely to cover all of the material that might be included on the exam. This book is a great source of information and can be used as a foundation for your study plan. In addition, use your study materials, notes, exams, and texts from your real estate course.

Using This Book

In addition to this chapter and the LearningExpress Test Preparation System in Chapter 2, this book contains three content and review chapters and four practice exams. We suggest that you take the first practice exam (Chapter 3) before moving on to the content and review material. This way, you will be able to better assess your personal strengths and weaknesses, allowing you to direct your time where you need it the most.

Chapter 4, the Massachusetts Real Estate Refresher Course, is an overview of real estate concepts and criteria that will be covered on the exam.

Chapter 5 is dedicated to Real Estate Math Review. This chapter reviews the types of problems and computations you will face on the exam, allowing you to practice and polish your math skills.

Chapter 6 is a Real Estate Glossary, providing an excellent list of real estate terminology needed for the exam and your career.

Although you should focus most of your efforts on the areas where you need the most improvement, you should read all of the chapters in this book to ensure that you do not miss out on valuable information. You will find that some of the information and terminology in Chapters 4 through 6 is repeated, but this will only help to reinforce your knowledge.

Use the other three practice tests in the book (Chapters 7, 8, and 9) to gauge your progress as you go along, so you can continue to focus your concentration where needed. Based on the exam content and time allotted for the actual exam, the practice tests in this book are multiple choice and each have 110 questions.

Do not forget about the bonus CD-ROM included with this book. It includes practice questions, so you can practice on a computer if you wish. The CD-ROM is designed to be user friendly; however, please consult the "How to Use the CD-ROM" section located in the back of the book, should you have any questions.

▶ Important Note

This book covers the most commonly used key terms and concepts that are likely to be covered on the exam. However, it would be impossible to include everything; thus, we suggest that you utilize a variety of study materials. Please note that real estate laws and regulations change from time to time, so it is important that you be aware of the most up-to-date information (consult the Board of Registration of Real Estate Brokers and Salespersons). Our book is intended to be just one of the many study tools you will use, and is designed to reinforce and round out your knowledge of real estate sales. In addition, information about application processes, fees, and practices may change. For the most accurate information, visit the Board's website at www.mass.gov/dpl/boards/re/index.htm.

▶ The Path to Success

Each person has his or her own personal goals and individual path to take to achieve those goals. Desire, dedication, and know-how are essential, no matter what path you take. You have already shown that you have the desire and dedication, just by reading this chapter. You are well on your way to a new career in real estate! You have shown that you are serious; now let this book help give you the know-how you need to pass your exam.

The LearningExpress Test Preparation System

CHAPTER SUMMARY

Taking the Massachusetts Real Estate Sales Exam can be tough. It demands a lot of preparation if you want to achieve a top score. Your career depends on your passing the exam. The LearningExpress Test Preparation System, developed exclusively for LearningExpress by leading test experts, gives you the discipline and attitude you need to be a winner.

FACT: TAKING THE real estate licensing exam is not easy, and neither is getting ready for it. Your future career as a real estate salesperson depends on your getting a passing score, but there are all sorts of pitfalls that can keep you from doing your best on this exam. Here are some of the obstacles that can stand in the way of your success:

- being unfamiliar with the format of the exam
- being paralyzed by test anxiety
- leaving your preparation to the last minute
- not preparing at all!
- not knowing vital test-taking skills: how to pace yourself through the exam, how to use the process of elimination, and when to guess
- not being in tip-top mental and physical shape
- arriving late at the test site, having to work on an empty stomach, or shivering through the exam because the room is cold

What's the common denominator in all these test taking pitfalls? One word: control. Who's in control, you or the exam?

Here's some good news: The LearningExpress Test Preparation System puts you in control. In nine easy-to-follow steps, you will learn everything you need to know to make sure that you are in charge of your preparation and your performance on the exam. Other test takers may let the test get the better of them; other test takers may be unprepared or out of shape, but not you. You will have taken all the steps you need to take to get a high score on the real estate licensing exam.

Here's how the LearningExpress Test Preparation System works: Nine easy steps lead you through everything you need to know and do to get ready to master your exam. Each step discussed in this chapter includes both reading about the step and one or more activities. It's important that you do the activities along with the reading, or you won't be getting the full benefit of the system. Each step tells you approximately how much time that step will take you to complete.

Step 1. Get Information	50 minutes
Step 2. Conquer Test Anxiety	20 minutes
Step 3. Make a Plan	30 minutes
Step 4. Learn to Manage Your Time	10 minutes
Step 5. Learn to Use the Process of Elimination	20 minutes
Step 6. Know When to Guess	20 minutes
Step 7. Reach Your Peak Performance Zone	10 minutes
Step 8. Get Your Act Together	10 minutes
Step 9. Do It!	10 minutes
Total	3 hours

We estimate that working through the entire system will take you approximately three hours, although it's perfectly okay if you work faster or slower. If you take an afternoon or evening, you can work through the whole LearningExpress Test Preparation System in one sitting. Otherwise, you can break it up, and do just one or two steps a day for the next several days. It's up to you—remember, you are in control.

► Step 1: Get Information

Time to complete: 50 minutes

Activity: Read Chapter 1, The Massachusetts Real Estate Sales Exam.

Knowledge is power. The first step in the LearningExpress Test Preparation System is finding out everything you can about the Massachusetts Real Estate Sales Exam. Once you have your information, the other steps in the LearningExpress Test Preparation System will show you what to do about it.

Part A: Straight Talk about the Massachusetts Real Estate Sales Exam

Why do you have to take this exam, anyway? You have already been through your pre-license course; why should you have to go through a rigorous exam? It's simply an attempt on the part of your state to be sure you have the knowledge and skills necessary for a licensed real estate agent. Every profession that requires practitioners to exercise financial and fiduciary responsibility to clients also requires practitioners to be licensed—and licensure requires an exam. Real estate is no exception.

It's important for you to remember that your score on the Massachusetts Real Estate Sales Exam does not determine how smart you are, or even whether you will make a good real estate agent. There are all kinds of things an exam like this can't test: whether you have the drive and determination to be a top salesperson, whether you will faithfully exercise your responsibilities to your clients, or whether you can be trusted with confidential information about people's finances. Those kinds of things are hard to evaluate, while a computer-based test is easy to evaluate.

This is not to say that the exam is not important! The knowledge tested on the exam is knowledge you will need to do your job. And your ability to enter the profession you've trained for depends on your passing this exam. And that's why you are here—using the LearningExpress Test Preparation System to achieve control over the exam.

Part B: What's on the Test

If you haven't already done so, stop here and read Chapter 1 of this book, which gives you an overview of the Massachusetts Real Estate Sales Exam.

► Step 2: Conquer Test Anxiety

Time to complete: 20 minutes

Activity: Take the Test Stress Quiz.

Having complete information about the exam is the first step in getting control of the exam. Next, you have to overcome one of the biggest obstacles to test success: test anxiety. Test anxiety not only impairs your performance on the exam itself, but also keeps you from preparing! In Step 2, you will learn stress management techniques that will help you succeed on your exam. Learn these strategies now, and practice them as you work through the exams in this book, so they will be second nature to you by exam day.

You need to worry about test anxiety only if it is extreme enough to impair your performance. The following questionnaire will provide a diagnosis of your level of test anxiety. In the blank before each statement, write the number that most accurately describes your experience.

0 = Never   1 = Once or twice   2 = Sometimes   3 = Often

___ I have gotten so nervous before an exam that I simply put down the books and didn't study for it.

___ I have experienced disabling physical symptoms such as vomiting and severe headaches because I was nervous about an exam.

___ I did not show up for an exam because I was scared to take it.

___ I have experienced dizziness and disorientation while taking an exam.

___ I have had trouble filling in the little circles because my hands were shaking too hard.

___ I have failed an exam because I was too nervous to complete it.

___ **Total: Add up the numbers in the blanks above.**

Your Test Stress Score

Here are the steps you should take, depending on your score. If you scored:

0–2: Your level of test anxiety is nothing to worry about; it's probably just enough to give you that little extra edge.

3–6: Your test anxiety may be enough to impair your performance, and you should practice the stress management techniques listed in this section to try to bring your test anxiety down to manageable levels.

7+: Your level of test anxiety is a serious concern. In addition to practicing the stress management techniques listed in this section, you may want to seek additional help.

Combating Test Anxiety

The first thing you need to know is that a little test anxiety is a good thing. Everyone gets nervous before a big exam—and if that nervousness motivates you to prepare thoroughly, so much the better. It's said that Sir Laurence Olivier, one of the foremost British actors of this century, felt ill before every performance. His stage fright didn't impair his performance; in fact, it probably gave him a little extra edge—just the kind of edge you need to do well, whether on a stage or in an examination room.

Above is the Test Stress Quiz. Stop and answer the questions to find out whether your level of test anxiety is something you should worry about.

Stress Management before the Test

If you feel your level of anxiety getting the best of you in the weeks before the test, here is what you need to do to bring the level down again:

- **Get prepared.** There's nothing like knowing what to expect and being prepared for it to put you in control of test anxiety. That's why you are reading this book. Use it faithfully, and remind yourself that you are better prepared than most of the people taking the test.

- **Practice self-confidence.** A positive attitude is a great way to combat test anxiety. This is no time to be humble or shy. Stand in front of the mirror and say to your reflection, "I am prepared. I am full of self-confidence. I am going to ace this test. I know I can do it." Say it into a tape recorder and play it back once a day. If you hear it often enough, you will believe it.

- **Fight negative messages.** Every time someone starts telling you how hard the exam is or how it's almost impossible to get a high score, start saying your self-confidence messages above. Don't listen to the negative messages. Turn on your tape recorder and listen to your self-confidence messages.

- **Visualize.** Imagine yourself reporting for duty on your first day as a real estate salesperson. Think of yourself talking with clients, showing homes, and best of all, making your first sale. Visualizing success can help make it happen—and it reminds you of why you are going to all this work in preparing for the exam.

- **Exercise.** Physical activity helps calm your body down and focus your mind. Besides, being in good physical shape can actually help you do well on the exam. Go for a run, lift weights, go swimming—and do it regularly.

Stress Management on Test Day

There are several ways you can bring down your level of test anxiety on test day. They will work best if you practice them in the weeks before the test, so you know which ones work best for you.

- **Deep breathing.** Take a deep breath while you count to five. Hold it for a count of one, then let it out on a count of five. Repeat several times.

- **Move your body.** Try rolling your head in a circle. Rotate your shoulders. Shake your hands from the wrist. Many people find these movements very relaxing.

- **Visualize again.** Think of the place where you are most relaxed: lying on the beach in the sun, walking through the park, or whatever. Now close your eyes and imagine you are actually there. If you practice in advance, you will find that you need only a few seconds of this exercise to experience a significant increase in your sense of well-being.

When anxiety threatens to overwhelm you right there during the exam, there are still things you can do to manage the stress level:

- **Repeat your self-confidence messages.** You should have them memorized by now. Say them silently to yourself, and believe them!

- **Visualize one more time.** This time, visualize yourself moving smoothly and quickly through the test answering every question right and finishing just before time is up. Like most visualization techniques, this one works best if you have practiced it ahead of time.

- **Find an easy question.** Find an easy question, and answer it. Getting even one question finished gets you into the test-taking groove.

- **Take a mental break.** Everyone loses concentration once in a while during a long test. It's normal, so you shouldn't worry about it. Instead, accept what has happened. Say to yourself, "Hey, I lost it there for a minute. My brain is taking a break." Put down your pencil, close your eyes, and do some deep breathing for a few seconds. Then you will be ready to go back to work.

Try these techniques ahead of time, and see if they work for you!

▶ Step 3: Make a Plan

Time to complete: 30 minutes
Activity: Construct a study plan.

Maybe the most important thing you can do to get control of yourself and your exam is to make a study plan. Too many people fail to prepare simply because they fail to plan. Spending hours on the day before the exam poring over sample test questions not only raises your level of test anxiety, but is simply no substitute for careful preparation and practice over time.

Don't fall into the cram trap. Take control of your preparation time by mapping out a study schedule. On the following pages are two sample schedules, based on the amount of time you have before you take the Massachusetts Real Estate Sales Exam. If you are the kind of person who needs deadlines and assignments to motivate you for a project, here they are. If you are the kind of person who doesn't like to follow other people's plans, you can use the suggested schedules here to construct your own.

Even more important than making a plan is making a commitment. You can't review everything you learned in your real estate courses in one night. You have to set aside some time every day for study and practice. Try for at least 20 minutes a day. Twenty minutes daily will do you much more good than two hours on Saturday.

Don't put off your study until the day before the exam. Start now. A few minutes a day, with half an hour or more on weekends, can make a big difference in your score.

Schedule A: The 30-Day Plan

If you have at least a month before you take the Massachusetts Real Estate Sales Exam, you have plenty of time to prepare—as long as you don't waste it! If you have less than a month, turn to Schedule B.

TIME	PREPARATION
Days 1–4	Skim over the written materials from your training program, particularly noting 1) areas you expect to be emphasized on the exam and 2) areas you don't remember well. On Day 4, concentrate on those areas.
Day 5	Take the first practice exam in Chapter 3.
Day 6	Score the first practice exam. Use "Exam I for Review" on page 45 to see which topics you need to review most. Identify two areas that you will concentrate on before you take the second practice exam.
Days 7–10	Study the two areas you identified as your weak points. Don't forget, there is the Massachusetts Real Estate Refresher Course in Chapter 4, the Real Estate Math Review in Chapter 5, and the Real Estate Glossary in Chapter 6. Use these chapters to improve your score on the next practice test.
Day 11	Take the second practice exam in Chapter 7.
Day 12	Score the second practice exam. Identify one area to concentrate on before you take the third practice exam.
Days 13–18	Study the one area you identified for review. Again, use the Refresher Course, Math Review, and Glossary for help.
Day 19	Take the third practice exam in Chapter 8.
Day 20	Once again, identify one area to review, based on your score on the third practice exam.
Days 20–21	Study the one area you identified for review. Use the Refresher Course, Math Review, and Glossary for help.
Days 22–25	Take an overview of all your training materials, consolidating your strengths and improving on your weaknesses.
Days 26–27	Review all the areas that have given you the most trouble in the three practice exams you have taken so far.
Day 28	Take the fourth practice exam in Chapter 9. Note how much you have improved!
Day 29	Review one or two weak areas by studying the Refresher Course, Math Review, and Glossary.
Day before the exam	Relax. Do something unrelated to the exam and go to bed at a reasonable hour.

Schedule B: The 10-Day Plan

If you have two weeks or less before you take the exam, use this ten-day schedule to help you make the most of your time.

TIME	PREPARATION
Day 1	Take the first practice exam in Chapter 3 and score it using the answer key at the end. Use "Exam I for Review" on page 45 to see which topics you need to review most.
Day 2	Review one area that gave you trouble on the first practice exam. Use the Massachusetts Real Estate Refresher Course in Chapter 4, the Real Estate Math Review in Chapter 5, and the Real Estate Glossary in Chapter 6 for extra practice in these areas.
Day 3	Review another area that gave you trouble on the first practice exam. Again, use the Refresher Course, Math Review, and Glossary for extra practice.
Day 4	Take the second practice exam in Chapter 7 and score it.
Day 5	If your score on the second practice exam doesn't show improvement on the two areas you studied, review them. If you did improve in those areas, choose a new weak area to study today.
Day 6	Take the third practice exam in Chapter 8 and score it.
Day 7	Choose your weakest area from the third practice exam to review. Use the Refresher Course, Math Review, and Glossary for extra practice.
Day 8	Review any areas that you have not yet reviewed in this schedule.
Day 9	Take the fourth practice exam in Chapter 9 and score it.
Day 10	Use your last study day to brush up on any areas that are still giving you trouble. Use the Refresher Course, Math Review, and Glossary.
Day before the exam	Relax. Do something unrelated to the exam and go to bed at a reasonable hour.

▶ Step 4: Learn to Manage Your Time

Time to complete: 10 minutes to read, many hours of practice!
Activity: Practice these strategies as you take the sample tests in this book.

Steps 4, 5, and 6 of the LearningExpress Test Preparation System put you in charge of your exam by showing you test-taking strategies that work. Practice these strategies as you take the sample tests in this book, and then you will be ready to use them on test day.

First, you will take control of your time on the exam. It's a terrible feeling to know there are only five minutes left when you are only three-quarters of the way through the test. Here are some tips to keep that from happening to *you*.

- **Follow directions.** Since the Massachusetts Real Estate Sales Exam is given on the computer, you should take your time taking the tutorial before the exam. Read the directions carefully and ask questions before the exam begins if there's anything you don't understand.
- **Pace yourself.** There is a timer on the screen as you take the exam. This will help you pace yourself. For example, when one-quarter of the time has elapsed, you should be a quarter of the way through the test, and so on. If you are falling behind, pick up the pace a bit.
- **Keep moving.** Don't waste time on one question. If you don't know the answer, skip the question and move on. You can always go back to it later.
- **Don't rush.** Although you should keep moving, rushing won't help. Try to keep calm and work methodically and quickly.

▶ Step 5: Learn to Use the Process of Elimination

Time to complete: 20 minutes
Activity: Complete worksheet on Using the Process of Elimination.

After time management, your next most important tool for taking control of your exam is using the process of elimination wisely. It's standard test-taking wisdom that you should always read all the answer choices before choosing your answer. This helps you find the right answer by eliminating wrong answer choices. And, sure enough, that standard wisdom applies to your exam, too.

Let's say you are facing a question that goes like this:

Alicia died, leaving her residence in town and a separate parcel of undeveloped rural land to her brother Brian and her sister Carrie, with Brian owning one-quarter interest and Carrie owning three-quarters interest. How do Brian and Carrie hold title?

- **a.** as tenants in survivorship
- **b.** as tenants in common
- **c.** as joint tenants
- **d.** as tenants by the entirety

You should always use the process of elimination on a question like this, even if the right answer jumps out at you. Sometimes, the answer that jumps out isn't right after all. Let's assume, for the purpose of this exercise, that you are a little rusty on property ownership terminology, so you need to use a little intuition to make up for what you don't remember. Proceed through the answer choices in order.

So you start with answer **a.** This one is pretty easy to eliminate; this tenancy doesn't have to do with survivorship. Since the Massachusetts Real Estate Sales Exam is given on a computer, you won't be able to cross out answer choices; instead, make a mental note that answer choice **a** is incorrect.

Choice **b** seems reasonable; it's a kind of ownership that two people can share. Even if you don't remember much about tenancy in common, you could tell it's about having something "in common." Make a mental note, "Good answer, I might use this one."

Choice **c** is also a possibility. Joint tenants also share something in common. If you happen to remember that joint tenancy always involves equal ownership rights, you mentally eliminate this choice. If you don't, make a mental note, "Good answer" or "Well, maybe," depending on how attractive this answer looks to you.

Choice **d** strikes you as a little less likely. Tenancy by the entirety doesn't necessarily have to do with two people sharing ownership. This doesn't sound right, and you have already got a better answer picked out in choice **b.** If you are feeling sure of yourself, you can mentally elimnate this choice.

If you're pressed for time, you should choose answer **b.** If you have got the time to be extra careful, you could compare your answer choices again. Then, choose one and move on.

If you are taking a test on paper, like the practice exams in this book, it's good to have a system for marking good, bad, and maybe answers. We recommend this one:

X = bad
✓ = good
? = maybe

If you don't like these marks, devise your own system. Just make sure you do it long before test day—while you're working through the practice exams in this book—so you won't have to worry about it just before the exam.

Even when you think you are absolutely clueless about a question, you can often use process of elimination to get rid of one answer choice. If so, you are better prepared to make an educated guess, as you will see in Step 6. More often, the process of elimination allows you to get down to only two possibly right answers. Then you are in a strong position to guess. And sometimes, even though you don't know the right answer, you find it simply by getting rid of the wrong ones, as you did in the previous example.

Try using your powers of elimination on the questions in the worksheet Using the Process of Elimination. The questions aren't about real estate work; they're just designed to show you how the process of elimination works. The answer explanations for this worksheet show one possible way you might use the process to arrive at the right answer.

The process of elimination is your tool for the next step, which is knowing when to guess.

Using the Process of Elimination

Use the process of elimination to answer the following questions.

1. Ilsa is as old as Meghan will be in five years. The difference between Ed's age and Meghan's age is twice the difference between Ilsa's age and Meghan's age. Ed is 29. How old is Ilsa?
   a. 4
   b. 10
   c. 19
   d. 24

2. "All drivers of commercial vehicles must carry a valid commercial driver's license whenever operating a commercial vehicle." According to this sentence, which of the following people need NOT carry a commercial driver's license?
   a. a truck driver idling his engine while waiting to be directed to a loading dock
   b. a bus operator backing her bus out of the way of another bus in the bus lot
   c. a taxi driver driving his personal car to the grocery store
   d. a limousine driver taking the limousine to her home after dropping off her last passenger of the evening

3. Smoking tobacco has been linked to
   a. increased risk of stroke and heart attack.
   b. all forms of respiratory disease.
   c. increasing mortality rates over the past ten years.
   d. juvenile delinquency.

4. Which of the following words is spelled correctly?
   a. incorrigible
   b. outragous
   c. domestickated
   d. understandible

Answers

Here are the answers, as well as some suggestions as to how you might have used the process of elimination to find them.

1. d. You should have eliminated answer **a** right away. Ilsa can't be four years old if Meghan is going to be Ilsa's age in five years. The best way to eliminate other answer choices is to try plugging them in to the information given in the problem. For instance, for answer **b**, if Ilsa is 10, then Meghan must be 5. The difference in their ages is 5. The difference between Ed's age, 29, and Meghan's age, 5, is 24. Does 24 equal 2 times 5? No. Then answer **b** is wrong. You could eliminate answer **c** in the same way and be left with answer **d**.

2. c. Note the word not in the question, and go through the answers one by one. Is the truck driver in choice **a** "operating a commericial vehicle"? Yes, idling counts as "operating," so he needs to have a commercial driver's license. Likewise, the bus operator in answer **b** is operating a commercial vehicle; the question doesn't say the operator has to be on the street. The limo driver in **d** is operating a commercial vehicle, even if it doesn't have passenger in it. However, the cabbie in answer **c** is not operating a commercial vehicle, but his own private car.

3. a. You could eliminate answer **b** simply because of the presence of the word *all*. Such absolutes hardly ever appear in correct answer choices. Choice **c** looks attractive until you think a little about what you know—aren't fewer people smoking these days, rather than more? So how could smoking be responsible for a higher mortality rate? (If you didn't know that *mortality rate* means the rate at which people die, you might keep this choice as a possibility, but you would still be able to eliminate two answers and have only two to choose from.) And choice **d** is not logical, so you could eliminate that one, too. And you are left with the correct choice, **a**.

4. a. How you used the process of elimination here depends on which words you recognized as being spelled incorrectly. If you knew that the correct spellings were *outrageous*, *domesticated*, and *understandable*, then you were home free. You probably knew that at least one of those words was wrong!

▶ Step 6: Know When to Guess

Time to complete: 20 minutes
Activity: Complete worksheet on Your Guessing Ability.

Armed with the process of elimination, you are ready to take control of one of the big questions in test taking: Should I guess? The first and main answer is *yes*. Some exams have what's called a "guessing penalty," in which a fraction of your wrong answers is subtracted from your right answers—but the Massachusetts Real Estate Sales Exam doesn't work like that. The number of questions you answer correctly yields your raw score. So you have nothing to lose and everything to gain by guessing.

The more complicated answer to the question "Should I guess?" depends on you—your personality and your "guessing intuition." There are two things you need to know about yourself before you go into the exam:

- Are you a risk-taker?
- Are you a good guesser?

You will have to decide about your risk-taking quotient on your own. To find out if you are a good guesser, complete the worksheet Your Guessing Ability. Frankly, even if you are a play-it-safe person with lousy intuition, you're still safe in guessing every time. The best thing would be if you could overcome your anxieties and go ahead and mark an answer. But you may want to have a sense of how good your intuition is before you go into the exam.

Your Guessing Ability

The following are ten really hard questions. You are not supposed to know the answers. Rather, this is an assessment of your ability to guess when you don't have a clue. Read each question carefully, just as if you did expect to answer it. If you have any knowledge at all of the subject of the question, use that knowledge to help you eliminate wrong answer choices.

1. September 7 is Independence Day in
   a. India.
   b. Costa Rica.
   c. Brazil.
   d. Australia.

2. Which of the following is the formula for determining the momentum of an object?
   a. $p = mv$
   b. $F = ma$
   c. $P = IV$
   d. $E = mc^2$

3. Because of the expansion of the universe, the stars and other celestial bodies are all moving away from each other. This phenomenon is known as
   a. Newton's first law.
   b. the big bang.
   c. gravitational collapse.
   d. Hubble flow.

4. American author Gertrude Stein was born in
   a. 1713.
   b. 1830.
   c. 1874.
   d. 1901.

5. Which of the following is NOT one of the Five Classics attributed to Confucius?
   a. the *I Ching*
   b. the *Book of Holiness*
   c. the *Spring and Autumn Annals*
   d. the *Book of History*

6. The religious and philosophical doctrine that holds that the universe is constantly in a struggle between good and evil is known as
   a. Pelagianism.
   b. Manichaeanism.
   c. neo-Hegelianism.
   d. Epicureanism.

7. The third Chief Justice of the U.S. Supreme Court was
- **a.** John Blair.
- **b.** William Cushing.
- **c.** James Wilson.
- **d.** John Jay.

8. Which of the following is the poisonous portion of a daffodil?
- **a.** the bulb
- **b.** the leaves
- **c.** the stem
- **d.** the flowers

9. The winner of the Masters golf tournament in 1953 was
- **a.** Sam Snead.
- **b.** Cary Middlecoff.
- **c.** Arnold Palmer.
- **d.** Ben Hogan.

10. The state with the highest per capita personal income in 1980 was
- **a.** Alaska.
- **b.** Connecticut.
- **c.** New York.
- **d.** Massachusetts.

Answers

Check your answers against the correct answers below.

1. c.
2. a.
3. d.
4. c.
5. b.
6. b.
7. b.
8. a.
9. d.
10. a.

► How Did You Do?

You may have simply gotten lucky and actually known the answer to one or two questions. In addition, your guessing was more successful if you were able to use the process of elimination on any of the questions. Maybe you didn't know who the third Chief Justice was (question 7), but you knew that John Jay was the first. In that case, you would have eliminated answer **d** and, therefore, improved your odds of guessing right from one in four to one in three.

According to probability, you should get $2\frac{1}{2}$ answers correct, so getting either two or three right would be average. If you got four or more right, you may be a really terrific guesser. If you got one or none right, you may be a really bad guesser.

Keep in mind, though, that this is only a small sample. You should continue to keep track of your guessing ability as you work through the sample questions in this book. Circle the numbers of questions you guess on as you make your guesses; or, if you don't have time while you take the practice exams, go back afterward and try to remember which questions you guessed on. Remember, on an exam with four answer choices, your chances of getting a right answer is one in four. So keep a separate "guessing" score for each exam. How many questions did you guess on? How many did you get right? If the number you got right is at least one-fourth of the number of questions you guessed on, you are at least an average guesser, maybe better—and you should always go ahead and guess on the real exam. If the number you got right is significantly lower than one-fourth of the number you guessed on, you would, frankly, be safe in guessing anyway, but maybe you would feel more comfortable if you guessed only selectively, when you can eliminate a wrong answer or at least have a good feeling about one of the answer choices.

▶ Step 7: Reach Your Peak Performance Zone

Time to complete: 10 minutes to read, weeks to complete!
Activity: Complete the Physical Preparation Checklist.

To get ready for a challenge like a big exam, you have to take control of your physical, as well as your mental, state. Exercise, proper diet, and rest will ensure that your body works with, rather than against, your mind on test day, as well as during your preparation.

Exercise

If you don't already have a regular exercise program going, the time during which you are preparing for an exam is actually an excellent time to start one. And if you are already keeping fit—or trying to get that way—don't let the pressure of preparing for an exam fool you into quitting now. Exercise helps reduce stress by pumping wonderful good-feeling hormones called endorphins into your system. It also increases the oxygen supply throughout your body, including your brain, so you will be at peak performance on test day.

A half hour of vigorous activity—enough to raise a sweat—every day should be your aim. If you are really pressed for time, every other day is okay. Choose an activity you like, and get out there and do it. Jogging with a friend always makes the time go faster, or take a radio.

But don't overdo it. You don't want to exhaust yourself. Moderation is the key.

Diet

First of all, cut out the junk. Go easy on caffeine and nicotine, and eliminate alcohol and any other drugs from your system at least two weeks before the exam. Promise yourself a binge the night after the exam, if need be.

What your body needs for peak performance is simply a balanced diet. Eat plenty of fruits and vegetables, along with protein and carbohydrates. Foods high in lecithin (an amino acid), such as fish and beans, are especially good "brain foods."

The night before the exam, you might "carbo-load" the way athletes do before a contest. Eat a big plate of spaghetti, rice and beans, or your favorite carbohydrate.

Rest

You probably know how much sleep you need every night to be at your best, even if you don't always get it. Make sure you do get that much sleep, though, for at least a week before the exam. Moderation is important here, too. Extra sleep will just make you groggy.

If you are not a morning person and your exam will be given in the morning, you should reset your internal clock so that your body doesn't think you are taking an exam at 3:00 A.M. You have to start this process well before the exam. The way it works is to get up half an hour earlier each morning, and then go to bed half an hour earlier that night. Don't try it the other way around; you will just toss and turn if you go to bed early without having gotten up early. The next morning, get up another half an hour earlier, and so on. How long you will have to do this depends on how late you are used to getting up. Use the Physical Preparation Checklist on the next page to make sure you are in tip-top form.

► Step 8: Get Your Act Together

Time to complete: 10 minutes to read, time to complete will vary
Activity: Complete Final Preparations worksheet.

You are in control of your mind and body; you are in charge of test anxiety, your preparation, and your test-taking strategies. Now it's time to take charge of external factors, like the testing site and the materials you need to take the exam.

Find Out Where the Exam Is and Make a Trial Run

Do you know how to get to the testing site? Do you know how long it will take to get there? If not, make a trial run, preferably on the same day of the week at the same time of day. Make note, on the Final Preparations worksheet on page 26, of the amount of time it will take you to get to the exam site. Plan on arriving 30–45 minutes early so you can get the lay of the land, use the bathroom, and calm down. Then figure out how early you will have to get up that morning, and make sure you get up that early every day for a week before the exam.

Gather Your Materials

The night before the exam, lay out the clothes you will wear and the materials you have to bring with you to the exam. Plan on dressing in layers; you won't have any control over the temperature of the examination room. Have a sweater or jacket you can take off if it's warm. Use the checklist on the Final Preparations worksheet to help you pull together what you will need.

Don't Skip Breakfast

Even if you don't usually eat breakfast, do so on exam morning. A cup of coffee doesn't count. Don't do doughnuts or other sweet foods, either. A sugar high will leave you with a sugar low in the middle of the exam. A mix of protein and carbohydrates is best: Cereal with milk and just a little sugar, or eggs with toast, will do your body a world of good.

► Step 9: Do It!

Time to complete: 10 minutes, plus test-taking time
Activity: Ace the Massachusetts Real Estate Sales Exam!

For the week before the exam, write down 1) what physical exercise you engaged in and for how long and 2) what you ate for each meal. Remember, you are trying for at least half an hour of exercise every other day (preferably every day) and a balanced diet that's light on junk food.

Exam minus 7 days

Exercise: _____ for _____ minutes
Breakfast: _____
Lunch: _____
Dinner: _____
Snacks: _____

Exam minus 6 days

Exercise: _____ for _____ minutes
Breakfast: _____
Lunch: _____
Dinner: _____
Snacks: _____

Exam minus 5 days

Exercise: _____ for _____ minutes
Breakfast: _____
Lunch: _____
Dinner: _____
Snacks: _____

Exam minus 4 days

Exercise: _____ for _____ minutes
Breakfast: _____
Lunch: _____
Dinner: _____
Snacks: _____

Exam minus 3 days

Exercise: _____ for _____ minutes
Breakfast: _____
Lunch: _____
Dinner: _____
Snacks: _____

Exam minus 2 days

Exercise: _____ for _____ minutes
Breakfast: _____
Lunch: _____
Dinner: _____
Snacks: _____

Exam minus 1 day

Exercise: _____ for _____ minutes
Breakfast: _____
Lunch: _____
Dinner: _____
Snacks: _____

Fast-forward to exam day. You are ready. You made a study plan and followed through. You practiced your test-taking strategies while working through this book. You are in control of your physical, mental, and emotional state. You know when and where to show up and what to bring with you. In other words, you are better prepared than most of the other people taking the Massachusetts Real Estate Sales Exam with you. You are psyched.

Just one more thing. When you are done with the exam, you will have earned a reward. Plan a celebration. Call up your friends and plan a party, or have a nice dinner for two—whatever your heart desires. Give yourself something to look forward to.

Final Preparations

Getting to the Exam Site

Location of exam: _____

Date: _____

Departure time: _____

Do I know how to get to the exam site? Yes _____ No _____
If no, make a trial run.

Time it will take to get to exam site: _____

Things to Lay Out the Night Before

Clothes I will wear	_____
Sweater/jacket	_____
Watch	_____
Photo ID	_____
No. 2 pencils	_____
Calculator	_____
_____	_____
_____	_____

And then do it. Go into the exam, full of confidence, armed with test-taking strategies you have practiced until they're second nature. You are in control of yourself, your environment, and your performance on the exam. You are ready to succeed. So do it. Go in there and ace the exam. And look forward to your future career as a real estate salesperson!

Massachusetts Real Estate Sales Exam I

CHAPTER SUMMARY

This is the first of four practice tests in this book based on the Massachusetts Real Estate Sales Exam. Take this test to see how you would do if you took the exam today, and to get a handle on your strengths and weaknesses.

IKE THE OTHER practice tests in this book, this test is based on the actual Massachusetts Real Estate Sales Exam. See Chapter 1 for a complete description of this exam.

Take this exam in as relaxed a manner as you can, without worrying about timing. You can time yourself on the other three exams. You should, however, make sure that you have enough time to take the entire exam in one sitting. Find a quiet place where you can work without interruptions.

The answer sheet you should use is on the following page, followed by the exam. After you have finished, use the answer key and explanations to learn your strengths and your weaknesses. Then use the scoring section at the end of this chapter to see how you did overall.

▶ Massachusetts Real Estate Sales Exam I Answer Sheet

1.	ⓐ	ⓑ	ⓒ	ⓓ	38.	ⓐ	ⓑ	ⓒ	ⓓ	75.	ⓐ ⓑ ⓒ ⓓ
2.	ⓐ	ⓑ	ⓒ	ⓓ	39.	ⓐ	ⓑ	ⓒ	ⓓ	76.	ⓐ ⓑ ⓒ ⓓ
3.	ⓐ	ⓑ	ⓒ	ⓓ	40.	ⓐ	ⓑ	ⓒ	ⓓ	77.	ⓐ ⓑ ⓒ ⓓ
4.	ⓐ	ⓑ	ⓒ	ⓓ	41.	ⓐ	ⓑ	ⓒ	ⓓ	78.	ⓐ ⓑ ⓒ ⓓ
5.	ⓐ	ⓑ	ⓒ	ⓓ	42.	ⓐ	ⓑ	ⓒ	ⓓ	79.	ⓐ ⓑ ⓒ ⓓ
6.	ⓐ	ⓑ	ⓒ	ⓓ	43.	ⓐ	ⓑ	ⓒ	ⓓ	80.	ⓐ ⓑ ⓒ ⓓ
7.	ⓐ	ⓑ	ⓒ	ⓓ	44.	ⓐ	ⓑ	ⓒ	ⓓ	81.	ⓐ ⓑ ⓒ ⓓ
8.	ⓐ	ⓑ	ⓒ	ⓓ	45.	ⓐ	ⓑ	ⓒ	ⓓ	82.	ⓐ ⓑ ⓒ ⓓ
9.	ⓐ	ⓑ	ⓒ	ⓓ	46.	ⓐ	ⓑ	ⓒ	ⓓ	83.	ⓐ ⓑ ⓒ ⓓ
10.	ⓐ	ⓑ	ⓒ	ⓓ	47.	ⓐ	ⓑ	ⓒ	ⓓ	84.	ⓐ ⓑ ⓒ ⓓ
11.	ⓐ	ⓑ	ⓒ	ⓓ	48.	ⓐ	ⓑ	ⓒ	ⓓ	85.	ⓐ ⓑ ⓒ ⓓ
12.	ⓐ	ⓑ	ⓒ	ⓓ	49.	ⓐ	ⓑ	ⓒ	ⓓ	86.	ⓐ ⓑ ⓒ ⓓ
13.	ⓐ	ⓑ	ⓒ	ⓓ	50.	ⓐ	ⓑ	ⓒ	ⓓ	87.	ⓐ ⓑ ⓒ ⓓ
14.	ⓐ	ⓑ	ⓒ	ⓓ	51.	ⓐ	ⓑ	ⓒ	ⓓ	88.	ⓐ ⓑ ⓒ ⓓ
15.	ⓐ	ⓑ	ⓒ	ⓓ	52.	ⓐ	ⓑ	ⓒ	ⓓ	89.	ⓐ ⓑ ⓒ ⓓ
16.	ⓐ	ⓑ	ⓒ	ⓓ	53.	ⓐ	ⓑ	ⓒ	ⓓ	90.	ⓐ ⓑ ⓒ ⓓ
17.	ⓐ	ⓑ	ⓒ	ⓓ	54.	ⓐ	ⓑ	ⓒ	ⓓ	91.	ⓐ ⓑ ⓒ ⓓ
18.	ⓐ	ⓑ	ⓒ	ⓓ	55.	ⓐ	ⓑ	ⓒ	ⓓ	92.	ⓐ ⓑ ⓒ ⓓ
19.	ⓐ	ⓑ	ⓒ	ⓓ	56.	ⓐ	ⓑ	ⓒ	ⓓ	93.	ⓐ ⓑ ⓒ ⓓ
20.	ⓐ	ⓑ	ⓒ	ⓓ	57.	ⓐ	ⓑ	ⓒ	ⓓ	94.	ⓐ ⓑ ⓒ ⓓ
21.	ⓐ	ⓑ	ⓒ	ⓓ	58.	ⓐ	ⓑ	ⓒ	ⓓ	95.	ⓐ ⓑ ⓒ ⓓ
22.	ⓐ	ⓑ	ⓒ	ⓓ	59.	ⓐ	ⓑ	ⓒ	ⓓ	96.	ⓐ ⓑ ⓒ ⓓ
23.	ⓐ	ⓑ	ⓒ	ⓓ	60.	ⓐ	ⓑ	ⓒ	ⓓ	97.	ⓐ ⓑ ⓒ ⓓ
24.	ⓐ	ⓑ	ⓒ	ⓓ	61.	ⓐ	ⓑ	ⓒ	ⓓ	98.	ⓐ ⓑ ⓒ ⓓ
25.	ⓐ	ⓑ	ⓒ	ⓓ	62.	ⓐ	ⓑ	ⓒ	ⓓ	99.	ⓐ ⓑ ⓒ ⓓ
26.	ⓐ	ⓑ	ⓒ	ⓓ	63.	ⓐ	ⓑ	ⓒ	ⓓ	100.	ⓐ ⓑ ⓒ ⓓ
27.	ⓐ	ⓑ	ⓒ	ⓓ	64.	ⓐ	ⓑ	ⓒ	ⓓ	101.	ⓐ ⓑ ⓒ ⓓ
28.	ⓐ	ⓑ	ⓒ	ⓓ	65.	ⓐ	ⓑ	ⓒ	ⓓ	102.	ⓐ ⓑ ⓒ ⓓ
29.	ⓐ	ⓑ	ⓒ	ⓓ	66.	ⓐ	ⓑ	ⓒ	ⓓ	103.	ⓐ ⓑ ⓒ ⓓ
30.	ⓐ	ⓑ	ⓒ	ⓓ	67.	ⓐ	ⓑ	ⓒ	ⓓ	104.	ⓐ ⓑ ⓒ ⓓ
31.	ⓐ	ⓑ	ⓒ	ⓓ	68.	ⓐ	ⓑ	ⓒ	ⓓ	105.	ⓐ ⓑ ⓒ ⓓ
32.	ⓐ	ⓑ	ⓒ	ⓓ	69.	ⓐ	ⓑ	ⓒ	ⓓ	106.	ⓐ ⓑ ⓒ ⓓ
33.	ⓐ	ⓑ	ⓒ	ⓓ	70.	ⓐ	ⓑ	ⓒ	ⓓ	107.	ⓐ ⓑ ⓒ ⓓ
34.	ⓐ	ⓑ	ⓒ	ⓓ	71.	ⓐ	ⓑ	ⓒ	ⓓ	108.	ⓐ ⓑ ⓒ ⓓ
35.	ⓐ	ⓑ	ⓒ	ⓓ	72.	ⓐ	ⓑ	ⓒ	ⓓ	109.	ⓐ ⓑ ⓒ ⓓ
36.	ⓐ	ⓑ	ⓒ	ⓓ	73.	ⓐ	ⓑ	ⓒ	ⓓ	110.	ⓐ ⓑ ⓒ ⓓ
37.	ⓐ	ⓑ	ⓒ	ⓓ	74.	ⓐ	ⓑ	ⓒ	ⓓ		

► Massachusetts Real Estate Sales Exam I

1. An agent who works with and not for the buyer or seller is a
   a. general agent.
   b. dual agent.
   c. facilitator.
   d. licensee.

2. The MA Mandatory Licensee-Consumer Relationship Disclosure requires that which of the following parties be given the agency disclosure?
   a. seller
   b. buyer
   c. both
   d. none of the above

3. Using the gross rent multiplier method of evaluation, what would be the value of a three-family house that had an annual gross income of $40,000 if the average selling price of a three-family house in the community is $300,000 and the average annual gross income of the property is $30,000?
   a. $400,000
   b. $40,000
   c. $600,000
   d. $300,000

4. The type of deed in which the grantee receives the premises with the promise that it will be free of any encumbrances is
   a. a quitclaim deed.
   b. a warranty deed.
   c. a certificate of title.
   d. a trust deed.

5. In a cooperative sale, what is the legal theory in which the principal may be held responsible for the acts of his agent and subagent?
   a. *caveat emptor*
   b. vicarious liability
   c. escheat
   d. licensee

6. The municipality permit that allows habitation of a property is a/an
   a. building permit.
   b. deed.
   c. lease.
   d. occupancy permit.

7. Real estate taxes for the year are $4,800 and are due on June 24 of the year. If the property is sold on March 11 of that year, which of the following is correct?
   a. The prorated amount is $946.67.
   b. debit to seller
   c. credit to buyer
   d. all of the above

8. The exculpatory clause in a lease relieves the landlord from
   a. the back rent.
   b. the security deposit.
   c. the liability for a tenant's personal injury in common areas.
   d. the repairs to the unit.

9. A lease in Massachusetts, to be valid, must be
   a. oral.
   b. written.
   c. a percentage of rent collected.
   d. none of the above

10. Continuing education classes in Massachusetts
  a. can be taken in a classroom setting.
  b. can be taken on the Internet.
  c. can be taken once every three years.
  d. are not required.

11. Instructors for salesperson and broker licensing must
  a. be authorized by the Board of Registration.
  b. hold a current broker's license.
  c. both **a** and **b**
  d. none of the above

12. What approach method is essential in almost every appraisal of the value of a property?
  a. cost
  b. market data
  c. income
  d. none of the above

13. A seller wants to net $330,000 from the sale of property and the broker's commission is 5%. What should the listing price be?
  a. $347,368
  b. $346,500
  c. $345,313
  d. $330,000

14. Fiduciary relationship means that the broker owes trust and confidence to
  a. all the parties.
  b. none of the parties.
  c. only to the seller.
  d. to the party who hired him.

15. A property sells for $85,000 and the total commission is 5%. The broker pays a 20% referral fee to the listing agent and a 40% fee to the selling agent. How much does the broker net from the sale?
  a. $4,250
  b. $1,700
  c. $850
  d. $6,000

16. RESPA is required to be given by the broker
  a. at the signing of the Purchase and Sales Agreement.
  b. at the time of the loan application.
  c. at the time of settlement.
  d. none of the above

17. If the total of the buyer's debits is $335,305 and the total of the credits is $297,460, which of the following is correct?
  a. due from buyers to close—$37,845
  b. due from sellers to close—$37,000
  c. Buyers do not owe any monies.
  d. Sellers owe buyers $37,845.

18. The purpose of which of the following laws is to inform mortgage applicants of the cost of obtaining the loan?
  a. Sherman Anti-trust Law
  b. Truth-in-Lending Law
  c. Berra-Mantle Law
  d. Taft-Hartly Law

19. What would have the greatest effect on a person's interest rate?
  a. the discount rate
  b. the person's credit score
  c. Regulation Z
  d. private mortgage insurance

20. What type of ownership is becoming a greater factor in real estate sales?
   a. adverse possession
   b. cooperatives
   c. licenses
   d. condominiums

21. In a cooperative, the buyer of a unit becomes the
   a. unit owner.
   b. stockholder in the cooperative.
   c. adverse tenant.
   d. estoppel tenant.

22. A cap rate is used in what type of appraisal?
   a. reproduction
   b. income approach
   c. tax assessment
   d. competitive market analysis

23. In order to sell timesharing, a person
   a. does not need to be licensed.
   b. must be licensed as a salesperson.
   c. must hold a broker's license.
   d. must be an appraiser.

24. An income property has a gross income of $36,638 and operating expenses of $23,910. If you want to achieve a 9% capitalization rate, what is the maximum price you should pay for the property?
   a. $142,500
   b. $142,000
   c. $141,800
   d. $141,422

25. Which of the following would be considered part of the real estate?
   a. a ceiling fan permanently installed by the tenant
   b. a poster hanging in the den
   c. a bird bath sitting on the back lawn
   d. a bookcase standing in the living room

26. Most Purchase and Sale Agreements will have a clause stating the title shall be free from all
   a. appurtenances.
   b. encumbrances.
   c. riparian.
   d. torrens.

27. It is best for an owner to have the mortgage taken over as
   a. an amortization.
   b. subject to the mortgage.
   c. an assumption.
   d. a wraparound.

28. Which of the following would be considered an indirect cost of real estate ownership?
   a. financing
   b. real estate taxes
   c. homeowners insurance
   d. home inspection costs

29. A minor is
   a. barred from making contracts.
   b. able to make a voidable contract.
   c. exempt from making a contract.
   d. has no business making a contract.

30. An agent who has been hired by a seller and allows another agent to be a subagent
- **a.** is liable for the other agent's statements.
- **b.** is not liable for the other agent's statements.
- **c.** is a facilitator in the transaction.
- **d.** would be a buyer's agent in the transaction.

31. A buyer-agent
- **a.** always has to be paid directly by the buyer.
- **b.** is not entitled to any compensation.
- **c.** can be paid his or her compensation from the proceeds of the sale.
- **d.** can be paid his or her compensation by the lessor.

32. An agent has two listings from the same owner. One listing is located at 9 Mason Street and the other at 4 Mason Street. This agent would be known as
- **a.** a dual agent.
- **b.** a single agent.
- **c.** a special agent.
- **d.** a general agent.

33. Sunday contracts for sale of residential property in Massachusetts are
- **a.** valid.
- **b.** void.
- **c.** voidable.
- **d.** unenforceable.

34. The allodial system gives an individual
- **a.** the right to own personal property.
- **b.** the right to own real property.
- **c.** the right of personality.
- **d.** the right to a mortgage.

35. A ticket to a ball game would be considered
- **a.** a license.
- **b.** a freehold.
- **c.** fee simple.
- **d.** a non-freehold.

36. Which of the following are required for a property manager?
- **a.** must have a real estate salesperson's license
- **b.** must have a college degree
- **c.** must be hired by a property owner
- **d.** must have a broker's license

37. An owner who sells his land and remains as a tenant of the new owner is an example of
- **a.** a freehold.
- **b.** a sale and leasehold.
- **c.** secondary financing.
- **d.** an installment contract.

38. If the selling price of a property is $300,000 and the bank requires a $60,000 down payment, then the loan-to-value ratio would be
- **a.** 80%.
- **b.** 70%.
- **c.** 40%.
- **d.** 10%.

39. A community has an annual budget of $1,206,000 and a total assessed value of $24,500,000. What is the tax rate per thousand?
- **a.** $42
- **b.** $49.22
- **c.** $20.31
- **d.** $203

40. On the sale of a single-family primary residence, an individual has a capital gain exclusion of
   a. $250,000.
   b. $500,000.
   c. $750,000.
   d. zero.

41. At the closing, who has the obligation to provide a "good and marketable" title?
   a. the buyer
   b. the buyer's attorney
   c. the home inspector
   d. the seller

42. Who CANNOT recommend a home inspector?
   a. the buyer's agent
   b. the buyer's brother
   c. the buyer's friend
   d. the seller's agent

43. A property is three-quarters of a mile in length, half a mile in width, and sells for $25,000 per acre. What is the selling price?
   a. $60,000
   b. $550,175
   c. $6,000,000
   d. $3,750,000

44. A mortgage that pledges more than one parcel of property as a security for a debt would be
   a. a purchase money mortgage.
   b. an open-end mortgage.
   c. a blanket mortgage.
   d. a package mortgage.

45. What type of mortgage is a form of financing in which the buyer makes a down payment and the seller finances the balance?
   a. a wraparound mortgage
   b. a closed mortgage
   c. an open-end mortgage
   d. a purchase money mortgage

46. A condition in the lease in which the tenant is entitled to peaceful possession is called
   a. prevention of waste.
   b. quiet enjoyment.
   c. escheat.
   d. tenancy at sufferance.

47. The three-day right of rescission does NOT apply in which of the following situations?
   a. first mortgage
   b. home equity loan
   c. refinancing of the loan
   d. none of the above

48. If a buyer withdraws an offer to purchase after it has been accepted by the seller,
   a. the buyer is entitled to reimbursement of the earnest money.
   b. the buyer forfeits the earnest money.
   c. the buyer owes the broker a commission.
   d. the buyer must pay the advertising expenses.

49. If a person runs an ad in a newspaper offering a reward for his lost dog, this would be an example of
   a. an executory contract.
   b. an executed contract.
   c. a unilateral contract.
   d. a bilateral contract.

50. To give constructive notice of ownership, the buyer must
 a. comply with RESPA requirements.
 b. record the deed.
 c. be a beneficiary.
 d. sign the deed.

51. The income approach to value can also be called the
 a. market data approach.
 b. capitalization approach.
 c. cost approach.
 d. comparison approach.

52. An investment property was bought for $385,000. The land value was $140,000. If the useful life of the property is thirty years, what is the annual depreciation?
 a. $12,833
 b. $4,667
 c. $8,167
 d. $17,500

53. The role of the broker at the closing
 a. is to prepare the deed.
 b. is to prepare the mortgage.
 c. is to prepare the closing statement.
 d. The broker has no official role.

54. When the broker principal appoints an agent to work specifically with one seller, this is an example of
 a. a facilitator.
 b. a dual agency.
 c. a designated agency.
 d. a buyer agency.

55. An agent working as a facilitator
 a. must present each property honestly and accurately to the buyer.
 b. works only for the seller.
 c. works only for the buyer.
 d. is not allowed.

56. An agency disclosure MUST be presented to the buyer
 a. at the time of closing.
 b. by the bank's attorney.
 c. at the first personal meeting with a buyer to discuss a specific property.
 d. at the time of the offer.

57. In Massachusetts, an agent who has an inactive license MUST do which of the following to activate the license?
 a. Retake the licensing test.
 b. Complete 12 hours of continuing education.
 c. Complete 24 hours of continuing education.
 d. Complete 30 hours of continuing education.

58. In order to be a qualified real estate instructor in Massachusetts, a person is required to
 a. be a college graduate.
 b. have a broker's license for five years.
 c. be approved and authorized by the Board of REALTORS®.
 d. be approved and authorized by the Board of Registration.

59. At a meeting, a group of brokers agrees that they will not charge less than a 5% commission on their listings. This would be an example of
 a. price fixing.
 b. adverse negotiation.
 c. a commission split.
 d. a bilateral contract.

60. In arriving at the final opinion of value, the appraiser
  a. averages the methods.
  b. analyzes the approaches and bases the value on the most appropriate approach.
  c. will always use the market approach.
  d. will use the assessed value of the property.

61. The Federal Fair Housing Act of 1968 prohibits
  a. blockbusting.
  b. steering.
  c. redlining.
  d. discrimination based on race.

62. When dealing with zoning laws, the real estate agent
  a. needs to join the Board of Appeals.
  b. does not need to be familiar with them.
  c. needs a thorough knowledge of the bylaws of the local communities.
  d. should give gifts to the inspectors and become friendly with them.

63. An insurance claims representative would use what appraisal method to determine the amount of damage to an insured's home?
  a. market data
  b. cost approach
  c. income approach
  d. all of the above

64. A seller wishes to net $285,000 from the sale of his property. He agrees to a 5% commission plus $500 for advertising. What should the selling price be?
  a. $300,526
  b. $299,250
  c. $299,775
  d. $315,810

65. Which of the following applies to a security deposit in Massachusetts?
  a. It cannot exceed one month's rent.
  b. It must be deposited in an interest-bearing escrow account.
  c. Both **a** and **b** are correct.
  d. Neither **a** nor **b** is correct.

66. Kasper has received a "Notice to Quit" from his landlord. How long does he have to vacate the apartment?
  a. 14 days
  b. 30 days
  c. 50 days
  d. He must vacate immediately.

67. A period of time over which an asset is expected to remain economically feasible to an owner is called its
  a. salvage value.
  b. cost basis.
  c. useful life.
  d. accelerated life.

68. A listing in which an owner instructs an agent NOT to sell to a woman would be classified as
  a. an easement.
  b. restrictive.
  c. an avulsion.
  d. a demise.

69. In Massachusetts, the Smoke Detector Law requires that
  a. buyers must inspect the property.
  b. local fire departments must inspect and test the units.
  c. brokers have to pay the cost of inspection.
  d. No inspection is required.

70. A 1031 tax-deferred exchange allows an investor to
a. avoid capital gain taxes.
b. sell and buy another like property.
c. do an installment sale.
d. do a market comparison.

71. The equity in a property that has a market value of $389,000 and is owned free and clear would be
a. none.
b. $125,000.
c. $389,000.
d. none of the above

72. The term "cloud on title" means
a. the title is free and clear.
b. the seller must pay the broker's commission.
c. the title is encumbered.
d. a title search does not have to be done.

73. A projected annual operating statement that shows anticipated income, expenses, and net income is
a. a balance sheet.
b. a closing statement.
c. an appraisal.
d. a pro forma statement.

74. Which of the following would NOT be considered an element of value?
a. comparison
b. utility
c. scarcity
d. demand

75. A trust of at least 100 persons that is chartered to acquire and develop real estate is
a. a real estate trust.
b. REIT.
c. a cooperative.
d. tenants in partnership.

76. Purchasing property by reinvesting proceeds from refinancing already owned properties is called
a. appreciation.
b. steering.
c. pyramiding.
d. riparian.

77. Qualifying the buyer for a mortgage is the function of
a. the broker.
b. the principal.
c. the mortgagor.
d. the mortgagee.

78. A statement that is made with the intent to deceive, with the knowledge that it is untrue, is considered to be
a. misrepresentation.
b. *caveat emptor*.
c. execution.
d. ethical.

79. It is mandatory for a real estate broker in Massachusetts to have
a. an errors and omissions policy.
b. a surety bond.
c. a comprehensive insurance policy.
d. mortgage insurance.

80. Tenant Ford is leasing a store in the Burlington Mall, and she has to pay a fixed amount of rent for the space plus a certain amount of the gross receipts. This would be called a
a. gross lease.
b. net lease.
c. triple net lease.
d. percentage lease.

81. A Purchase and Sales Agreement would be an example of what type of contract?
a. unconscionable
b. executory
c. executed
d. all of the above

82. Mr. Rivera executed a deed to his nephew citing the consideration as $1.00. The deed is
a. voidable.
b. incomplete.
c. valid.
d. void.

83. Broker James received an offer of $195,000 on a property listed at $200,000. Before he presents the offer to the seller, he receives another offer from a different buyer for $202,000. What must broker James do?
a. Call the first buyer and reject the offer of $195,000.
b. Present only the highest offer.
c. Present both offers.
d. Decide which is the best offer for the sale.

84. What is required for a deed to be recorded?
a. It must be signed by the mortgagor.
b. It must have the signature of the grantors and acknowledgement of the same.
c. It must have the signature of the grantee and acknowledgement of the same.
d. A title search must be done.

85. The amortization of a mortgage means
a. the amount of each monthly payment applied to interest remains the same.
b. mortgagor can prepay the loan without a penalty.
c. payments will be constant and will pay off the principal and interest.
d. only interest will be paid off.

86. A mortgage in which the seller will deliver a deed upon receipt of the final mortgage payment is
a. a purchase money mortgage.
b. a secondary mortgage.
c. a land sales contract.
d. an equity mortgage.

87. Insurance in which the insuring company is obligated to take action to defend the title, take action to perfect it, or to compensate the insured for loss is
a. mandatory.
b. called title insurance.
c. escheat.
d. provided by the seller.

88. The relationship of a broker to a buyer in an exclusive buyer agency contract is that of a
a. principle agent.
b. single agent.
c. facilitator.
d. dual agent.

89. Appraiser Patrick appraised a property at $350,000, which reflected a 30% drop in value. What was the original purchase price of this property?
- **a.** $269,231
- **b.** $245,000
- **c.** $455,000
- **d.** $500,000

90. What is the purpose of the closing statement?
- **a.** to show the title search
- **b.** to show the financial obligations of the buyer and seller
- **c.** to show the liability of the lessee
- **d.** none of the above

91. If a landlord failed to provide water and the tenants moved out for their own protection, this would be considered
- **a.** actual eviction.
- **b.** constructive eviction.
- **c.** eminent domain.
- **d.** subleasing.

92. The city of Boston leased a three-acre parcel of real estate to Jennifer Jones for 99 years. This is what type of lease?
- **a.** net lease
- **b.** escalation lease
- **c.** ground lease
- **d.** sale and lease back

93. You are appraising a mobile home park that is on a major highway, which has been developing into a commercial area. Which concept would you have to apply?
- **a.** highest and best use
- **b.** insurable value
- **c.** salvage value
- **d.** replacement cost

94. If a large manufacturing plant was allowed to construct a new plant near a new subdivision, the depreciation for the subdivision would be considered
- **a.** substitution.
- **b.** physical.
- **c.** functional.
- **d.** economic.

95. Most states exempt which of the following types of property from real estate taxes?
- **a.** properties owned by veterans
- **b.** properties owned by elderly
- **c.** properties owned by farmers
- **d.** properties owned by non-profit hospitals

96. In Massachusetts, when there is a change of business address, who must notify the Board of Registration of Real Estate Brokers and Salespersons?
- **a.** the licensee
- **b.** the broker
- **c.** both **a** and **b**
- **d.** neither **a** nor **b**

97. A non-resident of Massachusetts must do which of the following to obtain a Massachusetts real estate license?
- **a.** move into the state
- **b.** conform to the same examination requirements as a Massachusetts resident
- **c.** be sponsored by an out-of-state broker
- **d.** be sponsored by a Massachusetts broker

98. What type of mortgage would be most beneficial to a buyer?
- **a.** subject to mortgage
- **b.** assumable mortgage
- **c.** junior mortgage
- **d.** closed mortgage

99. A multiple-listing property sells for $319,000. The shared commission is 5%: 2.5% to the listing office, 2.5% to the buyer agent. The listing salesperson earns 40% of the commission. What does his broker principal of the listing office earn?
  a. $15,950
  b. $7,975
  c. $6,000
  d. $4,785

100. What is the name of the decision of the Massachusetts Supreme Court which states that "if a buyer defaults, a contract is not consummated"?
  a. Tristam's Landing
  b. Martha's Vineyard
  c. Sherman Anti-trust Law
  d. Landfall Act

101. In real estate agency relationships, the agreement between a seller and his agent is known as
  a. a listing agreement.
  b. a sales agreement.
  c. a binder.
  d. a purchase offer.

102. Janet Jones, a sales agent, placed an advertisement in the newspaper. She advertised her name, her office address, her telephone number, and her educational background. What was one important item she was missing?
  a. the area she services
  b. her areas of specialty
  c. her experience
  d. her broker's and agency's name

103. Regardless of who sells the house, the broker will collect a commission. This type of listing offers the most protection, therefore, to the broker. This is called
  a. an open listing.
  b. a net listing.
  c. an exclusive right to sell listing.
  d. an exclusive agency listing.

104. The remaining balance on Shari Larson's mortgage is $185,500. The interest rate is 8.5%, and the monthly payment is $1,425.50. How much of her next monthly payment will be applied to principal?
  a. $1,426.50
  b. $112.54
  c. $113.96
  d. $43.79

105. Jason is eager to sell his house quickly and tells his listing agent to offer a bonus to the agent who sells that house. His listing agent tells him
  a. "That's great. It will sell much faster."
  b. "No, it's illegal to offer a bonus."
  c. "We can only offer a bonus to the selling agency; agents can only collect commission from their own broker."
  d. "I don't do that."

106. A variety of land uses will add to property value as long as the uses are in
  a. conformity.
  b. balance.
  c. progress.
  d. decline.

107. The buyer of a cooperative apartment receives shares in the cooperative and a
   a. proprietary lease.
   b. bargain and sale deed.
   c. joint tenancy.
   d. limited partnership.

108. An owner may sell his or her home and not pay a commission, even though it is exclusively listed with an agency, when he or she has a(n)
   a. exclusive right to sell listing agreement.
   b. exclusive agency listing.
   c. net listing.
   d. open listing.

109. The annual real estate taxes on a property are $2,400. The seller pays taxes in arrears in two installments, on June 1 and October 1. If the closing is scheduled for August 28, what taxes will be due and how will the information appear on the HUD-1?
   a. Credit seller $1,596 and debit buyer $1,596.
   b. Credit buyer $2,400 and debit seller $2,400.
   c. Debit seller $804 and credit buyer $804.
   d. Credit buyer $2,796 and debit seller $2,796.

110. In inflationary times, a property manager would NOT want a long-term lease based on
   a. graduated payments.
   b. the consumer price index.
   c. a fixed rate.
   d. a cost-of-living index.

▶ Answers

1. **c.** A facilitator assists the buyer and seller to reach an agreement without representing either the buyer or the seller in the transaction.

2. **c.** The MA Mandatory Licensee-Consumer Relationship Disclosure is for both the seller and the buyer.

3. **a.** The gross multiplier is determined by dividing the average selling price by the annual income: $300,000 ÷ $30,000 = gross multiplier of 10; gross multiplier of 10 × $40,000 = $400,000.

4. **b.** The seller grants the title to the grantee free of encumbrances in a warranty deed.

5. **b.** A principal maybe held liable for the acts of his agent and subagents through vicarious liability.

6. **d.** An occupancy permit is the city or town permit which establishes habitability of a property.

7. **d.** Adjustment is $947.67 based on the following: $4,800 ÷ 360 days = daily rate of $13.33 × 71 (the number of days seller owned the property – January and February 30 days each, plus 11 days for March) = $946.67. The sellers owned it, so it is a debit to the sellers. The buyers receive it, so it is a credit to the buyers.

8. **c.** An exculpatory clause relieves the landlord from liability for a tenant's personal injury in a common area.

9. **b.** All leases in Massachusetts must be written.

10. **a.** Continuing education classes in Massachusetts must be taken in a classroom, every two years.

11. **c.** Instructors must be authorized by the Board and hold a current license.

12. **b.** The market data approach is essential in almost every appraisal.

13. **a.** 100% − 5% = 95%; 330,000 ÷ .95 = 347,368.

14. **d.** Loyalty is to the person that hires the broker above all others.

15. **b.** The total commission is $4,250.
    | 20% to listing agent | 4,250 × .20 = 850 |
    | 40% to selling agent | 4,250 × .40 = 1,700 |
    | 40% to broker | 4,250 × .40 = 1,700 |

16. **d.** The broker is not required to give the RESPA.

17. **a.** 335,305 − 297,460 = 37,845 and is owed by the buyers.

18. **b.** The Truth-in-Lending Law requires disclosure to mortgage applicants.

19. **a.** The federal discount rate has the greatest effect. The Federal Reserve Board will adjust its rate to encourage or discourage member banks to increase the supply of money.

20. **d.** Because of affordability and lifestyle, condominiums have become more popular.

21. **b.** They have no individual ownership.

22. **b.** Capitalization rate is an analysis of how much investors are willing to spend in a certain neighborhood in return for a certain amount of income.

23. **a.** A real estate license is not required to sell timesharing.

24. **d.** The maximum price should not exceed $141,422.
    | Gross Income | $36,638 |
    | Operating Expenses | − 23,910 |
    | Net Income | $12,728 |

    12,728 ÷ .09 = 141,422

25. **a.** The ceiling fan became real property when it was permanently attached.

26. b. Most Purchase and Sale Agreements expressly state that title should be free of all encumbrances.

27. c. This is because the buyer agrees to assume and make himself personally responsible for payment.

28. a. Financing is an indirect cost of ownership.

29. b. Minors are capable of making a voidable contract.

30. a. In a subagency relationship, the listing agent is liable for the subagent's statements.

31. c. The buyer-agent can be paid by the buyer or from the proceeds of the sale.

32. d. The general agent has received multiple authorization from the same owner.

33. a. Sunday contracts for residential properties are valid and enforceable.

34. b. The allodial system gives the individual the right to own land.

35. a. It is a license that gives the individual the non-exclusive right of usage.

36. c. Property managers are not required to have a specific license, nor is a college education required.

37. b. When an owner sells land and remains as a tenant, this is an example of a sale and leasehold.

38. a. The loan-to-value ratio is the percent the bank lends. The amount of the loan is $240,000; 240,000 ÷ 300,000 = 80%.

39. b. 1,206,000 ÷ 24,500,000 = .04922 × 1,000 = 49.22.

40. a. An individual has an exclusion of $250,000.

41. d. It is the seller's obligation to provide a clear and marketable title.

42. d. The seller's agent cannot recommend a home inspector.

43. c. $\frac{3}{4}$ of a mile = 3,960 feet
$\frac{1}{2}$ of a mile = 2,640 feet
3,960 feet × 2,640 feet = 10,454,400 square feet
10,454,400 square feet ÷ 43,560 square feet in an acre = 240 acres × 25,000 = $6,000,000

44. c. A blanket mortgage is the mortgage that pledges more than one parcel of property as collateral.

45. d. In a purchase money mortgage, the seller finances the sale of the property by lending the money to the buyer.

46. b. Quiet enjoyment gives the tenant the right to peaceful possession.

47. a. The three-day right of rescission applies only when a lien can be placed on a person's home that he already owns.

48. b. This situation constitutes a liquidating damage.

49. c. It is a unilateral contract because only one person is promising to perform.

50. b. The recording of the deed gives constructive notice of ownership.

51. b. The capitalization approach is also known as the income approach.

52. c. Annual depreciation is based on the cost of the building less the land value, which equals the value of the building, divided by 30 years of useful life.
cost of the building $385,000
value of the land   − 140,000
                              $245,000 ÷ 30 = $8,167

53. d. The broker does not prepare any of the closing documents.

54. c. Designated agency is accomplished by appointing an agent to work exclusively for that seller.

55. a. A facilitator does not represent either the buyer or the seller and must present every property honestly and accurately.

56. **c.** The agency disclosure must be given at the first meeting to discuss a specific property.

57. **b.** The agent must complete 12 hours of continuing education to activate the license. In Massachusetts, re-testing is not required.

58. **d.** The inspector must be approved and authorized by the Board of Registration of Real Estate Brokers and Salespersons.

59. **a.** Price fixing is illegal.

60. **b.** The appraiser does not average. He will analyze and place the weight on the most appropriate approach.

61. **d.** The Federal Fair Housing Act of 1968 prohibits discrimination based on race only.

62. **c.** The real estate agent must have a thorough knowledge of the local bylaws in order to assist all parties with confidence.

63. **b.** This method is used because damage would be determined by the replacement cost.

64. **a.** $285,000 plus the advertising fee of $500 equals $285,500, which equals 100%. Subtract the 5% commission and we have 95%. Divide $285,500 by 95%, and the resulting figure is $300,526.

65. **c.** In Massachusetts, the security deposit cannot exceed one month's rent and must be deposited in an interest-bearing escrow account.

66. **b.** The notice to quit requires a 30-day notice.

67. **c.** Useful life is the period of years over which a building can be depreciated.

68. **b.** In Massachusetts, a restrictive listing may not be taken by a real estate agent.

69. **b.** In Massachusetts, the local fire departments must inspect and test the units at the owner's expense.

70. **b.** The 1031 tax-deferred exchange allows an investor the ability to defer the capital gain by investing in another like property.

71. **c.** The equity would be the difference between the market value and the liens. Since it is owned free and clear, the equity would be $389,000.

72. **c.** A "cloud" means that the title is not clear.

73. **d.** This is a projected annual operating statement.

74. **a.** The other three (utility, scarcity, and demand) are all elements of value.

75. **b.** REIT is also known as a Real Estate Investment Trust, which is the vehicle by which at least 100 persons can acquire and develop real estate.

76. **c.** Pyramiding is the process of reinvesting proceeds from refinanced properties, which are already owned, into additional properties.

77. **d.** The mortgagee lends the money, and it is the mortgagee's responsibility to qualify the buyer.

78. **a.** Misrepresentation is a statement that is known to be untrue and is made with the intent to deceive.

79. **b.** The broker is only required to have a surety bond.

80. **d.** In a percentage lease the tenant pays a fixed amount plus a percentage of the gross sales.

81. **b.** This is true because the parties have agreed to all of the terms.

82. **c.** $1.00 is considered to be valid consideration.

83. **c.** All offers must be presented to the seller.

84. **b.** Only the grantor(s) sign the deed and the signature(s) must be notarized for the deed to be recorded.

85. **c.** Amortization means making constant payments to pay off the principal and interest.

86. **c.** The deed is not executed until the final loan payment is made.

87. **b.** Title insurance is purchased by the borrower.

88. **b.** If the buyer hires an agent to perform a specific act, the agent hired is a single agent.

89. **d.** 100% − 30% = 70%; $350,000 ÷ .70 = $500,000

90. **b.** The purpose of the closing statement is to show the financial obligations of the parties.

91. **b.** If a landlord fails to provide services and the premises becomes uninhabitable, constructive eviction occurs when the tenant vacates.

92. **c.** A ground lease is a lease that is for more than 50 years.

93. **a.** Utilization of this concept would likely produce the highest net return over a period of years.

94. **d.** Economic obsolescence relates to loss of value from causes outside the property.

95. **d.** Non-profit organizations do not have to pay real estate taxes.

96. **c.** Both the licensee and the broker must notify the Board of a change of business address.

97. **b.** Non-residents do not have to move into the state, nor be sponsored by a Massachusetts broker, but they must meet the same examination requirements.

98. **a.** A buyer purchasing property with a subject to mortgage is not liable for any deficiency.

99. **d.** $319,000 × .05 = $15,950 (total commission) $15,950 × .5 = $7,975 (which is the 50% which goes to the listing office) The broker principal is entitled to 60% of $7,975 ($7,975 × .6), which equals $4,785.

100 **a.** The Tristam's Landing decision states that a contract is not consummated if a buyer defaults.

101. **a.** The agreement that an agent has with his seller is called a listing agreement; when the agent has a buyer-client, the document that they both sign is called a buyer-agency agreement.

102. **d.** All agent advertising must include the name of the broker and the agency, which must be prominently displayed.

103. **c.** An exclusive right to sell listing agreement is the listing that is encouraged by most brokers. It should also provide the homeowner with the most extensive advertising, as the broker will be entitled to the commission regardless of how someone hears about the house.

104. **b.** ($185,500 × 0.085) ÷ 12 = $1,313.96 interest for month; $1,426.50 − $1,313.96 = $112.54.

105. **c.** Bonuses are still commissions; commissions may be paid only by the employing broker; in this case, the selling broker's agency.

106. **b.** A range of land uses will contribute to value.

107. **d.** A co-op apartment is personal property, not real estate, and no deed is involved. The owners become shareholders in the overall organization and have a proprietary lease to their apartments.

108. **b.** An exclusive agency listing is one in which the owner retains the right to sell the property on his or her own without owing a commission.

109. **d.** $2,400 ÷ 2 = $1,200; $2,400 ÷ 12 = $200; $2,400 ÷ 356 = $7; half year at $1,200 plus 7 months at $200 equals $1,400; 28 days at $7 equals $196 for a total $2,796, to be credited to buyer and debited to seller on the HUD-1.

110. **c.** With a fixed-rate lease, the property manager would not have the ability to raise the rent as the market dictates.

Scoring

Evaluate how you did on this practice exam by first finding the number of questions you answered correctly. Only the number of correct answers is important—questions you skipped or got wrong don't count against your score. At the time this book was printed, a passing score for the exam was 70%, although the test you take may have more or fewer than 110 questions. On this practice exam, a passing score would be 77 correct answers.

Use your scores in conjunction with the LearningExpress Test Preparation System in Chapter 2 of this book to help you devise a study plan using the Massachusetts Real Estate Refresher Course in Chapter 4, the Real Estate Math Review in Chapter 5, and the Real Estate Glossary in Chapter 6. You should plan to spend more time on the sections that correspond to the questions you found hardest and less time on the lessons that correspond to areas in which you did well.

For now, what is much more important than your overall score is how you performed on each of the areas tested by the exam. You need to diagnose your strengths and weaknesses so that you can concentrate your efforts as you prepare. The different question types are mixed in the practice exam, so in order to diagnose where your strengths and weaknesses lie, you will need to compare your answer sheet with the following table, which shows which of the categories each questions falls into.

Once you have spent some time reviewing, take the second practice exam in Chapter 7 to see how much you have improved.

EXAM I FOR REVIEW

Test I Subject Area	Question Numbers (Questions 1–110)
Real Estate Principles and Practices	4, 6, 20, 21, 25, 26, 34, 40, 50, 57, 58, 61, 67, 70, 72, 73, 75, 76, 82, 84, 95, 107
Property Valuation/Appraisal	3, 12, 22, 24, 51, 60, 63, 74, 93, 94, 106
Financing	18, 19, 27, 28, 37, 38, 44, 45, 47, 77, 85, 86, 98
Contacts/Agency Relationship	2, 14, 29, 30, 33, 49, 56, 81, 83, 100, 101
Law, Definition, and Nature of Agency Relationships, Type of Agencies and Agents	1, 5, 31, 48, 54, 55, 88, 102, 103, 105, 108
Settlement/Transfer of Property	16, 17, 41, 53, 71, 90, 109
Business Practices	10, 11, 23, 42, 59, 62, 68, 78, 87, 96, 97
Property Management	8, 9, 35, 36, 46, 65, 66, 79, 80, 91, 92, 110
Real Estate Math	7, 13, 15, 39, 43, 52, 64, 89, 99, 104

CHAPTER

4 ▶ Massachusetts Real Estate Refresher Course

CHAPTER SUMMARY

If you want to review real estate concepts for your exam, this is the chapter you need. Using this chapter, you can review just what you need to know for the test. How you use this chapter is up to you. You may want to proceed through the entire course in order, or perhaps, after taking the first practice exam, you know that you need to brush up on just one or two areas. In that case, you can concentrate only on those areas. Following are the major sections of the real estate refresher course and the page on which you can begin your review of each one. (This list of items covered in the Massachusetts Real Estate Sales Exam is from the Board of Registration of Real Estate Brokers and Salespersons and can be found online at www.mass.gov/dpl/boards/re/contedu/sal00.htm.)

Property/Property Rights/Ownership

Condominiums/Cooperatives/Time Sharing Leases and Options

Contracts/Deeds

Financing/Mortgages

▶ Property/Property Rights/Ownership

Real versus Personal Property

Property can be divided into two classes: **real property** and **personal property**. **Real property** (also know as **real estate** or **realty**) is land and that which is permanently attached to the land (i.e., buildings, shrubs, trees). **Land** includes the earth's surface, the minerals and water below the surface (**mineral rights**), and the air space above the surface (**air rights**).

Personal property (also known as **chattel**) is movable items not attached to land. Ownership of personal property is transferred by a **bill of sale**.

There are two types of personal property:

- **tangibles** such as a car, refrigerator, or chandelier
- **intangibles** such as a patent, which is considered intellectual property

Items Affixed to the Property

Fixtures are man-made additions to real property, such as fences, lights, and other improvements. When an item of personal property is permanently attached to real estate, it becomes real property and is identified as a fixture. Fixtures become **appurtenances** and remain with the property when ownership transfers to a new owner. An exception occurs when a commercial tenant installs a business fixture to be used in the business for which the space has been leased. In the absence of a contract between the landlord and tenant stating otherwise, **trade fixtures** remain the property of the tenant and may be removed by the tenant at the end of the lease. The tenant is obligated to repair any damage caused by the removal of a trade fixture.

The determination of a fixture is made by asking and answering the following questions:

1. How is the item attached?
2. Have the improvements been modified to accommodate the item?
3. What was the intent of the parties?
4. Is there a contractual agreement that defines the item as a fixture or as a chattel?

Growing things can be real property or personal property, depending on how they are grown. Plants and trees that occur naturally or as part of the landscaping are part of the real estate. **Emblements** are annually cultivated crops and are personal property. Corn would be considered personal property, but orange trees would be considered real property, as trees are perennial. The oranges may be considered personal property if commercially grown.

Property Rights

The **bundle of rights of ownership** interest in real property includes the **right of possession, control, enjoyment, and disposition** (transfer title to someone else by **sale, gift, will,** or **exchange**). **Corporeal** rights affect the physical land themselves (i.e., the right to use the land and build on it). **Incorporeal** rights are not tangible (i.e., the right to grant others an easement).

Limits to Property Rights

Government Rights

Eminent domain is the right of government to take ownership of privately held land. Typically, land is taken for schools, freeways, parks, public housing, urban renewal, economic development, and other social and public purposes. When direct negotiations with the property owner are unsuccessful, the legal proceeding involved in exercising the right of eminent domain is called **condemnation**. The property owner must be paid the fair market value of the property taken.

An **inverse condemnation** is a proceeding brought about by a property owner demanding that a government entity purchase his land. A property owner might choose this proceeding if his land has been adversely affected by the taking of neighboring land. For instance, homeowners at the ends of airport runways may try to force airport authorities to buy their homes because of the noise of aircraft during takeoffs.

The government may enact laws and enforce them to protect the safety, health, morals, and general welfare of the public. The government's right to control the owner's use of private property is called **police power**. Examples of police power are **zoning laws** and **building codes**.

Zoning ordinances designate which land parcels in a city can be used for specific property uses (i.e., single family homes, multi-family home, commercial uses). A **non-confirming** use is a use that was in existence before the current zoning regulation went into effect. Such property improvements typically will be allowed to remain, although subject to strict rules regarding future modifications. A **conditional use permit** or **special permit** allows a property use that is not specified for the zoned area but is nevertheless considered for the public good.

All new construction or modification of existing structures must comply with the **setback** requirements (the minimum distance from property boundaries or other buildings).

A **variance** may be granted for a deviation from a zoning requirement. Normally variances need approval by the local **zoning board of appeals**.

Building codes are minimum construction standards for building, framing, plumbing, and electrical wiring.

All of these laws restrict the property owner's use of their land but do not constitute a taking (see **Eminent Domain**). Consequently, there is no payment to the property owner who suffers a loss of value through the exercise of police power.

Taxation

The government has the right to collect property taxes from property owners to provide funds for services such as schools, fire and police protection, parks, and libraries. The federal government does not tax property, relying on income taxes for operating revenues, but cities levy taxes on real property. These taxes are levied according to the value of the property and are called *ad valorem* taxes.

Estates

Estates in real property are **freehold** (an ownership interest in the property) or **non-freehold** (a rental interest in the property).

Types of Freehold Estates

Fee simple is the highest and best form of ownership. Also known as **fee simple absolute**, the owner has the right to:

- occupy, rent, or mortgage the property
- sell, dispose of, or transfer ownership of the property
- build on the property (or destroy buildings already part of the property)
- mine or extract oil, gas, and minerals
- restrict or allow the use of the property to others

A **fee simple determinable estate** ends whenever a specific event happens (or does not happen) and the real property automatically reverts back to the grantor or their heirs. **Fee upon condition** gives the grantor the right to take back the property upon a particular event, but the property does not automatically revert to the grantor.

A **life estate** lasts only for the lifetime of the holder of the estate (or another identified living person, when a life estate *pur autre vie* is created).

The holder of a **life estate** has all the responsibilities of ownership while the estate is in effect and may not destroy the premises unless the vested holder of the life estate grants permission. The vested holder is the party that will own the property after the life estate holder is deceased.

A life estate is not inheritable unless it is a life estate *pur autre vie* and the person against whose life the estate is measured survives the original holder of the life estate.

At the completion of the life estate, the property normally passes to a third party called a **remainderman**. If no remainder interest was created, the property returns by reversion (**life estate in reversion**) to the creator of the life estate or their heirs.

Forms of Ownership

There are many different entities that can acquire ownership in real property: an individual, a group of individuals, a large corporation, a government entity (at any level of government), and others. In addition, there are many different forms of ownership. **Estate in severalty** (sole ownership) occurs when property is held by one person or a single legal entity. The individual's interest is severed from everyone else's.

Concurrent ownership is ownership by more than one party.

Tenancy in common involves two or more individuals who own an undivided interest in real property without rights to survivorship. Undivided means that each tenant has an interest in the entire property.

The interest in the estate can vary among the tenants in common. One party can have 40%, another 25%, and another 35%. If a deed conveying property is made out to two people but does not stipulate their relationship, they are presumed to be tenants in common with equal interest. A party can freely dispose of his or her interest by sale, gift, devise, or descent without affecting the rights of the other owners. The new owner will be a **tenant in common** with the other owners.

Joint tenancy also involves two or more people but includes a right of survivorship. Four unities must exist to create a valid joint tenancy:

1. Unity of time—All tenants must acquire their interest at the same moment. This means that no new tenants can be added at a later time.
2. Unity of title—All tenants must acquire their interest from the same source—the same deed, will, or other conveyance.
3. Unity of interest—Each tenant has an equal percentage ownership.
4. Unity of possession—Each tenant enjoys the same undivided interest in the whole property and right to occupy the property.

Joint tenancy also includes the **right of survivorship**. This means that a joint tenant cannot will his or her ownership interest; when a co-owner dies, the surviving co-owners share equally in the deceased owner's interest. The last survivor becomes the sole owner.

Tenancy by the entirety is a form of joint tenancy specifically for married couples. Neither spouse can sell the property independently; both must sign the deed in order to transfer the property. **Tenancy by the entirety**, like a joint tenancy, provides the right of survivorship for the remaining spouse.

Transfer of Rights

Deeds

A **deed** is a written document that conveys property from the **grantor** (owner) to the **grantee** (buyer). The requirements for a valid deed are as follows:

- It must be in writing.
- The grantor(s) must be of sound mind (legally capable).
- It must identify the parties (grantor and grantee).
- It must identify the property adequately, preferably with a full legal description.
- It must contain a **granting clause**—also called words of conveyance—that contains the appropriate words ("I hereby grant, transfer, and convey").
- It must state the **consideration** (something of value like money) given.
- It must be signed by the grantor(s).
- It must be **delivered** to and **accepted** by the grantee.

Note: For more, go to page 59 under Contract/Deeds.

Will or Inheritance

A person who dies with a will, **testate**, will have their property distributed as specified in the will. An owner who has died without a will has died **intestate**. When someone dies intestate, their possessions will be distributed based on the **laws of descent**:

- A transfer of personal property by will is called a **bequest** or **legacy** (money).
- A transfer of real estate by will is called a **devise**.

Escheat is the state's right to claim ownership of property when a person dies and leaves no heirs and no will. Ownership of the property reverts to the state. This reversion to the state is called *escheat*, from the Anglo-French word meaning "to fall back."

Adverse possession may be used to acquire title to property against the owner's will. The occupancy must be **open, notorious** (not secretive), **continuous**, and **without permission**. Adverse possession can only be used against private property, not public property.

Eminent domain is the right of the government (federal or state) to take private property for a public purpose.

Foreclosure is the legal act of selling property because the terms of a note were not met (normally for non-payment).

Encumbrances and Liens

An **encumbrance** is a right or interest in a property that does not belong to an owner or tenant. An encumbrance is **voluntary** if it is imposed with the consent of the owner. It is **involuntary** if it can be imposed without the consent of the owner. Encumbrances consist of **liens** (a claim to property to ensure payment of a debt to another) and items that affect the use and physical condition of the property, such as **encroachments** or **easements**.

An **encroachment** occurs when a property improvement extends onto an adjoining parcel of land. An encroachment may be so slight as to be unnoticeable or unobjectionable, as with a fence line that deviates by only one or a few inches from the defined property boundary. The remedy may be removal of the encroachment or money damages. If no legal action is taken (or permission granted) by the owner of the burdened land, such action may become a **claim of adverse possession**.

Easements grant a right to use a portion of a property owner's land for a specific purpose. The **dominant tenement** is a parcel of land that benefits from an easement over an adjoining or adjacent parcel. An **easement appurtenant** is one that runs with the land because it is transferred when title to the dominant tenement is transferred. The **servient tenement** is the parcel of land that is burdened with the easement; that is, the parcel over which the owner of the dominant tenement is allowed to travel.

An **easement in gross** does not benefit any one parcel of real estate but rather benefits a number of parcels to bring such things as utilities.

An easement may be acquired by:

- **express grant** in a deed
- **easement by necessity** when a parcel is landlocked and there is no method of ingress or egress other than over someone else's land
- **easement by prescription**—obtained in a manner similar to that of adverse possession. The right to be obtained is a right of use rather than ownership, but the use must be without the permission of the property owner, open and notorious, and must continue for a statutory number of years.

Unlike an easement, which is permanent, a **license** is the temporary permission to come onto someone's land. The holder of a ticket for a baseball game has a license to enter the stadium for the game. A license can be revoked by the licensor.

If a married person owns property in their name only, upon their death, their surviving spouse is entitled to a one-third life interest in the property. If the surviving spouse is the wife, the right is called dower. If the surviving spouse is the husband, the right is called **courtesy** (sometimes spelled *curtesy*).

Liens

Liens are claims against property that secure payment of a financial obligation owed by the property or the property owner. They come in many varieties. Liens may be created voluntarily or by operation of law. A **specific lien** is a lien on one specific property such as a mortgage or city tax lien. A **general lien** is a lien on all of a person's property such as a judgment or IRS tax lien. A **mechanic's lien** is an example of an involuntary lien. In general, a mechanic's lien is available to anyone who provides material or labor for an improvement to real estate if they have not been paid for their services or materials.

Water Rights

Water rights are defined by state law and depend on the water source and use.

Riparian rights—On a navigable body of water, the property owner's boundary will extend to the water's edge or the accretion line of the water. On a non-navigable body of water, the property owner's boundary will extend to the center of the body of water.

Littoral rights—the rights of a landowner whose property borders on a non-flowing body of water, such as a lake, ocean, or other body of still water

Accretion—the gradual addition of land resulting from the natural deposit of soil by streams, lakes, or rivers

Avulsion—the sudden loss of land when a stream or other body of water suddenly changes its course

Erosion—the gradual loss of land by wind, water, and other natural processes

Reliction—the gradual adding of land due to the withdrawal of water

Alluvion—the soil carried by a moving body of water that is deposited on someone's land

Accession—acquiring ownership of land due to the deposit of soil by natural forces (wind or water)

▶ Condominiums/Cooperatives/Time Sharing Leases and Options

Condominiums

In Massachusetts, a condominium is created under the provisions of **Massachusetts General Laws** (MGL), Chapter 183A, that permit a multi-unit building to be divided into separate units that can be owned by an individual fee simple estate.

The condominium is created by a master deed, which identifies the property, each unit, and the percentage ownership that the individual owns in the land and the **common areas** of the structures. The master deed is recorded at the appropriate registry of deeds. A **unit deed** is recorded for each sale of an individual unit. Each unit owner agrees to be bound by the **bylaws** and rules and regulations of the condominium. The **bylaws** (**Declaration of Trust**) establish the condominium association and define its legal authority. It defines the role of the **trustees** and their authority. It is also recorded.

Condominium fees are determined by the annual operating **budget** of the condominium. Normally, fees are due monthly and are based on the unit's percentage of ownership.

Some of the **common areas** are for the use of all of the unit owners (for example, the foundation, elevator, pool), while some of the common areas will be defined as limited common elements and will be designated for the exclusive use of a specific unit, such as a balcony.

An advantage of condominium ownership over cooperative ownership is that a default in payment of taxes, mortgage payment, or monthly assessment affects only the specific unit. Each unit is defined as a separate parcel of real estate and is owned fee simple.

If a unit owner fails to pay their monthly condominium fee, the association has the right under the **Condo Super Lien Bill** (Chapter 400 of M.G.L. 183A) to impose a "priority" lien (a lien that would take precedence over the first mortgage holder).

In order to transfer a condominium unit to another owner in Massachusetts, the current owner must procure a certificate (known as a **6(d) certificate**) from the association, which states that all of the condominium fees are paid through the end of the current month. The current owner also needs to procure an **insurance certificate** showing that the new owner (and their mortgage holder) will be covered under the condominium master insurance policy.

Cooperatives

Cooperatives are apartments owned by a corporation that holds titles to the entire cooperative property, holds a blanket mortgage on the entire property, and is responsible for the *ad valorem* taxes for the entire property. The cooperative is taxed as one entity.

Each purchaser of an apartment unit is a stockholder in the corporation and receives a **stock certificate** in the corporation. The purchaser obtains the right to occupy through a **proprietary unit lease** for the life of the corporation. Each block of stock is tied to a specific right to occupy and carries a lease payment financial obligation that represents a *pro rata* share of the total cost of the operations expense and mortgage payments on the building.

A disadvantage of cooperative ownership over condominium ownership is that default of the monthly payment by a shareholder affects the entire cooperative and the other shareholders must make up the deficiency.

Time Sharing

Time shares are when multiple owners own a proportional interest in a single condominium unit with the exclusive right to use and occupy the unit for a specified period of time each year. The individual owners pay common expense, maintenance costs, and management fees based on the ratio between the ownership period and the total number of ownership periods available in the property. This type of ownership can be either a fee simple or leasehold interest. Time share owners can participate in an **exchange program** (either in-house for affiliated resorts or external) and exchange their time share for another location.

Leases

Freehold versus Non-Freehold

Estates in real property are **freehold** (an ownership interest in the property) or **non-freehold** (a rental interest in the property).

A **non-freehold** estate gives the holder of the estate a right to occupy the property until the end of the lease when the right will revert to the fee simple holder. The **lessor** permits the **lessee** to use the property for the period and under the **terms** specified in the **lease**. **Demise** is another legal term meaning to lease.

Types of Tenancy

TYPE	CHARACTERISTIC	EXAMPLE
Estate/Tenancy for Years	a lease with a definite termination date	1-year residential apartment lease
Tenancy for Period to Period	a lease with an automatic renewal option	90-day house lease that will renew for another 90 days unless proper notice is given by either party
Tenancy at Will	a lease without a termination date. It terminates when proper notice is given by either party.	A residential apartment lease that continues indefinitely until either party gives property notice (normally 30 days)
Tenancy at Sufferance	also called holdover tenant. The tenant remains in possession of the property after the termination of a lease. If the lessor accepts rent from the holdover tenant, a tenancy at will is created; otherwise the tenant at sufferance may be evicted.	A residential apartment lease has ended, but the tenant has not vacated the property.

Common Leases

Leases must be signed by the landlord and the tenant but need not be recorded to be enforceable. An individual who wishes to notify the public of a leasehold interest may record a **memorandum of lease**.

A lease must include a sufficient property description. A legal description as used in a deed is appropriate, although in certain residential leases a street address and apartment number are sufficient.

There are several kinds of leases:

- A **gross lease** specifies that the landlord pay all expenses: property taxes, insurance, and maintenance. This kind of lease is often used for apartments and other residential properties.
- A **net lease** specifies that the tenant pay certain expenses. The most common arrangement requires the tenant to pay property taxes, insurance, and maintenance. This is called a **net, net, net** or **triple net** lease.
- A **percentage lease** requires the tenant to pay a percentage of gross sales as rent in addition to a base rental amount specified in the lease. Percentage leases are often used in shopping centers.
- A **graduated lease** calls for periodic, stated changes in rent during the term of the lease.
- A **ninety-nine year lease** is a long-term land lease typically used for commercial development when the lessee prefers to spend their money on capital improvements or the owner does not want to sell (often used by fast food restaurants).

When a lease is **assigned**, the original lessee transfers the remaining interest in a lease to a new party. With a **sublet**, only a portion of the lease is transferred. In both instances, the original lessee remains responsible. With **novation**, a new lease is substituted for the original lease, removing responsibility from the original lessee. Some leases expressly prohibit the lessee's interest to be transferred.

When a property sells and there are existing leases, the **leases are binding** on the new owner.

Obligation of Parties

The lessor (property owner or landlord) is obligated to provide:

- **utility services** (although the lessee may be required to pay for these services under the terms of the lease)
- a property that is **fit for habitation**
- **free of sanitary and building code violations**

The lessor of residential property will not be allowed to interfere with the tenant's **quiet enjoyment** of the leased property. This means that the lessor must recognize the tenant's right of possession of the property.

If the unit becomes unfit for habitation or the lessor interferes with the tenant's quiet enjoyment of the property, the lessee may vacate the apartment by **constructive eviction**.

The lessee is obligated to **avoid waste**, which means that they will use the property in the proper manner. The lessee is also obligated to:

- keep the leased property clean and dispose of trash in a sanitary manner
- use fixtures and appliances in a safe and sanitary manner, and in the rooms designated for their use
- not damage, deface, or otherwise destroy the property, or permit anyone else to do so

If a lessor takes a **security deposit**, they must hold the money in a separate, interest-bearing account. If the lessee lives in the apartment for one year or more, they are entitled to 5% interest (or the actual interest paid by the bank, whichever is less) on the security deposit.

Options

An **option** is a unilateral contract. An option to purchase enables a purchaser to purchase a property at a set price within a given time frame. An option may also be used with a lease. To create a valid option, the property owner must be paid some cash (valuable consideration), the option must be in writing, and time is of the essence. Options may be **assigned** without the consent of the optionor.

A **right of first refusal** gives the optionee the right to match another offer or rescind their option.

Property Management

The range of services that the property manager can perform for the landlord (property owner) includes marketing, leasing, maintenance, bill payment, preparing reports on monthly income and operating expenses, and rent collection.

▶ Contracts/Deeds

Real Estate Contracts

A **listing** is a hiring contract between a real estate brokerage and the owner of a property for the sale of a specific property, spelling out the terms and consideration due.

In a real estate sale, the Commonwealth of Massachusetts uses two different contracts to spell out the terms of the agreement between the buyer and seller. The first is called an **Offer to Purchase**. The offer is normally a fill-in-the-blank form in which the buyer spells out the price and terms he or she is willing to pay for the property. The offer normally includes contingencies for a home inspection and mortgage financing. The second contract is called the **Purchase and Sale Agreement** (P & S). This agreement is normally signed after the buyer has completed their home inspection. The Purchase and Sale takes the basic terms of the agreement from the Offer to Purchase and spells out each party's responsibilities more thoroughly. Although both are legally binding documents, the Purchase and Sale is a more explicit contract.

A **lease** is a contract for the rental (possession) of property. The lessor permits the lessee to use the property for the period and under the terms specified in the lease.

A **deed** conveys title to real property. It must be in writing, executed, and delivered to transfer ownership of property.

The **mortgage note** is a primary financing instrument. The borrower agrees to pay the loan off according to a schedule of payments at a certain interest rate over a specified period of time (an IOU).

The **mortgage deed** is a pledge of property to secure the repayment of a debt (collateral). If the debt is not repaid as agreed between the lender and borrower, the lender can force the sale of the pledged property and apply the proceeds toward repayment of the debt.

A **bilateral contract** is one in which both parties exchange promises to do or refrain from doing something. A real estate sales contract is bilateral because both sides have an obligation to perform—the turning over of title to the property in exchange for money or other considerations.

A **unilateral contract** is one in which one party makes a promise and the other party does not promise, but can make the contract a binding agreement by taking some action.

An **option** is a unilateral contract. An option to purchase enables a purchaser to purchase a property at a set price within a given time frame. To create a valid option, the property owner must be paid some cash (valuable consideration), the option must be in writing, and time is of the essence.

A contract is **executory** when it has not yet been fully performed.

A contract is **executed** when all contract terms have been met and the transaction is completed.

Essential Elements of Contracts

A contract is a legally enforceable agreement between two parties to do something (**performance**) or to refrain from certain acts (**forbearance**). A contract must:

- have **offer** and **acceptance** (mutual assent)
- include **consideration** (does not need to be money)
- have a **lawful objective**
- involve **legally competent parties**
- be in writing as required by the **Statute of Frauds** (One notable exception is a lease for one year or less.)
- be signed by the parties to the agreement signifying their **consent** to the contract

If a notary witnesses the parties' signatures, the notary certifies that neither party is acting under duress and is signing the contract of their own free act.

Termination of an Offer

The offer to purchase can be terminated by one of the following:

- death of either party
- expiration of the time frame listed in the offer
- revocation by the offeror before receiving notice of acceptance by offeree
- bankruptcy of either party
- condemnation or destruction of the property
- outright rejection or a counteroffer by the offeree (a counteroffer constitutes a rejection of the previous offer)

Valid/Void/Voidable Contracts

A contract can be construed by the courts to be valid, void, or voidable.

A **valid** contract meets all the requirements of law. It is binding upon its parties and legally enforceable in a court of law.

A **void** contract has no legal effect and, in fact, is not a contract at all. Even though the parties may have intended to enter into a contract, no legal rights are created and no party is bound. The word *void* means the absence of something. An example of a void contract is a contract to commit a crime.

A **voidable** contract binds one party but not the other. For example, when one party is guilty of fraud, the other party may void the contract. But if the offended party wishes to fulfill the contract, then the party who committed fraud is still bound to the terms of the contract. A contract with a minor is voidable at the option of the minor party.

Purchase and Sale Agreement

The Purchase and Sale Agreement includes the following:

- **names** of all parties to the transaction (seller is **vendor**, buyer is **vendee**)
- **description of the land**
- **sales price** (consideration)
- amount of buyer's earnest money **deposit** which will be held in an escrow account
- **date** of the contract
- **signatures** of the buyer(s) and seller(s)

The **Massachusetts Statute of Frauds** requires that a Purchase and Sale Agreement must be in writing. (Most contracts dealing with real estate must be in writing. An exception is a lease that will terminate one year or less from the date of the agreement. Even then, it is in the best interests of both landlord and tenant to have a written agreement.)

Once a contract to purchase has been signed by both parties, the buyer has **equitable title** in the property (interest in real property, but the transaction is not yet complete). **Legal title** is title that is fully vested in the owner as evidenced by a deed, will, or court document. Legal title to land and its appurtenances encompasses the entire bundle of rights that an owner possesses.

Most Purchase and Sale Agreements allow the buyer the **right to assign** the contract to another party. If the contract is assigned, the original buyer is not relieved of their obligations if the assignee does not fulfill the responsibilities under the contract.

Breach of Contract

When one party fails to perform as required by the contract, a breach of contract or default has occurred. The wronged or innocent party has the following possible remedies:

- sue for money **damages**—For example, if a seller cannot perform, but the buyer has already spent a large amount of money on inspections, appraisals, and so on, the buyer could sue to recover the money spent.
- sue for **specific performance**—Specific performance means fulfilling the terms of the contract.
- accept liquidated money damages—This remedy, available only to the seller, means **retaining the earnest money deposit.**
- mutually **rescind** the contract—Sometimes both parties are better off just walking away from the contract and canceling the agreement.

Deeds

A deed is a written document that conveys property from the **grantor** (owner) to the **grantee**. A deed does not need to be recorded at the **county registry of deeds** (the place where the public records of the county in which the property is located are stored) in order to be valid. Recording a deed provides **constructive notice** (assumed or publicly available notice) of the conveyance. Recorded deeds are organized in the registry of deeds according to the **book** and **page** reference number where it was recorded.

There are many different types of deeds:

- A general **warranty deed** (not used in Massachusetts) carries the grantor's **express** or **implied assurances** (called **warranties** or **covenants**) regarding the validity of the title.
- A **special warranty deed** (not used in Massachusetts) carries the grantor's assurances only as to the state of the title after the grantor acquired ownership.
- A **quitclaim deed** (used in Massachusetts) transfers whatever interest the grantor may own but does not warrant that the grantor actually has any interest in the described property.

Elements of a Deed

To be valid, a deed must have the following:

- **identification of all parties** (sometimes deeds will include the terms *et al* meaning "and others" and *et ux* meaning "and wife")
- **granting clause**—the appropriate words to transfer the property, such as "I hereby grant and convey"
- **consideration** (money or something of value)
- **explanation of the rights transferred**
- **legal description** of the property (metes and bounds, lot and block, government survey will be discussed in detail on page 63)
- **proper execution**—the deed must be signed by the grantor, sealed, and delivered to the grantee to be valid
- If a deed is going to be recorded at the registry of deeds, the deed must also be **acknowledged** (grantor states it is their free act and deed) and **notarized**.

Torrens System

The **Torrens System** (**Land Court**) is a system of registering land. With registered land, the title has been searched by the Land Court. Although most land in Massachusetts is recorded, some is registered. When purchasing registered land, instead of a deed, the grantee is given a numbered **certificate of title**.

Legal Descriptions of Property

In order to convey real property, the deed must include an unmistakable description of the property. To satisfy the requirement for legal description in the deed, one of the following methods may be used:

- **The metes and bounds system** is one of the oldest methods of land measurement and description used in this country. The **bounds** (boundary lines) of property are measured from a specified point of beginning along measurements called **metes**, with each change of direction marked by a compass angle. **Markers** denote each turning point; in modern description, **natural monuments** (the old oak tree) have been replaced by **benchmarks** (metal pins). The description ends with the return to the **point of beginning** (POB).
- **The lot and block system** uses parcel numbers noted on a subdivision map (**plat map**). The plat is divided into blocks by streets. The blocks are then separated into lots.
- **The government survey system** (rectangular survey system) was developed to have a more uniform method of delineating property boundaries. Property is identified by reference to the intersection of a **meridian (principal meridian)** running north-south and a baseline running east-west. Land is separated into rectangles called **townships** of six miles squared (six miles to a side, or 36 square miles). Townships are counted in **tiers** north or south of a baseline and ranges east or west of a meridian. A township is divided into 36 sections. A **section** is one mile squared (one square mile) and contains 640 acres. An **acre** contains 43,560 square feet.

Massachusetts Tax Stamps

The Commonwealth of Massachusetts charges **tax stamps** whenever real property changes hands. The amount of the tax stamps are based on the sales price of the property. Currently, tax stamps are $4.56 per $1,000.00 and are an expense paid by the seller at closing.

Title Search

A title search will reveal the chain of title, the history of conveyances, and encumbrances that can be found in the public records. The title search begins with the name of the present owner and the instrument that establishes title in that owner as the grantee. Working back through what is called the **grantee index**, the name of the grantor to the present owner is found on the deed in which that owner is the grantee. In this way, the person examining the title can go back to the first recorded document of the property. The **chain of title** is an account of the successive owners of the property. An **abstract of title** is a certified summary of the history of the recorded documents affecting the title.

▶ Financing/Mortgages

Real Estate Cycle

Although there are many steps to the real estate cycle, typically they include:

1. listing the real property
2. qualifying the buyer
3. showing the buyer properties
4. Offer/Purchase and Sale Agreement—the contracts between the buyer and seller
5. financing—most Offer/Purchase and Sale Agreements have a financing contingency
6. pass papers (also called a closing when title changes hands)

Financing Procedure

The first step to obtaining financing is submitting a **mortgage application**.

Bank Approval Steps

The lender wants to make sure that the borrower is a good credit risk. To ensure this, they look at several items:

- the property—the bank will send an appraiser to evaluate the property and ensure that the sales price is in line with other comparable properties that have recently sold nearby
- the borrower's ability to pay
- a check of the borrower's credit

The standard Purchase and Sale Agreement includes a **financing clause**. Since the majority of buyers of property in Massachusetts need financing in order to purchase real property, the standard contract includes a contingency allowing the buyer a specific period of time to receive a mortgage commitment. If the buyer does not receive their commitment by the deadline, they can withdraw from the transaction and receive their earnest money deposit back.

Types of Lending Institutions

There are many sources of financing available to the buyer of real property. The borrower can apply to a **savings and loan association**, a **commercial bank**, a **mutual savings bank** (owned by their depositors), a **cooperative bank**, a **credit union**, a **mortgage company** (which is different from a mortgage broker who does not actually loan money but brings borrowers and lenders together), a **life insurance company**, or a **private lender**.

Money as a Commodity

The discount rate is the interest rate the Federal Reserve Bank charges when it makes a loan to another financial institution. The **prime rate** is the interest rate charged by banks to their preferred borrowers. Many home equity loans are based on the prime rate published by the Federal Reserve Bank. **Mortgage rates** are market-driven for long-term loans and do not necessarily rise or fall with changes in either the short-term discount rate or prime rate.

Some loans include **origination points** or **discount points**. Each point is 1% of the amount borrowed, so one point on a $100,000 loan would be $1,000. **Origination points** are costs of the loan and are the usual way for mortgage brokers to be paid. When a borrower pays **discount points**, they are prepaying the lending institution money at the beginning of the loan to receive a lower interest rate over the life of the loan. This can also be called a **buydown** since the borrower is "buying down" the interest rate of the loan.

Types of Mortgages

With a **direct reduction** mortgage, a portion of the principal is paid off with each mortgage payment.

A **construction loan** is short-term financing used by a developer or builder. The funds are released based on a predetermined schedule as phases of the construction are completed. Upon completion, the developer must pay off the construction loan and secure long-term financing.

A **blanket mortgage** is used by a developer or contractor to purchase more than one lot of land. A defining feature of the blanket mortgage is a **release clause**, which lets the developer sell off a parcel of the land while retaining the blanket mortgage on the rest of the property.

A **package mortgage** uses not only real estate for collateral but also personal property.

A **demand mortgage** gives the lender the right to demand payment at any time.

With a **purchase money mortgage** the seller holds the financing for the borrower (seller financing).

A **junior** or **second mortgage** is an additional loan on top of the borrower's primary financing. It is a **junior** lien and, in the case of a default by the borrower, will not be paid unless the primary loan is covered in full.

An **open-end mortgage** allows the mortgagor to borrow additional funds from the lender, up to a specified amount, without rewriting the mortgage.

A **wraparound mortgage** combines a new loan wrapped around an existing mortgage. The borrower makes payment on both mortgages to the wraparound mortgagee who then forwards the payments on the first mortgage to the first mortgagee.

With a **variable-rate mortgage** (**adjustable-rate mortgage**), the interest rate will vary over the life of the loan. The rate is adjusted at specified intervals throughout the loan based on some predetermined indicator, such as Treasury Bill rates (known as the **index**). The **margin** is a predetermined amount added to the index rate to determine the interest rate. For the borrower's protection, there is a **cap**, or limit, on the amount the rate can be increased for each specified rate change period and a cap for how high the rate can go to over the life of the loan.

A **balloon loan** usually charges a lower interest rate than a regular fixed-rate loan. The loan will be structured as an amortized loan with a term of 30 years, but the loan will balloon after a certain period. That is, the loan becomes due and payable before the end of the amortization term. The loan may balloon in five, seven, or ten years, or however long the lender stipulates. At the end of the balloon period, the borrower must repay the loan and secure other financing.

In a **shared equity** loan, the lender give the borrower a lower interest rate in exchange for a percentage of the equity of the property.

Negative amortization occurs when an adjustable rate goes up, but the monthly payment stays the same. The monthly payment is no longer large enough to cover both the interest and the amount of principal due. The amount of the shortfall is added to the remaining principal balance.

An **equity loan** is a second mortgage used to access the equity (the difference between the market value of the property and what is owed) in a property.

Conventional loans are those made without any form of government-backed insurance or guarantee. The lender looks to the borrower and the **security** (the property) for assurance that the loan will be repaid by the borrower (or by forced sale of the property).

VA-guaranteed loans carry the assurance of the **Department of Veteran Affairs** (**VA**) (established in 1944) that the lender will be protected in the event of default by the borrower. (Note that the VA is not lending the money itself, but guaranteeing it.) Following are some specifics:

- The **certificate of eligibility** is the VA's statement that the veteran is eligible for the loan-guarantee program.
- The property must be appraised by a VA-approved appraiser and the VA will issue a **certificate of reasonable value** (**CRV**) based on that estimate.
- VA loans are for 1- to 4-family owner-occupied homes.
- The **funding fee** depends on the veteran's category and the amount of the down payment, which can range from zero (**100% financing**) to 10% or more.
- No prepayment penalty is allowed.
- The property may be sold and the **VA loan assumed** (even by a non-veteran), but the veteran must receive a written release of liability from the VA to be relived of personal obligation in the event of a future foreclosure and deficiency.
- The veteran's entitlement can be reused on a subsequent home purchase, although the amount of entitlement will be reduced if there has been an assumption of a prior loan guarantee.

The **Federal Housing Administration** (**FHA**), established in 1934, insures loans for any qualified buyer. It is administered through the **U.S. Department of Housing and Urban Development** (**HUD**). FHA-insured loans protect the lender in the event the borrower defaults on the mortgage. (Note that the FHA does not lend money itself, it insures the lender.) Following are some specifics:

- The FHA sets maximum loan amounts that it will lend depending on the state and county in which the property is located.
- The borrower makes a one-time insurance payment at the time of the closing of the sale.
- The borrower and the property must meet FHA guidelines.
- No prepayment penalty is allowed.
- FHA loans are for 1- to 4-family owner-occupied homes.
- An FHA loan may be assumed.
- Because of the FHA insurance, a lower-than-usual down payment may be possible.

Borrowers who make a down payment of less than 20% of the sales price may be required to purchase **private mortgage insurance** (**PMI**). The insurance **premium** usually is a monthly charge added to the loan payment. It can be eliminated (with the lender's approval) when the borrower's equity in the home is at least 20% of the home's value.

Depending on the loan, a buyer may be able to take over the seller's existing mortgage. If the buyer assumes the loan, then both the new owner and the seller are both responsible in the event of a deficiency after a foreclosure. If the buyer takes the loan **"subject to,"** then only the seller is responsible if there is a deficiency after a foreclosure.

Secondary Mortgage Market

The **primary market** sells loans directly to borrowers, while the **secondary market** sells the loans made in the primary market to investors.

The major purchasers of home loans are:

- The **Federal National Mortgage Association** (**Fannie Mae** or **FNMA**) is the largest purchaser of all types of home loans. The FNMA was originally a government agency, and then was converted to entirely private ownership and control.
- The **Federal Home Loan Mortgage Corporation** (**FHLMC** or **Freddie Mac**) is a federally chartered private corporation that primarily purchases conventional loans.
- The **Government National Mortgage Association** (**GNMA** or **Ginnie Mae**) is a government corporation, which is a division of HUD and is a major purchaser of government-backed (FHA and VA) mortgage loans.

These entities buy so many loans that they virtually control how the loan origination or primary market operates. A loan that meets Fannie Mae's guidelines is called a **conforming loan**. Most conventional loans will use uniform instruments for:

- loan applications
- appraisal reporting forms
- closing statements

Truth-in-Lending Law (Regulation Z)

The **Truth-in-Lending Act** (**TILA**), enacted by Congress in 1968, is part of the Consumer Protection Act. TILA is commonly referred to as **Regulation Z**. The law applies to creditors (lenders) involved in at least one of the following:

- more than 25 consumer credit transactions per year
- more than five transactions per year with a dwelling used as security
- credit is offered to consumers

- credit is offered on a regular basis
- the credit is subject to a finance charge
- the arrangement requires more than four installments
- the credit is primarily for personal, family, or household purposes

If credit is extended to a business, or for a commercial or an agricultural purpose, Regulation Z does not apply. The required truth-in-lending disclosures must be made in a **disclosure statement** that highlights certain information by using a box, boldface type, a different type style, or a different background color. The disclosure statement must be presented to the borrower within **three business days** of making the loan application; the day the application is completed by the borrower is not counted. Information to be disclosed includes (in addition to other items) the:

- amount financed
- finance charge
- annual percentage rate (**APR**)
- total amount that will be paid over the life of the loan
- prepayment penalties
- late-payment charges

When a consumer is refinancing a loan that qualifies under the Truth-in-Lending Act, which is enforced through Regulation Z as a consumer credit transaction, the borrower has three business days to **rescind** (or cancel) the mortgage (**right of rescission**).

Advertisements for consumer loans covered under Regulation Z must give the APR and provide other payment terms and conditions if specific credit terms are used. Remember, this is a disclosure law so consumers have a summary of the financial offer and can compare products available from other providers in the marketplace.

Mortgage Note and Mortgage Deed

A **mortgage deed** is a pledge of property made by a mortgagor (the borrower) to pledge collateral (the property) that may be sold at auction (foreclosure) when the borrower defaults and fails to fulfill the promises made in the mortgage instrument. The mortgage (pledge of the collateral) is given for the benefit of the mortgagee (the lender). Caution! Remember that in real estate terminology words ending in –*or* refer to the person giving something (the borrower gives the pledge) and the words ending in *ee* refer to the person receiving something (the lender receives the benefit of the pledge of the collateral). Forget about the fact that the lender gives the money, it is the pledge of collateral that is important in this discussion.

When a lender makes a loan, the borrower signs a **mortgage note** that promises to repay the loan and defines the terms of the repayment.

The **mortgage deed** pledges the property as collateral. When the loan has been paid in full, the **defeasance clause** in the mortgage deed requires the lender (mortgagee) to issue a **discharge** (showing the release of the debt) that should be recorded to remove the encumbrance affecting the title to the property.

A **due-on-sale** clause (also known as **alienation** or **assumption** clause) means that the loan must be paid off in full when the property is sold and the loan can not be assumed by another party.

A **subordination clause** states that the loan will be junior (subordinated) to another lien in the future.

A defaulting borrower faces penalties of varying severity. Late charges will be incurred if the borrower is late in making a payment. If the borrower remains in default, the lender may invoke an acceleration clause. An **acceleration clause** gives the lender the right to collect the balance of the loan immediately. Finally, if the debt remains unpaid, the **power of sale** clause in the mortgage deed allows the process of foreclosure to begin.

The mortgage deed is different from the **grantor/grantee deed**, which is the deed that transfers actual ownership (bundle of rights) from the grantor (seller) to the grantee (buyer).

Real Estate Settlement and Procedures Act (RESPA)

The **Real Estate Settlement Procedures Act** (**RESPA**), enacted by Congress in 1974, is the federal law that requires disclosures by lenders, mortgage brokers, and closing agents in federally related transactions involving the sale or transfer of a dwelling of one to four units. (Second mortgages, seller financing, also known as purchase money mortgages and construction loans are not subject to RESPA requirements.) The law requires:

- The lender or mortgage broker must provide the borrower with a copy of the special information booklet prepared by HUD within three business days of the loan application.
- The lender or mortgage broker must provide the borrower with a **good-faith estimate of closing costs**.
- A **Uniform Settlement Statement** (form **HUD-1**) must be made available to the borrower and seller at least one day prior to closing. The borrower and the seller will receive a copy of the form after the closing is completed.
- Fees, kickbacks, or other such payments to persons who do not actually provide loan services are strictly prohibited.
- Any affiliated business arrangement with an individual or entity offering settlement services must be disclosed.

Chapter 112: Section 87PP of the general laws of Massachusetts (see www.mass.gov/legis/laws/mgl/ 112-87pp.htm) defines a " 'Real estate broker,' hereinafter referred to as broker, as any person who for another person and for a fee, commission or other valuable consideration, or with the intention or in the expectation or upon the promise of receiving or collecting a fee, commission, or other valuable consideration, does any of the following: sells, exchanges, purchases, rents, or leases, or negotiates, or offers, attempts or agrees to negotiate the sale, exchange, purchase, rental, or leasing of any real estate, or lists or offers, attempts or agrees to list any real estate, or buys or offers to buy, sells or offers to sell or otherwise deals in options on real estate, or advertises or holds himself out as engaged in the business of selling, exchanging, purchasing, renting, or leasing real estate, or assists or directs in the procuring of prospects or the negotiation or completion of any agreement or transaction, which results or is intended to result in the sale, exchange, purchase, leasing, or renting of any real estate."

► Brokerage

Law of Agency

An **agent** is a person who represents the interest of another person or party (called the **principal**) in dealings with third persons. An agent acts as the fiduciary to their client.

In **single agency**, an agent is representing either the buyer or the seller. In **dual agency**, an agent is representing both the buyer and the seller. In Massachusetts, a dual agent is always required to have informed, written consent of both parties before acting as a dual agent. A dual agent cannot give both parties all of the fiduciary duties.

On July 1, 2005, Massachusetts enacted a new statute and regulation regarding agency. At the first personal meeting to discuss a specific property, a real estate agent must give a prospective buyer or seller the **Massachusetts Mandatory Licensee-Consumer Relationship Disclosure** form. This form discloses both the relationship of the agent with the prospective buyer or seller and the relationship of the buyer or seller with the other licensees in the agent's office.

There are two agency models for real estate companies:

- all agents in the firm have the same relationship with the consumer (**seller** or **buyer agency**, not **designated agency**)
- **designated agency**—only the real estate agent listed on the disclosure form (**designated seller** or **buyer agent**) represents the client and other agents affiliated with the real estate company do not represent that client and may represent another party in the real estate transaction

The Massachusetts Mandatory Licensee-Consumer Relationship Disclosure form also discloses the agent's relationship with the prospective buyer or seller. The relationship options are:

An agent's fiduciary duties to their client or principal (remember it as OLD CAR) are:

- **O**bedience
- **L**oyalty
- **D**isclosure (of material facts concerning the transaction)
- **C**onfidentiality
- **A**ccountability (of funds)
- **R**easonable care

- **Seller's agent**—an agent who works for the best interest of the seller (**client**) and owes the seller fiduciary duties. The majority of agents who list property work with the seller as the seller's agent. A seller's agent can work with a buyer, but as a **customer**, not a client. The buyer must understand that the agent owes their fiduciary duties to the seller.
- **Buyer's agent**—an agent who works for the best interest of the buyer and owes the buyer fiduciary duties.
- **Facilitator** (**non-agent**)—no agency relationship exists with either party in the transaction. The facilitator's job is to bring both parties together. A facilitator has a duty to present all real property honestly and accurately, disclosing known material defects and accounting for funds. The facilitator does not have fiduciary duties.
- **Designated seller's and buyer's agent**—a designated agent represents their client (either buyer or seller) and owes fiduciary duties to their client. With the client's permission, the agent can be **designated** by another agent (the appointing agent, normally the broker or office manager) to be the office's sole representative for that particular client. All other agents affiliated with the real estate company do not represent that client. If the appointing agent designates another agent in the office to represent the other party to the transaction, the appointing agent becomes a **dual agent** and must remain impartial, while the two designated agents (the **designated seller's** and **designated buyer's** agent) each represent their respective clients fully and owe their respective clients fiduciary duties. In Massachusetts, in order to practice designated agency, an agent must have the informed, written consent of their client.
- **Dual agent**—an agent who represents both the buyer and the seller. In Massachusetts, a dual agent is always required to have informed, written consent of both parties before acting as a dual agent. A dual agent cannot give both parties all of the fiduciary duties. **Undisclosed dual agency** is prohibited.

Creation of Agency

The listing agreement is the contract that establishes the **agency** relationship between an agent and their principal. These contracts can either be a listing agreement for the right to sell a property, or a buyer agency agreement for the right to help a buyer find a property. A written or oral listing agreement will establish an **express agency** (a hiring). **Implied agency** can be inferred by the conduct of the principal and agent (the parties act as if there had been an actual hiring). **Apparent authority** may establish an agency relationship. This occurs when a principal gives a third party reason to believe that another person is the principal's agent, even though that person is unaware of the appointment. If the third party accepts the principal's representation as true, the principal may have established ostensible authority and therefore may be bound by the acts of his agent. This may happen, for example, when a seller gives the keys for a property to an agent. Other agents may reasonably rely upon the first agent's statement that authority exists for the first agent to show the property.

Listing agreements in Massachusetts do not have to be in writing; however, it is a good business practice (especially if the agent wants to be paid).

Types of Listings

There are many types of listings:

- An **open listing** is an agreement that a commission will be paid to the listing broker only if they are the procuring cause of the sale. A seller may enter into an open listing with an unlimited number of brokers. If the property is sold by another broker or by the sellers themselves, the listing broker is not entitled to a commission.
- An **exclusive agency listing** means that only one listing broker represents the seller. If the property sells through the efforts of the broker or through cooperation with MLS, the listing broker receives a commission. However, the seller retains the right to sell the property on their own without paying a commission.
- An **exclusive right to sell listing** provides the greatest protection to the listing broker, who will be paid a commission no matter who sells the property.
- A **net listing** offers the property owner a guaranteed sales price, with the listing broker taking any part of the purchase price over that amount. Net listings are illegal in Massachusetts.
- The **multiple listing service** (**MLS**) is a system in which all members can share information regarding the properties they have for sale.

Duties of an Agent

The real estate listing agent owes the property owner (**principal**) the duties of a **fiduciary** if they are acting as a seller's agent. The agent must act in the owner's best interest. The buyer's agent owes the same responsibilities to the buyer.

When agents have a **personal interest in a property** and are selling or buying property for themselves, they must disclose that they are licensed real estate agents to the other party.

A broker must have a separate escrow bank account where all deposits for pending sales are kept in safekeeping. These funds must be kept separate from the broker's personal or business account. Any **commingling** of funds is prohibited.

Many properties sell through the cooperation offered in MLS. The agent working with the buyer is called a **co-broke**.

Subagency is normally found in a co-broke situation when a seller's agent works with a buyer as a customer. A **subagent** owes fiduciary duties to the seller and can only offer the buyer customer level services (fairness and honesty). In Massachusetts, in order to practice subagency, the listing broker must obtain written permission from the seller. The written permission must include the following disclosure regarding **vicarious liability**: "Vicarious liability is the potential for a seller to be held liable for a misrepresentation or an act or omission of the subagent and that the seller authorizes the broker or salesperson to offer subagency in the signing of the notice."

Termination of Agency

An agency contract can be terminated by:

- **completion of the objective**—either the property is sold or the buyer-client has bought a house
- **expiration of the time limit** specified in the contract
- **mutual consent (rescission)**
- **revocation**—by either principal or agent. The breaching party may have to pay damages.
- **death of the principal or broker** (since the agency contract is between the broker-owner of the real estate company and the principal, the agency relationship is not affected by the death of the agent)
- **destruction of the property**
- **bankruptcy of either party**

Commissions

The best way to ensure that an agent will be paid for the work they perform is to make sure that they are always working under a contract, a listing agreement, or a buyer-agency representation agreement.

Commissions are negotiable and are set through an agreement of the parties. The Sherman Anti-trust Law prohibits price-fixing among real estate offices.

Sometimes there is a dispute over a commission if a buyer has worked with more than one agent. The commission will be paid to the broker who is found to be the **procuring cause** in producing a ready, willing, and able buyer. (Determining procuring cause can be a difficult task because it is not necessarily the agent who was the first to show the property or the agent who wrote the offer.)

In 1975, the *Tristram's Landing versus Wait* decision ruled that a broker has earned the commission when they have procured a ready, willing, and able buyer if the sale is not completed due to the wrongful act or interference of the seller.

Broker versus Salesperson

Two kinds of agency relationships are common in real estate practice:

- **General agency**—Real estate brokers typically have agents who act as their agents in working with their principals.
- **Special agency**—A principal to a transaction (the seller or buyer) secures the advice and assistance of a real estate broker and the broker's agents. Although normally the agent signs the agency contract with the buyer or seller, the contract is between the broker owner of the real estate company and the principal.

Only the broker-owner can sue a principal, not an agent. The only agent's recourse is through the broker-owner.

A **REALTOR®** is a member of the National Association of REALTORS® and are the only real estate agents authorized to use the REALTOR® registered trademark. REALTORS® agree to abide by the Association's Code of Ethics.

Commission Splits

Commissions are split into many pieces when a property is sold. When a listing office submits a listing to MLS, they include the amount of commission they will offer to a co-broke who procures a buyer who successfully completes the transaction. The amount of the **commission split** is determined by the listing office's office policy. Many offices split the commission equally with the co-broke.

The remaining commission is now split between the broker-owner and the agent. The way a broker-owner shares a commission with an agent varies among different offices. Some offices take a percentage of the commission to cover operating expenses, advertising, and administrative help. Other offices charge agents a set monthly desk fee to cover overhead and the agent retains most of the commission.

▶ Appraisal

Appraisal and Value

An **appraisal** is performed by a licensed, certified appraiser who gives an unbiased estimate of a property's **value** as of a certain time, based on supporting data. The **Uniform Standards of Professional Appraisal Practice** (**USPAP**) sets the minimum requirement for appraisals.

Market value is the most probable price that an informed buyer will be likely to pay and that an informed seller will be likely to accept in an arm's-length transaction, where neither party is acting under duress.

Establish Appraisal Purpose

Although real estate agents focus their attention on when a property owner wishes to sell, there are many other times when an owner wants to know the value of their property:

- **condemnation**—when the government takes private property by eminent domain, the owner must be paid fair market value for the property
- **assessed value**—determination for property tax purposes (the basis for taxation)
- **insurance purposes**—the maximum amount that an insurer would be willing to pay for an insured loss
- **estate settlement**—the value of the sum of a person's estate (real property and personal property) when they die
- **sales value for owner**—the price the property should bring in the open market
- **loan value**—the maximum loan that can be secured by the property
- **exchanges**—a transaction in which a property is traded for another property, rather than sold for money or other consideration

Elements of Value

An appraisal will specify the type of value sought. The elements that establish value can be remembered by the acronym **DUST**:

Demand for the type of property

Utility (desirable use) the property offers

Scarcity of properties available

Transferability of property to a new owner (lack of impediments to a sale)

Forces Affecting Value

Many forces can affect value:

- **social**—demographic and other trends that affect the demand for property
- **economic adjustments**—employment level, business start-ups, availability of credit, and other factors that influence the level of prosperity of a region
- **political/government regulations**—regulations that affect property use like zoning regulations, building codes, and environmental laws
- **physical**—changes caused by the elements, which can occur gradually or over a brief period of time

Economic Principles

Many principles of value underlie the appraisal process, including the following:

Supply and demand: as the number of properties available for sale goes up relative to the number of potential buyers, prices will fall. As the number of properties declines while the number of potential buyers remains the same or increases, prices will rise.

Change: forces to which all property is subject can either increase or decrease property values (these forces can be physical, political, economic, or social)

Substitution: the principle that the typical buyer will want to pay no more for a property than would be required to buy another, equivalent property

Highest and best use: the legally allowed property use that makes maximum physical use of a site and generates the highest income

Conformity: individual properties in a neighborhood tend to have a higher value when they are of similar architecture, design, age, and size

Progression: the benefit to a property of being located in an area of more desirable properties; a small, plain house on a street of mansions will benefit from proximity to them.

Regression: the detriment to a property of being located in a neighborhood of less desirable properties; a large, over-improved house on a street of small, plain houses will have a lower value than it would in a neighborhood of comparable houses.

Anticipation (of future betterments): value is the present worth of the expected future benefits to be derived from owning the property, operating it (if the property has a commercial aspect), and potential gains when it is sold

Assemblage (plottage): bringing a group of adjoining parcels under the same ownership, which may make them more valuable for a particular purpose, such as construction of a residential or commercial development

Law of decreasing returns: is in effect when property improvements no longer bring a corresponding increase in property value

Law of increasing returns: is in effect as long as property improvements bring a corresponding increase in property value

Contribution: the value of any component is measured by what it adds to the property as a whole. If an improvement is excessively expensive or excessively large for the surrounding area and land, it is called an overimprovement.

Competition: a potential for profit attracts competition to the market. When competition brings more sellers to the market, there is the potential for an oversupply of properties, resulting in lower prices. When competition brings more buyers to the market, there is the potential for a shortage of properties resulting in higher prices.

The Appraisal Process

Following are the steps in the appraisal process:

- *State the problem*—the nature of the appraisal assignment must be clearly understood. The assignment may be to find a market value of the subject property. If so, that should be stated.
- *Determine the kinds and sources of data necessary.*
  - What are the characteristics of the subject property?
  - What economic or other factors will play a role in determining property value?
  - What approach(es) will be most appropriate in this appraisal, and what kind of data will be necessary?
- *Determine the highest and best use of the site.*
- *Estimate the value of the site.*
- *Estimate the property's value by each of the appropriate approaches* (market data, cost, and/or income).
- *Reconcile the different values reached by the different approaches to estimate the property's most probable market value.* This process is called **reconciliation** or correlation.
- *Report the estimate of value to the client in writing.* There are several types of documents that may be prepared.
  - The **narrative appraisal report** provides a lengthy discussion of the factors considered in the appraisal and the reasons for the conclusion of value.
  - The **form report** is used most often for single-family residential appraisals. A **Uniform Residential Appraisal Report** (URAR) is required by various agencies and organizations.

Market Data Approach (Sales Comparison Approach)

If the property being appraised is a residential property, the most important determinant of value is the price that other similar properties have commanded in the open market. In using the market data approach, the appraiser will select **comparable properties** (**comps**) to compare to the property being appraised (subject property). An appraiser would prefer to have at least three comps for a market data appraisal and typically will only use sales within the last six months. The sales price of a comparable property is adjusted down to compensate for the market value of a desirable feature that is present in the comp but not the subject property. The sales price of a comp is adjusted up to allow for desirable features that are present in the subject property and not the comp.

Example: The house at 29 Milo Avenue is being appraised. Comparable A sold last month for $350,000. The comp has a detached garage and the subject property does not. The estimated value of the garage is $9,600, which is subtracted from the sales price of $350,000 to derive an adjusted sales price for the comp of $340,400. After analyzing the sales prices of three comps this way, and comparing the resulting adjusted figures, the appraiser estimates the value of the subject property at $340,000.

Land, whether or not it has any improvements (buildings), is often valued separately by using the market data approach.

Income Approach

If a property produces income in the form of rent and other **revenues**, its value is estimated by analyzing the amount and stability of the income it can produce. The income approach is used to value income-producing properties.

The formula for determining value by the income approach is

$$\text{Value} = \text{Net Operating Income} \div \text{Capitalization Rate}$$

Effective gross income is found by totaling income from all sources and subtracting an allowance for vacancy and collection losses.

Net operating income is found by subtracting **maintenance and operating expenses** from effective gross income. For appraisal purposes, operating expenses include variable expenses (such as salaries and utilities), fixed expenses (such as real estate taxes and insurance), and reserves for replacement (such as set-asides for a new roof and furnace), but not the costs of financing, income tax payments, depreciation deductions, and capital improvements.

The **capitalization rate** (**cap rate**) is the desired return on the investment. The cap rate is found by building its component parts. An investor expects to receive a profit on the capital invested, as well as to have the capital itself returned by the time the investment is unusable.

Example: Mary wants to purchase an apartment building that has a remaining economic life of 40 years. She wants 10% annually on her investment, as well as the return of the amount invested. The building's net operating income is $120,000 annually. This means that each year the investment will have to have a cap rate of 10% plus $2\frac{1}{2}$% (100% divided by 40 years), or $12\frac{1}{2}$%. If we divide the net income of $120,000 by the $12\frac{1}{2}$% cap rate, the value of the property to this investor can be estimated at $960,000.

A **gross rent multiplier** (GRM) based on monthly market rent typically is used in the appraisal of a rental house. To determine the gross rent multiplier an appraiser will determine the gross monthly rent of recently sold properties and then divide each property's sales price by the gross monthly rent.

Example: Building A produces monthly rent of $4,000 and sold recently for $400,000. Building B produces monthly rent of $3,200 and sold recently for $350,000. The GRM for Building A is $400,000 divided by $4,000 or 100. The GRM for Building B is $350,000 divided by $3,200 or 109.375. After analyzing several more properties, the appraiser concludes that a GRM of 100 is appropriate for the subject property. Applying that multiple to the subject property's monthly rent of $3,700, the appraiser reaches an estimate of value by this method of $370,000.

Cost Approach

When the property is not an income-producing property and it is difficult to find comparables, the cost approach to value is often used. This approach is most often used with unique properties and public service buildings (churches, a college campus, or a state capitol building).

The appraiser begins by estimating the replacement cost of the improvements. **Replacement cost** is the cost, at today's prices and using today's methods of construction, for an improvement having the same or equivalent usefulness as the subject property. Or, the appraiser may estimate the **reproduction cost**, the cost of creating an exact replica of the improvements. This would show the value of a new building. Since the subject property is not new, adjustments must be made for depreciation. There are three types of depreciation:

1. **Physical deterioration** is the effect of the elements and ordinary wear-and-tear. It is generally curable.
2. **Functional obsolescence** highlights features that are no longer considered desirable in design, manner of construction, or layout. A house with four bedrooms and only one bathroom suffers from functional obsolescence. It can be curable or incurable.
3. **Economic obsolescence** results from factors outside of the property over which the owner has no control such as economic, locational, or environmental influences. It is generally incurable.

The **value of the land** must be considered in determining value by the cost approach. The value of the land is established as though it were vacant, using the market data approach. While land value can decrease, land does not depreciate.

The formula for determining value using the cost approach is as follows:

Value = Replacement or Reproduction Cost − Accrued Depreciation + Land Value

Example: An appraiser has determined that the reproduction cost of a building is $500,000. There is $60,000 of accrued depreciation and the land is valued at $200,000. The market value would be determined by taking $500,000 (the replacement cost) and subtracting $60,000 (the accrued depreciation) and then adding $200,000 (the land value). The appraiser would estimate the value to be $640,000.

▶ Fair Housing/Consumer Protection

Basic Concepts

Federal and state fair housing laws were enacted to allow all people an equal opportunity to enjoy the benefits of owning real property.

A **protected class** is any group of people designated as such by the Department of Housing and Urban Development (HUD) in consideration of federal and state civil rights legislation. Protected classes currently include color, race, religion or creed, ancestry or national origin, gender, handicap, and familial status. It is prohibited to discriminate against someone in a protected class, perceived to be in a protected class, or because of their association with a protected class.

A **complainant** alleging a violation of fair housing laws may file a complaint with HUD or the office of the U.S. Attorney General. After receiving a complaint, **testers** may be sent out to confirm the validity of the complaint. When testers are used, one set of testers is matched to the same protected class as the complainant. Care is taken to ensure that the test is legitimate and not entrapment. The **respondent** in the complaint can be a property owner, real estate agent or agency, or management company.

Federal Civil Rights Act of 1866

The **Civil Rights Act of 1866** prohibits discrimination on the basis of race in the sale, lease, or other transfer of real or personal property. This act has no exceptions. It applies to individual home sellers as well as to real estate agencies.

Federal Fair Housing Act of 1968 (Title VIII)

The **Federal Fair Housing Act** (**Title VIII of the Civil Rights Act of 1968**) and its amendments broadened the prohibitions against discrimination in housing to include sex, race, color, religion, national origin, handicap (mental and physical), and familial status in connection with the sale or rental of housing or vacant land offered for residential construction or use. The law specifically prohibits the following discriminatory acts:

- refusing to sell to, rent to, or negotiate with any person who is a member of a protected class, or otherwise making a dwelling unavailable to such a person
- changing terms, conditions, or services for different individuals as a means of discrimination against a member of a protected class
- practicing discrimination through any statement or advertisement that restricts the sale or rental of residential property

- representing to any person, as a means of discrimination, that a dwelling is unavailable for sale or rental
- **blockbusting**—making a profit by inducing owners of housing to sell or rent by representing that persons of a protected class are moving into the neighborhood
- **redlining**—altering the terms or conditions of a home loan to any person, or otherwise denying such a loan as a means of discrimination
- denying persons membership or limiting their participation in any multiple listing service, real estate brokers' organization, or other facility related to the sale or rental of dwellings
- **steering**—the practice of directing home seekers to or away from particular neighborhoods based on protected class. Steering includes both efforts to exclude minorities from one area of a city and efforts to direct minorities to minority or changing areas.
- attributing an impact on value due to any of the prohibited practices listed above in an appraisal report
- making notations indicating discriminatory preferences
- coercing, intimidating, or interfering with any person in the exercise of their rights

Familial status includes prohibiting discriminations against children (those under 18), families with children (whether headed by a parent or guardian), persons who are in the process of obtaining custody of a child, and pregnant women.

The Fair Housing Act prohibits the following discriminations against a handicapped person:

- refusal to make reasonable accommodations in policies
- refusal to permit reasonable modifications of existing premises at the handicapped person's expense

After 1991, all new (or rehab) four-family homes or larger must be designed so the first floor units include handicapped accessibility. If upper floors are serviced by elevators, these units must have accessibility, too.

The 1968 Fair Housing Act covers only residential property. Any type of residential property is covered under the act if the sale is handled by a real estate agent (depending on the type of property, liability may be only for the broker), if discriminatory advertising is used, or if any written notice or statement indicates a discriminatory preference.

A single-family house is also covered under fair housing laws if one of the following is true:

- It is not privately owned (corporate).
- It is owned by a private individual who owns more than three houses (a dealer) or who, in any two-year period, sells more than one property.

A multi-family dwelling is covered if one of the following is true:

- It consists of five units or more.
- It consists of two to four units, and the owner does not reside in one of the units.

Title VIII does not cover:

- the sale or rental of a single-family home by a private individual who owns three or less properties as long as they sell without a broker, with no discriminatory advertising, and have not sold another house in two years
- the rental of rooms or units in owner-occupied multi-family dwellings of two to four units, as long as discriminatory advertising and the services of a real estate agent are not used
- the sale, rental, or occupancy of dwellings owned or operated by a religious organization for a non-commercial purpose to persons of the same religion, as long as membership in that religion is not restricted on account of race, color, or national origin
- the rental or occupancy of lodgings operated by a private club for its members for other than commercial purposes
- housing for the elderly that meets certain Department of Housing and Urban Development (HUD) guidelines

A person who believes he or she has been discriminated against can:

- file a written complaint with HUD
- file a civil action directly in a U.S. District Court or state or local court

An **administrative law judge** may hear the case and can award damages.

The burden of proof is on the person filing the complaint. A person found guilty of a fair housing violation may face:

- civil penalties of up to $10,000 for the first offense, up to $25,000 for the second offense within a five-year period, and up to $50,000 for the third offense within a seven-year period
- monetary fines for actual and/or punitive damages caused by the discrimination
- an injunction to stop the sale or rental of the property to someone else, making it available to the complainant
- court costs
- criminal penalties against those who coerce, intimidate, threaten, or interfere with a person's buying, renting, or selling of housing
- state penalties including the loss of the real estate license

Massachusetts General Laws

Chapter 151B (Fair Housing)

Massachusetts General Law 151B regarding unlawful discrimination can be read in full online at www.mass.gov/legis/laws/mgl/gl-151b-toc.htm.

Massachusetts has three categories of protected classes. Protected classes in Category One in Massachusetts include race, color, religion, national origin, ancestry, sex, age, handicap, marital status, veteran history/military status, and sexual orientation. Massachusetts prohibits the same discriminatory practices as Title VIII.

Most residential properties are covered under the Massachusetts fair housing law. There are some exceptions that apply only to owners. (These exemptions do not apply to real estate agents.) Also, these exemptions do not apply if there has been discriminatory advertising:

- the lease of an owner-occupied two-family property
- elderly housing that receives federal or state funding is exempted on age only
- an approved "over 55" community that is on at least ten acres is exempted on age only

Protected classes in Category Two are people who receive public assistance or rental assistance. It is prohibited to discriminate in furnishing credit services or rental accommodations; also, to discriminate because of any requirement of such public assistance, rental assistance, or housing subsidy program. For rental subsidy recipients, discrimination may include the following: refusal to sign program lease, refusal to make modifications in unit to satisfy state sanitary code, requirement for security deposit in excess of program allowances. Discriminatory advertising is always prohibited. No properties are exempted.

Children are the protected class in Category Three. It is prohibited to refuse to rent, sell, or otherwise deny a property to someone with children (including a refusal based on the presence of lead paint or other safety concerns). It is also prohibited to use discriminatory advertising or to have different terms or conditions for someone with children.

There are three exemptions under Category Three:

1. a three-family house (or less) with an elderly (65 years or older) or infirm occupant for whom the presence of children would be a hardship
2. an owner/occupant temporary lease
3. a lease of an owner-occupied two-family house

A person who believes he or she has been discriminated against can:

- file a complaint with Massachusetts Commission Against Discrimination (MCAD)
- file a civil action

Remedies include injunctive relief, damages, affirmative relief, civil penalties, and attorneys' fees for prevailing complainants. An agent who is found to have violated Massachusetts fair housing law will have their license automatically suspended for **60 days**. If the agent has a second violation within two years, their license will be suspended for **90 days**.

If an agent meets with a seller who expresses discriminatory preferences, the agent should refuse the listing. Not only could taking the listing get the agent in trouble, but their broker-owner is also responsible for the actions of their agents.

Massachusetts Consumer Protection Law (Chapter 93A)

Real estate salespeople and brokers are subject to the **Massachusetts Consumer Protection Law** known as **Chapter 93A**. The law prohibits unfair and deceptive trade practices. An agent who is found guilty under Chapter 93A can be sued for up to triple damages plus attorney's fees.

Lead Paint Law

Sellers and real estate agents must comply with federal and Massachusetts's lead-based paint disclosure requirements. Before signing a Purchase and Sale Agreement on a property built before 1978, a prospective purchaser must be given the Department of Public Health Property Transfer Notification Certification in which the seller will state if they know of any lead-based paint on the property and give copies of any reports they have. The buyer has ten days to test for the presence of lead paint.

New tenants of a property built before 1978 must be given a Lead Paint Notification and Tenant Certification Form. If a child under six lives in the property, the owner shall delead.

In order to close on a property in Massachusetts, the local fire department must inspect the premises within 60 days of the closing and issue a smoke detector certificate verifying that the property is equipped with adequate smoke detectors. Three-family homes or larger must have hard-wired smoke detectors in the common areas. Six-family homes or larger must have hard-wired smoke detectors throughout the property. Some cities have stricter codes because every fire chief has the right to interpret the smoke detector code.

A **21E certificate** is used when a commercial property sells to certify that the property is not contaminated by hazardous waste. Other environmental risks like underground fuel storage tanks, the presence of asbestos or radon, or the prior use of chlordane (previously used to treat termite infestation) must be disclosed.

▶ Massachusetts License Law

The Board of Registration of Real Estate Brokers and Salespersons has put together a booklet called, "Massachusetts Real Estate License Law and Regulation." You can read it at www.mass.gov/dpl/boards/re/forms/lic_law_and_regulation_booklet.pdf.

Duties and Powers of the Real Estate Board of Registration

There are five members of the **Board of Registration of Real Estate Brokers and Salespersons** (**the Board**). The governor appoints the members of the Board. Three of the members are to be active real estate agents for at least seven years. The remaining two members are not licensed and are members to represent the public. The governor also appoints one of the members to be the chairperson. Each member serves for a five-year term. The Board holds at least four meetings a year and must have at least three members present for a quorum.

The Board has the power to:

- promulgate (announce) and administer Massachusetts license law
- conduct examinations
- examine records (such as escrow accounts and signed Massachusetts Mandatory Licensee-Consumer Relationship Disclosure forms)
- hold hearings and appeals to enforce the license law
- suspend, revoke, refuse to renew, and reinstate licenses

There are many ways for an agent to lose his or her license either temporarily or permanently. According to Massachusetts license law, the Board may suspend, revoke, or refuse to renew a license if an agent did any of the following:

- knowingly made any substantial misrepresentation
- acted in the dual capacity of broker and undisclosed principal in the same transaction
- acted as an undisclosed dual agent (without the knowledge and consent of both parties)
- failed to account for or remit funds within a reasonable time
- paid a commission to an unlicensed person
- accepted, gave or charged, any undisclosed commission, rebate, or profit on expenditures for a principal
- induced a party to break a contract (for the personal benefit of the licensee)
- commingled funds
- failed to provide a copy of real estate contracts to all parties
- performed any discriminatory practices
- took a net listing
- practiced real estate while impaired
- practiced real estate while his or her license was expired
- falsified a license application or renewal application
- failed to report a criminal conviction

When the Board holds a hearing regarding a person's license, the Board may summon witnesses and records. The licensee must receive at least **ten day's** written notice of the hearing (including a statement of the grounds and a copy of the complaint or charges). The licensee has the right to appear personally and with counsel and to cross-examine witnesses and to produce evidence. A licensee may appeal the Board's decision within **twenty days** to the superior court. A licensee has **seven days** to deliver their license to the Board once they have received notice that it has been suspended or revoked (even if an appeal is in process).

Licensing Requirements

The following real-estate related activities, when performed for another person and for a fee, require a real estate license in the state of Massachusetts:

- sales
- exchanges
- purchases
- rentals/leases
- negotiates
- offers
- listing
- options
- advertise real property
- prospecting
- loan negotiating
- apartment search

Types of Licenses

A **real estate broker** is any person who, for another person and for a fee, performs any of the previously mentioned activities.

A **real estate salesperson** also has the right to perform any of the previously mentioned activities, except they cannot complete negotiations. A salesperson cannot be self-employed. They must act under an employing broker.

When a corporation applies for a broker's license, at least one of its officers or partners shall be designated as the representative. This representative also needs an individual broker's license in their own name.

A **non-resident** can hold a Massachusetts real estate license; however, the non-resident must file a written power of attorney appointing the chairman of the Board as their attorney in fact for any legal proceedings issued to the non-resident.

Eligibility for Licensing

In order to receive a **salesperson's** license, a person must:

- be over 18 years old
- complete 24 hours of classroom instruction
- pass the exam

To receive a **broker's** license, a person must:

- be licensed as a salesperson and actively employed by a licensed real estate broker for at least one year
- complete 30 hours of classroom instruction
- pass the exam
- submit a surety bond to the Board for $5,000

In the event of the death of a licensed broker who is the sole proprietor of a real estate company, the Board shall, upon application by the sole proprietor's legal representative, issue a temporary license without examination to the broker's legal representative or to a designated individual. This license cannot be renewed and is valid for up to one year from the date of death of the sole proprietor.

Real estate licenses are valid for two years and renew on the person's birthday. A person must take twelve hours of continuing education classes within the two-year period prior to renewing either a salesperson or broker's license. If a person does not complete their continuing education requirements, they can place their license in an **inactive status**. A person with an inactive real estate license can collect referral fees, but cannot practice real estate. Currently the fee for renewing a salesperson's license is $93; and the fee for renewing a broker's license is $127. To renew a broker's license, a new surety bond must be posted.

There are some people who do not need a real estate license. They include:

- any individual acting for themselves
- a salaried employee or property manager employed by the property owner
- an licensed auctioneer
- a trustee
- a public official or public employee performing official duties
- a person acting as an attorney-in-fact under a power of attorney
- an attorney performing duties for a client
- a court appointee
- a bank, insurance company, or credit union and their employees

Statutory Requirements Governing Activities of Licensees

There following are the statutory requirements regarding **advertising**:

- A broker shall not advertise in any way that is false or misleading.
- No broker shall perform **blind advertising** by advertising real property to purchase, sell, rent, mortgage, or exchange through classified advertisement or otherwise unless they affirmatively disclose that they are a real estate broker. No broker shall insert advertisements in any advertising publication or other means where only a post office box number, telephone, facsimile, electronic mail number, or street address appears. All advertisements shall include the name of the real estate broker.

- **Salespeople are prohibited from advertising** the purchase, sale, rental, or exchange of any real property under their own name.
- No broker shall advertise to purchase, sell, rent, mortgage, or exchange any real property in any manner that indicates directly or indirectly unlawful **discrimination** against any individual or group.

A real estate salesperson can be hired by a real estate broker as an **employee** or as an **independent contractor**. A salesperson cannot be self-employed. They must be affiliated with a broker (and only one broker at a time). A salesperson can only accept a payment, fee, or commission from their broker. The broker is responsible for the actions of their agents. Because a salesperson works under a broker, they cannot sue a principal themselves. Only their employing broker can sue a principal. A salesperson can sue their broker.

A **commission** is a fee for brokerage services that is negotiated between the principal and broker.

An agent needs to disclose any potential conflict of interest. If they or their family member has a personal financial interest in a property (as either the seller or potential buyer), it must be disclosed in writing to all other parties and the other parties need to acknowledge the disclosure in writing.

All offers submitted to an agent must be conveyed as soon as possible to the owner of the property. Agents also have a responsibility to give copies of the real estate contract to all of the parties in the transaction.

One of the fiduciary responsibilities an agent owes their client is accountability of all funds. This means that all deposits (for both purchases and rentals) need to be deposited immediately into the broker's escrow account. The broker is accountable for all money held in the escrow account and must return the deposit at either the closing on the property or the termination of the sale. The broker needs to keep records of all funds deposited in their escrow account, including all information pertinent to the transaction. A copy of each check deposited into escrow needs to be kept for **three years**. The Board has the right to inspect these records and the escrow fund at any time.

A **net listing** offers the property owner a guaranteed sales price, with the listing broker taking any part of the purchase price over that amount. Net listings are illegal in Massachusetts.

The broker-owner must maintain a usual place of business and notify the Board of any change of location. The broker also needs to notify the Board of the relationship of all licensees affiliated with the company, and notify the Board when a new agent joins the office or an agent leaves the office. Each broker and salesperson must display a copy of their license in a conspicuous location that can be seen by the general public.

Agents are prohibited from advising against the use of an attorney in any real property transaction.

Promotional Sales of Out-of-State Real Property

There are several things to keep in mind regarding out-of-state property:

- No broker shall offer for sale in the Commonwealth an interest in real property that is located in a land development of another state unless the owner or developer of such land development **registers property with the Board**. It must be registered on the form and pay the fee prescribed by the Board. Such registration shall be renewed annually.
- The Board may **inspect** any out-of-state real property developments seeking registration or registered with it. The owner or developer must pay for the costs of any inspection. Following an inspection, the

Board shall issue a written report. This report must be kept on file both with the Board and in the owner or developer's files while the development is registered with the Board and for one year following the termination or expiration of the registration.

■ Once the Board registers an out-of-state real property development, the owner or developer must note the fact of the registration in all its advertisements in the state.

■ No interest in any real property located in an out-of-state real property development shall be subject to any promotional advertisement, offering for sale, or sold in the Commonwealth unless it is offered for sale and sold by a licensed Massachusetts broker. Promotional advertising as used herein means any advertising material offered through any means of communication in the Commonwealth.

■ A broker acting on behalf of an owner or developer of an out-of-state real property development shall notify the Board in writing of such status within **seven days** of accepting the client.

Apartment Rentals

Brokers and salespersons engaged in renting real property, whether by written agreement or not, shall provide each prospective tenant with a written notice which states whether the prospective tenant will pay any fee for such service, the amount of such fee, the manner and time in which it is to be paid, and whether or not any fee or any portion thereof will be payable by the tenant if a tenancy is not created. This written notice must be given by the real estate broker or salesperson at the first personal meeting between the broker or salesperson and a prospective tenant. It must be signed by the real estate broker or salesperson, contain the license number of such broker or salesperson, be signed by the prospective tenant, and contain the date such notice was given by the broker or salesperson to the prospective tenant. Where a prospective tenant declines to sign such written notice the real estate broker or salesperson must note on such written notice the tenant's name and the refusal to sign such notice.

A copy of the written notice shall be maintained by the real estate broker or salesperson for a period of three years from the date on which the notice was provided to the prospective tenant. Real estate brokers or salespersons shall furnish the notice to the Board, its investigators, or other agents upon request.

Brokers shall maintain all rental listings and written documents that demonstrate the availability of an apartment at the time it is advertised for rental for a period of **three years** from the date on which such apartment is rented.

Brokers shall maintain a copy of any check, money order, and written cash receipt for any fees, deposits, or payments made by a prospective tenant or actual tenant for a period of **three years** from the date of issuance. Brokers shall also maintain a copy of any check issued on an escrow account over which they have issuing authority for a period of **three years** from the date of issuance.

Any advertisement concerning the availability of an apartment shall disclose in print no smaller than that for the apartment itself that "The apartment advertised may no longer be available for rental."

No real estate broker shall charge any fee to a prospective tenant unless a tenancy is created or in those cases where no tenancy in real property is created unless the prospective tenant has agreed in writing to pay such a fee.

Real Estate
Math Review

CHAPTER SUMMARY

Real estate mathematics accounts for almost 10% of the Massachusetts Real Estate Sales Exam, so you should take this topic seriously. But even if math is not your favorite subject, this chapter will help you do your best. It not only covers arithmetic, algebra, geometry, and word problems, but also has practice problems for each of the real estate math topics.

ERE ARE THE types of math questions you will encounter on the exam:

- Percents
- Areas
- Property Tax
- Loan-to-Value Ratios
- Points
- Equity
- Qualifying Buyers
- Prorations
- Commissions

- Sale Proceeds
- Transfer Tax/Conveyance Tax/Revenue Stamps
- Competitive Market Analyses (CMA)
- Income Properties
- Depreciation

Keep in mind that although the math topics are varied, you will be using the same math skills to complete each question. But before you review your math skills, take a look at some helpful strategies for doing your best.

► Strategies for Math Questions

Answer Every Question

You should answer every single question, even if you don't know the answer. There is no penalty for a wrong answer, and you have a 25% chance of guessing correctly. If one or two answers are obviously wrong, the odds of selecting the correct one may be even higher.

Bring a Calculator

You are allowed to bring a calculator to your exam. **You must check with your exam center to find out exactly what type of calculator is permitted.** In general, permissible calculators are battery-operated, do not print, are not programmable, and do not have a keypad with letters. As a precaution, you should bring an extra battery with you to your exam. Try not to rely entirely on the calculator. Although using one can prevent simple adding and subtracting errors, it may take longer for you to use the calculator than to figure it out yourself.

Use Scratch Paper

Resist the temptation to "save time" by doing all your work on your calculator. The main pitfall with calculators is the temptation to work the problem all the way through to the end on the calculator. At this point, if none of the answers provided is correct, there is no way to know where the mistake lies. Use scratch paper to avoid this problem.

Check Your Work

Checking your work is always good practice, and it's usually quite simple. Even if you come up with an answer that is one of the answer choices, you should check your work. Test writers often include answer choices that are the results of common errors, which you may have made.

▶ Real Estate Math Review

Here's a quick review of some basic arithmetic, algebra, geometry, and word problem skills you will need for your exam.

Arithmetic Review

Symbols of Multiplication

When two or more numbers are being multiplied, they are called **factors**. The answer that results is called the **product**.

> *Example:*
> $5 \times 6 = 30$ 5 and 6 are **factors** and 30 is the **product**.

There are several ways to represent multiplication in the above mathematical statement.

- A dot between factors indicates multiplication:

  $5 \cdot 6 = 30$

- Parentheses around one or more factors indicates multiplication:

  $(5)6 = 30, 5(6) = 30,$ and $(5)(6) = 30$

- Multiplication is also indicated when a number is placed next to a variable:

  $5a = 30$ In this equation, 5 is being multiplied by a.

Divisibility

Like multiplication, division can be represented in a few different ways:

$8 \div 3$ $3\overline{)8}$ $\frac{8}{3}$

In each of the above, 3 is the divisor and 8 is the dividend.

If the number after the one you need to round to is 5 or more, make the preceding number one higher. If it is less than 5, drop it and leave the preceding number the same. (Information about rounding is usually provided in the exam instructions or in the exam bulletin.)

Example:
0.0135 = .014 or .01

Decimals

The most important thing to remember about decimals is that the first place value to the right begins with tenths. The place values are as follows:

1	2	6	8	•	3	4	5	7
THOUSANDS	HUNDREDS	TENS	ONES	DECIMAL POINT	TENTHS	HUNDREDTHS	THOUSANDTHS	TEN THOUSANDTHS

In expanded form, this number can also be expressed as . . .

$$1268.3457 = (1 \times 1,000) + (2 \times 100) + (6 \times 10) + (8 \times 1) + (3 \times .1) + (4 \times .01) + (5 \times .001) + (7 \times .0001)$$

Fractions

To do well when working with fractions, it is necessary to understand some basic concepts. Here are some math rules for fractions using variables:

$$\frac{a}{b} \times \frac{c}{d} = \frac{a \times c}{b \times d}$$

$$\frac{a}{b} + \frac{c}{b} = \frac{a + c}{b}$$

$$\frac{a}{b} \div \frac{c}{d} = \frac{a}{b} \times \frac{d}{c} = \frac{a \times d}{b \times c}$$

$$\frac{a}{b} + \frac{c}{d} = \frac{ad + bc}{bd}$$

Multiplication of Fractions

Multiplying fractions is one of the easiest operations to perform. To multiply fractions, simply multiply the numerators and the denominators, writing each in the respective place over or under the fraction bar.

Example:

$$\frac{4}{5} \times \frac{6}{7} = \frac{24}{35}$$

Division of Fractions

Dividing fractions is the same thing as multiplying fractions by their **reciprocals**. To find the reciprocal of any number, flip its numerator and denominator. For example, the reciprocals of the following numbers are:

$$\frac{1}{3} \rightarrow \frac{3}{1} = 3$$

$$x \rightarrow \frac{1}{x}$$

$$\frac{4}{5} \rightarrow \frac{5}{4}$$

$$5 \rightarrow \frac{1}{5}$$

When dividing fractions, simply multiply the dividend (the number being divided) by the divisor's (the number doing the dividing) reciprocal to get the answer.

Example:

$$\frac{12}{21} \div \frac{3}{4} = \frac{12}{21} \times \frac{4}{3} = \frac{48}{63} = \frac{16}{21}$$

Adding and Subtracting Fractions

To add or subtract fractions with like denominators, just add or subtract the numerators and leave the denominator as it is. For example,

$$\frac{1}{7} + \frac{5}{7} = \frac{6}{7} \quad \text{and} \quad \frac{5}{8} - \frac{2}{8} = \frac{3}{8}$$

To add or subtract fractions with unlike denominators, you must find the **least common denominator**, or LCD.

For example, if given the denominators 8 and 12, 24 would be the LCD because $8 \times 3 = 24$, and $12 \times 2 = 24$. In other words, the LCD is the smallest number divisible by each of the denominators.

Once you know the LCD, convert each fraction to its new form by multiplying both the numerator and denominator by the necessary number to get the LCD, and then add or subtract the new numerators.

Example:

$$\frac{1}{3} + \frac{2}{5} = \frac{5(1)}{5(3)} + \frac{3(2)}{3(5)} = \frac{5}{15} + \frac{6}{15} = \frac{11}{15}$$

Percent

A **percent** is a measure of a part to a whole, with the whole being equal to 100.

- To change a decimal to a percentage, move the decimal point two units to the right and add a percentage symbol.

  Example:
  .45 = 45%   .07 = 7%   .9 = 90%

- To change a fraction to a percentage, first change the fraction to a decimal. To do this, divide the numerator by the denominator. Then change the decimal to a percentage.

  Example:
  $\frac{4}{5}$ = .80 = 80%

  $\frac{2}{5}$ = .4 = 40%

  $\frac{1}{8}$ = .125 = 12.5%

- To change a decimal to a percentage, move the decimal point two units to the right and add a percentage symbol.
- To change a percentage to a decimal, simply move the decimal point two places to the left and eliminate the percentage symbol.

  Example:
  64% = .64   87% = .87   7% = .07

- To change a percentage to a fraction, divide by 100 and reduce.

  Example:
  64% = $\frac{64}{100}$ = $\frac{16}{25}$

  75% = $\frac{75}{100}$ = $\frac{3}{4}$

  82% = $\frac{82}{100}$ = $\frac{41}{50}$

- Keep in mind that any percentage that is 100 or greater will need to reflect a whole number or mixed number when converted.

  Example:
  125% = 1.25 or $1\frac{1}{4}$

  350% = 3.5 or $3\frac{1}{2}$

Here are some conversions you should be familiar with:

Fraction	Decimal	Percentage
$\frac{1}{2}$	.5	50%
$\frac{1}{4}$	.25	25%
$\frac{1}{3}$	.333 ...	$33.\overline{3}$%
$\frac{2}{3}$	.666 ...	$66.\overline{6}$%
$\frac{1}{10}$	.1	10%
$\frac{1}{8}$	.125	12.5%
$\frac{1}{6}$	.1666 ...	$16.\overline{6}$%
$\frac{1}{5}$	.2	20%

Algebra Review

Equations

An **equation** is solved by finding a number that is equal to an unknown variable.

Simple Rules for Working with Equations

1. The equal sign separates an equation into two sides.
2. Whenever an operation is performed on one side, the same operation must be performed on the other side.
3. Your first goal is to get all of the variables on one side and all of the numbers on the other.
4. The final step often will be to divide each side by the coefficient, leaving the variable equal to a number.

Checking Equations

To check an equation, substitute the number equal to the variable in the original equation.

Example:

To check the equation below, substitute the number 10 for the variable x.

$$\frac{x}{6} = \frac{x+10}{12}$$

$$\frac{10}{6} = \frac{10+10}{12}$$

$$\frac{10}{6} = \frac{20}{12}$$

$$1\frac{2}{3} = 1\frac{2}{3}$$

$$\frac{10}{6} = \frac{10}{6}$$

Because this statement is true, you know the answer $x = 10$ must be correct.

Special Tips for Checking Equations

1. If time permits, be sure to check all equations.
2. Be careful to answer the question that is being asked. Sometimes, this involves solving for a variable and then performing an operation.

Example:

If the question asks the value of $x - 2$, and you find $x = 2$, the answer is not 2, but $2 - 2$. Thus, the answer is 0.

Algebraic Fractions

Algebraic fractions are very similar to fractions in arithmetic.

Example:

Write $\frac{x}{5} - \frac{x}{10}$ as a single fraction.

Solution:

Just like in arithmetic, you need to find the LCD of 5 and 10, which is 10. Then change each fraction into an equivalent fraction that has 10 as a denominator.

$$\frac{x}{5} - \frac{x}{10} = \frac{x(2)}{5(2)} - \frac{x}{10}$$
$$= \frac{2x}{10} - \frac{x}{10}$$
$$= \frac{x}{10}$$

Geometry Review

Area	the space inside a two-dimensional figure
Circumference	the distance around a circle
Perimeter	the distance around a figure
Radius	the distance from the center point of a circle to any point on the arc of a circle

Area

Area is the space inside of the lines defining the shape.

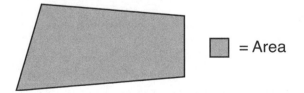

= Area

This geometry review will focus on the area formula for three main shapes: circles, rectangles/squares, and triangles.

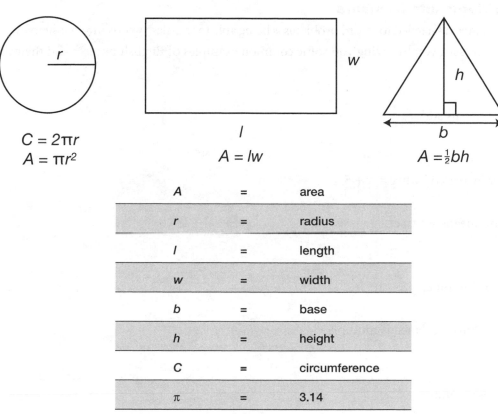

Circle	Rectangle	Triangle
$C = 2\pi r$		
$A = \pi r^2$	$A = lw$	$A = \frac{1}{2}bh$

A	=	area
r	=	radius
l	=	length
w	=	width
b	=	base
h	=	height
C	=	circumference
π	=	3.14

Perimeter

The perimeter of an object is simply the sum of all of its sides.

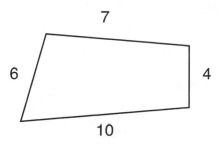

Perimeter = 6 + 7 + 4 + 10 = 27

The circumference is the perimeter of a circle.

$C = 2\pi r$

Word Problem Review

Since many of the math problems on the Massachusetts Real Estate Sales Exam will be word problems, pay extra attention to the following review.

Translating Words into Numbers

The most important skill needed for word problems is being able to translate words into mathematical operations. The following will assist you by giving you some common examples of English phrases and their mathematical equivalents.

- "Increase" means add.

    Example:
    A number increased by five $= x + 5$.

- "Less than" means subtract.

    Example:
    10 less than a number $= x - 10$.

- "Times" or "product" means multiply.

    Example:
    Three times a number $= 3x$.

- "Times the sum" means to multiply a number by a quantity.

    Example:
    Five times the sum of a number and three $= 5(x + 3)$.

- Two variables are sometimes used together.

    Example:
    A number y exceeds five times a number x by ten.
    $y = 5x + 10$

- "Of" means multiply.

    Example:
    10% of 100 is 10 $= 10\% \times 100 = 10$.

- "Is" means equals.

Example:
15 is 14 plus 1 becomes 15 = 14 + 1.

Assigning Variables in Word Problems

It may be necessary to create and assign variables in a word problem. To do this, first identify an unknown and a known. You may not actually know the exact value of the "known," but you will know at least something about its value.

Examples:
Max is three years older than Ricky.
Unknown = Ricky's age = x.
Known = Max's age is three years older.
Therefore,
Ricky's age = x and Max's age = $x + 3$.

Heidi made twice as many cookies as Rebecca.
Unknown = number of cookies Rebecca made = x.
Known = number of cookies Heidi made = $2x$.

Jessica has five more than three times the number of books that Becky has.
Unknown = the number of books Becky has = x.
Known = the number of books Jessica has = $3x + 5$.

Percentage Problems

There is one formula that is useful for solving the three types of percentage problems:

$$\frac{\#}{\text{whole}}^{\text{part}} = \frac{\%}{100}$$

When reading a percentage problem, substitute the necessary information into the above formula based on the following:

- 100 is always written in the denominator of the percentage sign column.
- If given a percentage, write it in the numerator position of the number column. If you are not given a percentage, then the variable should be placed there.
- The denominator of the number column represents the number that is equal to the whole, or 100%. This number always follows the word *of* in a word problem.

- The numerator of the number column represents the number that is the percent.
- In the formula, the equal sign can be interchanged with the word *is*.

Examples:

- Finding a percentage of a given number:

What number is equal to 40% of 50?

$$\frac{\overset{\#}{x}}{50} = \frac{\overset{\%}{40}}{100}$$

Cross multiply:

$100(x) = (40)(50)$

$100x = 2,000$

$\frac{100x}{100} = \frac{2,000}{100}$

$x = 20$ Therefore, 20 is 40% of 50.

- Finding a number when a percentage is given:

40% of what number is 24?

$$\frac{\overset{\#}{24}}{x} = \frac{\overset{\%}{40}}{100}$$

Cross multiply:

$(24)(100) = (40)(x)$

$2,400 = 40x$

$\frac{2,400}{40} = \frac{40x}{40}$

$60 = x$ Therefore, 40% of 60 is 24.

- Finding what percentage one number is of another:

What percentage of 75 is 15?

$$\frac{\overset{\#}{15}}{75} = \frac{\overset{\%}{x}}{100}$$

$$\textbf{Rate} = \frac{x \text{ units}}{y \text{ units}}$$

A percentage problem simply means that y units are equal to 100. This is important to remember that a percentage problem may be worded using the word *rate*.

Cross multiply:

$15(100) = (75)(x)$

$1,500 = 75x$

$\frac{1,500}{75} = \frac{75x}{75}$

$20 = x$ Therefore, 20% of 75 is 15.

Rate Problems

You may encounter a couple of different types of rate problems on the Massachusetts Real Estate Sales Exam: cost per unit, interest rate, and tax rate. Rate is defined as a comparison of two quantities with different units of measure.

$$\textbf{Rate} = \frac{x \text{ units}}{y \text{ units}}$$

Examples: $\frac{\text{dollars}}{\text{square foot}}, \frac{\text{interest}}{\text{year}}$

Cost Per Unit

Some problems on your exam may require that you calculate the cost per unit.

Example:

If 100 square feet cost $1,000, how much does 1 square foot cost?

Solution:

$\frac{\text{Total Cost}}{\text{\# of square feet}} = \frac{1,000}{100} = \$10$ per square foot

Interest Rate

The formula for simple interest is Interest = Principal × Rate × Time, or $I = PRT$. If you know certain values, but not others, you can still find the answer using algebra. In simple interest problems, the value of T is usually 1, as in 1 year. There are three basic kinds of interest problems, depending on which number is missing.

Equivalencies

Here are some equivalencies you may need to use to complete some questions. Generally, any equivalencies you will need to know for your exam are provided to you.

Equivalencies

12 inches (in. or ") = 1 foot (ft. or ')

3 feet or 36 inches = 1 yard (yd.)

1,760 yards = 1 mile (mi)

5,280 feet = 1 mile

144 square inches (sq. in. or in.^{2}) = 1 square foot (sq. ft. or ft.^{2})

9 square feet = 1 square yard

43,560 feet = 1 acre

640 acres = 1 square mile

Percents

You may be asked a basic percentage problem.

Example:

What is 86% of 1,750?

Solution:

Start by translating words into math terms.

$x = (86\%)(1,750)$

Change the percent into a decimal by moving the decimal point two spaces to the left.

$86\% = .86$

Now you can solve.

$x = (.86)(1,750)$

$x = 1,505$

Other percentage problems you may find on the Massachusetts Real Estate Sales Exam will come in the form of rate problems. Keep reading for more examples of these problems.

Interest Problems

Let's take a look at a problem in which you have to calculate the interest rate (R). Remember, the rate is the same as the percentage.

Example:

Mary Valencia borrowed $5,000, for which she is paying $600 interest per year. What is the rate of interest being charged?

Solution:
Start with the values you know.
Principal = $5,000
Interest = $600
Rate = x
Time = 1 year
Using the formula $I = PRT$, insert the values you know, and solve for x.
$600 = 5,000(x)(1)$
$600 = 5,000x$
$\frac{600}{5,000} = \frac{x}{5,000}$
$.12 = x$
To convert .12 to a percent, move the decimal point two places to the right.
$.12 = 12\%$

Area

Some of the problems on your exam may ask you to calculate the area of a piece of land, a building, or some other figure. Here are some formulas and how to use them.

Rectangles

Remember the formula: **Area** = (length)(width).

Example:
A man purchased a lot that is 50 feet by 10 feet for a garden. How many square feet of land does he have?

Solution:
Using the formula, Area = (length)(width), you have:
$A = (50)(10) = 500$ square feet

Example:
The Meyers family bought a piece of land for a summer home that was 2.75 acres. The lake frontage was 150 feet. What was the length of the lot?

Solution:
When you take your sales exam, you may be provided with certain equivalencies. You will need to refer to the "Equivalencies" list on the previous page to answer this question. First, find the area of the land in square feet.
$(2.75)(43,560) = 119,790$ square feet

In the previous example, you were given the length and the width. In this example, you are given the area and the width, so you are solving for the length. Since you know the area and the width of the lot, use the formula to solve.

Area = (length)(width)

$119,790 = (x)(150)$

Divide both sides by 150.

$\frac{119,790}{150} = \frac{(x)(150)}{150}$

$x = \frac{119,790}{150}$

$x = 798.6$ feet

Triangles

Although it may not be as common, you may be asked to find the area of a triangle. If you don't remember the formula, see page 97.

Example:

The Baron family is buying a triangular piece of land for a gas station. It is 200 feet at the base, and the side perpendicular to the base is 200 feet. They are paying $2.00 per square foot for the property. What will it cost?

Solution:

Start with the formula Area = $\frac{1}{2}$(base)(height).

Now, write down the values you know.

Area = x

Base = 200

Height = 200

If it's easier, you can change $\frac{1}{2}$ to a decimal.

$\frac{1}{2} = .5$

Now you can plug these values into the formula.

$x = (.5)(200)(200)$

$x = (.5)(40,000)$

$x = 20,000$ square feet

Don't forget that the question is not asking for the number of square feet, but for the *cost* of the property per square foot. This is a rate problem, so you need to complete one more step:

(20,000 square feet)($2 per square foot) = $40,000

Example:

Victor and Evelyn Robinson have an outlot that a neighbor wants to buy. The side of the outlot next to their property is 86 feet. The rear line is perpendicular to their side lot, and the road frontage is 111 feet. Their plat shows they own 3,000 square feet in the outlot. What is the length of the rear line of the outlot? Round your answer to the nearest whole number.

Solution:

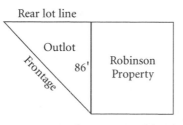

It helps to draw the figure to conceive shapes. The rear lot line is perpendicular to the side lot line. This makes the side lot line the base and the rear lot line the height (altitude).

Area $= \frac{1}{2}$(base)(height)

Area = 3,000 square feet

Base = 86 feet

Height = x

If it's easier, you can change $\frac{1}{2}$ to a decimal.

$\frac{1}{2} = .5$

Now you can plug these values into the formula.

$3,000 = (.5)(86)(x)$

$3,000 = (43)(x)$

Divide both sides by 43.

$\frac{3,000}{43} = \frac{(43)(x)}{43}$

$x = 69.767$ feet

Don't forget the question says to round your answer to the nearest whole number. The answer is 70 feet.

Circles

Remember the formula Area $= \pi r^2$.

Example:

Murray Brodman, a contractor, has been awarded the job to put up a circular bandstand in the town square. The radius of the circular area for the bandstand is 15 feet. What is the area of the bandstand? Use 3.14 for π.

Solution:

Area = πr^2

Start with the values you know.

Area = x

$\pi = 3.14$

radius = 15

Now plug these values into the formula.

Area = $(3.14)(15)(15) = 706.5$ sq. ft.

▶ Property Tax

To solve property tax questions, you will be using percents and rates.

Example:

The tax rate in your county is $4.17 per hundred of assessed valuation, and Mr. Brown, a possible client, has told you his taxes are $1,100. What is his property assessment? (Round your answer to the nearest 10 cents.)

Solution:

Start off with the values you know.

Taxes = $1,100

Assessment = x

Tax rate = $4.17 per hundred (%)

If you remember the definition of percent as being an amount per hundred, then $4.17 per hundred is actually 4.17%. To make this equation more manageable, convert this percent to a decimal by moving the decimal point two spaces to the left. Now the tax rate is .0417.

.0417 of the assessed value of the house is $1,100. Translate the words into math terms. This means: $(.0417)(x) = 1,100$.

To solve the equation, divide both sides by .0417.

$$\frac{.0417x}{.0417} = \frac{1,100}{.0417}$$

$x = \$26,378.896$

Remember, the question asks you round to the nearest 10 cents. That means that .896 needs to be rounded up to 90. So the answer is $26,378.90.

Example:

Mr. Smith knew his own taxes were $975 and his property assessment was $17,000 for the house and $6,000 for the land. He wanted to know the tax rate (%).

Solution:

Start with the values you know.

Tax = $975

Assessment for house = $17,000 plus assessment for land = $6,000. Therefore, total = $23,000.

Rate (%) = x

According to the question, $23,000 at a rate of x is $975. Convert this statement into an equation.

($23,000)($x$) = 975.

Solve the equation by dividing both sides by 23,000.

$$\frac{23,000x}{23,000} = \frac{975}{23,000}$$

$x = .0423913$

To make this equation more simple, round the answer to .0424.

Remember that you are looking for the rate. Therefore, you need to convert this decimal to a percent by moving the decimal point two places to the right. The rate is 4.24%. (This can also be expressed as $4.24 per hundred.)

Loan-to-Value Ratios

These problems often deal with percentages.

Example:

A mortgage loan for 10% is at a 75% loan-to-value ratio. The interest on the original balance for the first year is $6,590. What is the value of the property securing the loan? Round to the nearest one cent.

Solution:

First, find out the loan amount.

$6,590 is 10% of the loan amount. Let x equal the loan amount. Now, translate these words into math terms.

$6,590 = (10%)($x$)

Change 10% into a decimal by moving the decimal point two places to the left.

10% = .1

Now you have:

$6,590 = (.1)($x$)

Divide both sides by (.1).

$x – $65,900

Now that you know the loan amount ($65,900), use this information to find the value of the property.

Write down the values you know.

Loan amount = $65,900

Loan-to-value ratio = 75%

Value = x

We know that 75% of the value is $65,900.

Translate this into math terms.

$(75\%)(x) = \$65,900$

Change the percent into a decimal (75% = .75) and solve.

$(.75)(x) = 65,900$

Divide both sides by .75.

$$\frac{(.75)(x)}{(.75)} = \frac{65,900}{(.75)}$$

$x = 87,866.66666$

When rounded to the nearest one cent, the answer is $87,866.67.

Points

Loan discounts are often called **points**, or loan placement fees, one point meaning 1% of the face amount of the loan. The service fee of one percent paid by buyers of government backed loans is called a **loan origination fee**.

Example:

A homebuyer may obtain a $50,000 FHA mortgage loan, provided the seller pays a discount of five points. What is the amount of the discount?

Solution:

The definition of one point is 1% of the face amount of the loan.

Therefore, 5 points = 5% of the face of the loan. First, change the percent to a decimal.

5% = .05

Now you can use these values to solve.

Amount of discount = x

Points = .05

Amount of loan = $50,000

So, $x = (.05)(50,000)$.

$x = \$2,500$

Example:

A property is listed at $74,000. An offer is made for $72,000, provided the seller pays three points on a loan for 80% of the purchase price. The brokerage commission rate is 7%. How much less will the seller receive if he accepts the offer than he would have received if he sold at all cash at the original terms?

Solution:

Here are the values you know:

Sold for original terms—price	$74,000	
Less 7% commission	− 5,180	(.07)(74,000) = 5,180
Seller's net	$68,820	

This question becomes more difficult, because in order to find the seller's net on the offered price, you must calculate the discount. The provision is that the seller pays 3 points (or .03) on a loan for 80% (or .8) of the price.

Start by finding 80% of the price.

(.8)(72,000) = $57,600

Now, the points are applied to this amount. This means .03 of $57,600 is the discount.

So, (.03)(57,600) = discount = 1,728.

You know these values:

Sold at offered terms—price	$72,000	
Less 7% Commission	− 5,040	(.07)(72,000) = 5,040
Less discount	1,728	
Seller's net	$65,232	

$72,000	Sales price		Net at original	$68,820
× .80	Loan-to-value ratio		Net at offered	− 65,232
$57,600	Loan amount		Difference	$ 3,588
× .03	Points			
$ 1,728	Discount			

Equity

Example:

If a homeowner has a first mortgage loan balance of $48,350, a second mortgage loan balance of $18,200, and $26,300 equity, what is the value of her home?

Solution:

In this case, the value of the home is determined by the total loan balance plus the equity. Add the three numbers to find the value of the home.

$48,350 loan balance + $18,200 loan balance + $26,300 = value of the home

$92,850 = value of the home

Qualifying Buyers

Example:

A buyer is obtaining a conventional loan that requires 29/33 ratios. He earns $66,000 a year, and has a $1,350 car payment. What is his maximum PITI payment?

a. $1,612.50

b. $1,812.50

c. $21,750.00

d. $2,475.00

Solution:

$66,000 divided by 12 = $5,500 monthly income

($5,500)(.29) = $1,595 front end qualifier

($5,500)(.33) = $1,850 − $1,350 debt = $500 back end qualifier

Maximum PITI (Principal, Interest, Taxes, and Insurance) is the lower of these two qualifiers, $500.

Prorations

At the time of settlement, there must be a reconciliation or adjustment of any monies owed by either party as of that date. The important fact to bear in mind is that *the party who used the service pays for it.* If you will keep this firmly in mind, you will not have any difficulty deciding who to credit and who to debit.

Example:

Mr. Seller's taxes are $1,200 a year paid in advance on a calendar year. He is settling on the sale of his house to Mr. Buyer on August 1. Which of them owes how much to the other?

Solution:

Ask yourself some questions:

How many months has the seller paid for?	12	($1,200)
How many months has the seller used?	7	($700)
How many months should the seller be reimbursed for?	5	($500)
How many months will the buyer use?	5	($500)
How many months has he paid for?	0	($0)
How many months should he reimburse the seller for?	5	($500)

Credit Mr. Seller $500

Debit Mr. Buyer $500

What would the answer be if the taxes were paid in arrears? In other words, the seller has used the service for seven months but hasn't paid anything. The buyer will have to pay it all at the end of the year. In that case, the seller owes the buyer for seven months, or $700.

Commissions

Let's look at a commission problem. They are typically rate (percentage) problems.

Example:

Broker Jones sold the Smith house for $65,000. The total commission came to $4,000. What was Jones's commission rate? Round to the nearest whole percent.

Solution:

You see the word *rate* and decide this is solved using percentages.

Start with the values you know.

Price of house = 65,000

Commission Rate = x

Commission = 4,000

Now, translate the word problem into an equation.

$65,000x = 4,000$

Divide both sides by 65,000.

$x = \frac{4,000}{65,000}$

$x = 0.061$

Convert the decimal to a percent by moving the decimal two places to the right. 0.061 becomes 6.1%.

Example:

An agent received a 3% commission on $\frac{1}{4}$ of her total sales. On the remainder, she received a 6% commission. What was her average commission for all of her sales?

Solution:

Start off by asking yourself: How many fourths (parts) were there? Four, naturally.

3%   6%   6%   6%

To find the average, you add up all the numbers, and divide by the number of items you add together. In this case, there are four numbers.

So, 3 + 6 + 6 + 6 = 21.

And 21% ÷ 4 = 5.25%.

Sale Proceeds

Example:

Salesman Garcia was trying to list a house. The owner said he wanted to clear (net) $12,000 from the sale of the house. The balance of the mortgage was $37,000. It would cost about $1,200 to fix up the house to sell. How much would the owner have to sell the house for if the 7% commission was included? (Round your answer to the nearest cent.)

Solution:

Use a chart to clarify the problem.

Expenses	In Dollars	In Percents
Seller's net	$12,000	
Loan balance	$37,000	
Repairs	$1,200	
Commissio		%
	$50,200	7%

If the sales price is 100% and the commission is 7% of the sales price, all the remaining items added together must make 93% of the sales price. The place where most people go wrong is in not including the seller's net when they add the expenses. The seller's net has to come out of the sales price. (Where else would it come from?) Therefore, it is part of the remaining 93%. You now have a percentage problem. As always, convert your percents to decimals.

Start with the values you know:

Expenses = $50,200

Sales price = x

Seller's net, loan balance, repairs = .93 of sales price

.93 of the sales price is $50,200.

Convert this statement into an equation.

$(.93)(x) = \$50,200$

Divide both sides by .93.

$\frac{(.93)(x)}{.93} = \frac{\$50,200}{.93}$

$x = \frac{\$50,200}{.93}$

$x = \$53,978.4945$

Don't forget to round to the nearest cent!

$x = \$53,978.49$

Transfer Tax/Conveyance Tax/Revenue Stamps

Here is a transfer tax question.

Example:

A property is sold for $135,800 in cash. The transfer tax is $441.35. If transfer taxes are calculated per $200 of value, what was the rate (per $200) of the transfer tax?

Solution:

Start with the values you know.

Selling price = $135,800

Transfer tax rate = x per $200

Transfer tax = $441.35

It's probably easiest to begin by dividing by $200 since the rate is calculated per $200 of value.

So, $\frac{\$135,800}{\$200} = \$679$.

You know that $441.35 is produced by multiplying $679 by some rate. Translate this into math terms.

$\$441.35 = (x)(\$679)$

Divide both sides by $679.

$\frac{\$441.35}{(\$679)} = \frac{(x)(\$679)}{(\$679)}$

$.65 = x$

Therefore, the transfer tax rate is $.65 per $200.

Competitive Market Analyses (CMA)

To solve these problems, you will use measurements and other hypothetical features of the comparable property to arrive at a value. Remember, a CMA is not an appraisal.

Example:

If Building A measures 52' by 106' and Building B measures 75' by 85', how much will B cost if A costs $140,000 and both cost the same per square foot to build?

Solution:

Area = (length)(width)

Area of Building A = (52)(106) = 5,512 square feet

Area of Building B = (75)(85) = 6,375 square feet

Cost of Building A per square foot = $\frac{140,000}{5,512}$ = $25.40

Cost of Building B = (6,375)($25.40) = $161,925

Example:

Carson's house (B), which is being appraised, is an exact twin of the houses on either side of it, built by the same builder at the same time. House A was appraised for $45,000, but it has a 14 × 20 foot garage, which was added at a cost of about $18 per square foot. House C was recently sold for $43,000, with central air valued at $3,000. What would be a fair estimate of the value of Carson's house?

Solution:

Comparable C	$43,000
– Air Conditioning	– 3,000
	40,000

Comparable A	$45,000	Garage:	14' × 20' = 280 sq. ft.
– Cost of Garage	– 5,040		280 sq. ft. × $18 = $5,040
	$39,960		

Answer: $40,000

Income Properties

Example:

An investor is considering the purchase of an income property generating a gross income of $350,000. Operating expenses constitute 70% of gross income. If the investor wants a return of 14%, what is the maximum he can pay?

Solution:

Gross income = $350,000

Expenses = 70% of gross income

Net income = Gross income – Expenses

Desired return = 14%

Maximum buyer can pay = x

This is a multi-step problem. Start by calculating the expenses, but remember you will need to stop to calculate the net income. First, change the percent to a decimal.

70% = .70

Now, you know that expenses are 70% of the gross income of $350,000. Change the words to mathematical terms.

Expenses = (.7)(350,000) = $245,000

Gross income − Expenses = Net income

$350,000 − $245,000 = $105,000

The buyer wants the net income ($105,000) to be 14% of what he pays for the property.

Change the percent to a decimal (14% = .14) and then convert this statement to an equation.

$105,000 = (.14)(x)

Divide both sides by .14.

$$\frac{\$105,000}{.14} = \frac{(.14)(x)}{.14}$$

$105,000 ÷ .14 = x

$750,000 = x

Depreciation

There are several methods of depreciation, but the only one you are likely to meet on your exam is the straight-line method. This method spreads the total depreciation over the useful life of the building in equal annual amounts. It is calculated by dividing the replacement cost by the years of useful life left.

$$\frac{\text{replacement cost}}{\text{years of useful life}} = \text{annual depreciation}$$

The depreciation rate may be given or may have to be calculated by the straight-line method. This means dividing the total depreciation (100%) by the estimated useful life given for the building.

$$\frac{100\%}{\text{years of useful life}} = \text{depreciated rate}$$

If a building has 50 years of useful life left, the depreciation rate would be computed as follows:

$$\frac{100\%}{50} = 2\%$$

In other words, it has a 2% depreciation rate annually.

Example:

The replacement cost of a building has been estimated at $80,000. The building is 12 years old and has an estimated 40 years of useful life left. What can be charged to annual depreciation? What is the total depreciation for 12 years? What is the present value of this building?

Solution:

Calculate the annual depreciation.

$$\frac{\text{replacement cost}}{\text{years of useful life}} = \text{annual depreciation}$$

$$\frac{\$80,000}{40} = \$2,000$$

Find the total depreciation over the 12 years.

Annual depreciation of $\$2,000 \times 12$ years $= \$24,000$.

Find the current value: replacement − depreciation = current value.

$\$80,000 − \$24,000 = \$56,000$

▶ Summary

Hopefully, with this review, you have realized that real estate math is not as bad as it seems. If you feel you need more practice, check out LearningExpress's *Practical Math Success in 20 Minutes a Day* or *1001 Math Problems*. Use the exams in the books to practice even more real estate math.

CHAPTER

6 ▶ Real Estate Glossary

CHAPTER SUMMARY

One of the most basic components in preparing for Massachusetts Real Estate Sales Exam is making sure you know all the terminology. This glossary provides a list of the most commonly used real estate terms and their definitions.

THESE TERMS WILL help you not only as you study for your real estate exam, but also after you pass your exam and are practicing in the field. The terms are listed in alphabetical order for easy reference.

▶ A

abandonment the voluntary surrender of a right, claim, or interest in a piece of property without naming a successor as owner or tenant.

abstract of title a certified summary of the history of a title to a particular parcel of real estate that includes the original grant and all subsequent transfers, encumbrances, and releases.

abutting sharing a common boundary; adjoining.

acceleration clause a clause in a note, mortgage, or deed of trust that permits the lender to declare the entire amount of principal and accrued interest due and payable immediately in the event of default.

acceptance the indication by a party receiving an offer that they agree to the terms of the offer. In most states the offer and acceptance must be reduced to writing when real property is involved.

accretion the increase or addition of land resulting from the natural deposit of sand or soil by streams, lakes, or rivers.

accrued depreciation (1) the amount of depreciation, or loss in value, that has accumulated since initial construction; (2) the difference between the current appraised value and the cost to replace the building new.

accrued items a list of expenses that have been incurred but have not yet been paid, such as interest on a mortgage loan, which are included on a closing statement.

acknowledgment a formal declaration before a public official, usually a notary public, by a person who has signed a deed, contract, or other document that the execution was a voluntary act.

acre a measure of land equal to 43,560 square feet or 4,840 square yards.

actual eviction the result of legal action brought by a landlord against a defaulted tenant, whereby the tenant is physically removed from rented or leased property by a court order.

actual notice the actual knowledge that a person has of a particular fact.

addendum any provision added to a contract, or an addition to a contract that expands, modifies, or enhances the clarity of the agreement. To be a part of the contract and legally enforceable, an addendum must be referenced within the contract.

adjacent lying near to but not necessarily in actual contact with.

adjoining contiguous or attached; in actual contact with.

adjustable-rate mortgage (ARM) a mortgage in which the interest changes periodically, according to corresponding fluctuations in an index. All ARMs are tied to indexes. For example, a seven-year, adjustable-rate mortgage is a loan where the rate remains fixed for the first seven years, then fluctuates according to the index to which it is tied.

adjusted basis the original cost of a property, plus acquisition costs, plus the value of added improvements to the property, minus accrued depreciation.

adjustment date the date the interest rate changes on an adjustable-rate mortgage.

administrator a person appointed by a court to settle the estate of a person who has died without leaving a will.

ad valorem **tax** tax in proportion to the value of a property.

adverse possession a method of acquiring title to another person's property through court action after taking actual, open, hostile, and continuous possession for a statutory period of time; may require payment of property taxes during the period of possession.

affidavit a written statement made under oath and signed before a licensed public official, usually a notary public.

agency the legal relationship between principal and agent that arises out of a contract wherein an agent is employed to do certain acts on behalf of the principal who has retained the agent to deal with a third party.

agent one who has been granted the authority to act on behalf of another.

agreement of sale a written agreement between a seller and a purchaser whereby the purchaser agrees to buy a certain piece of property from the seller for a specified price.

air rights the right to use the open space above a particular property.

alienation the transfer of ownership of a property to another, either voluntarily or involuntarily.

alienation clause the clause in a mortgage or deed of trust that permits the lender to declare all unpaid principal and accrued interest due and payable if the borrower transfers title to the property.

allodial system in the United States, a system of land ownership in which land is held free and clear of any rent or services due to the government; commonly contrasted with the feudal system, in which ownership is held by a monarch.

amenities features or benefits of a particular property that enhance the property's desirability and value, such as a scenic view or a pool.

amortization the method of repaying a loan or debt by making periodic installment payments composed of both principal and interest. When all principal has been repaid, it is considered fully amortized.

amortization schedule a table that shows how much of each loan payment will be applied toward principal and how much toward interest over the lifespan of the loan. It also shows the gradual decrease of the outstanding loan balance until it reaches zero.

amortize to repay a loan through regular payments that are comprised of principal and interest.

annual percentage rate (APR) the total or effective amount of interest charged on a loan, expressed as a percentage, on a yearly basis. This value is created according to a government formula intended to reflect the true annual cost of borrowing.

anti-deficiency laws laws used in some states to limit the claim of a lender on default on payment of a purchase money mortgage on owner-occupied residential property to the value of the collateral.

anti-trust laws laws designed to protect free enterprise and the open marketplace by prohibiting certain business practices that restrict competition. In reference to real estate, these laws would prevent such practices as price-fixing or agreements by brokers to limit their areas of trade.

apportionments adjustment of income, expenses, or carrying charges related to real estate, usually computed to the date of closing so that the seller pays all expenses to date, then the buyer pays all expenses beginning on the closing date.

appraisal an estimate or opinion of the value of an adequately described property, as of a specific date.

appraised value an opinion of a property's fair market value, based on an appraiser's knowledge, experience, and analysis of the property, based on comparable sales.

appraiser an individual qualified by education, training, and experience to estimate the value of real property. Appraisers may work directly for mortgage lenders, or they may be independent contractors.

appreciation an increase in the market value of a property.

appurtenance something that transfers with the title to land even if not an actual part of the property, such as an easement.

arbitration the process of settling a dispute in which the parties submit their differences to an impartial third party, on whose decision on the matter is binding.

ARELLO the Association of Real Estate License Law Officials.

assessed value the value of a property used to calculate real estate taxes.

assessor a public official who establishes the value of a property for taxation purposes.

assessment the process of assigning value on property for taxation purposes.

asset items of value owned by an individual. Assets that can be quickly converted into cash are considered "liquid assets," such as bank accounts and stock portfolios. Other assets include real estate, personal property, and debts owed.

assignment the transfer of rights or interest from one person to another.

assumption of mortgage the act of acquiring the title to a property that has an existing mortgage and agreeing to be liable for the payment of any debt still existing on that mortgage. However, the lender must accept the transfer of liability for the original borrower to be relieved of the debt.

attachment the process whereby a court takes custody of a debtor's property until the creditor's debt is satisfied.

attest to bear witness by providing a signature.

attorney-in-fact a person who is authorized under a power of attorney to act on behalf of another.

avulsion the removal of land from one owner to another when a stream or other body of water suddenly changes its channel.

▶ B

balloon mortgage a loan in which the periodic payments do not fully amortize the loan, so that a final payment (a balloon payment) is substantially larger than the amount of the periodic payments that must be made to satisfy the debt.

balloon payment the final, lump-sum payment that is due at the termination of a balloon mortgage.

bankruptcy an individual or individuals can restructure or relieve themselves of debts and liabilities by filing in federal bankruptcy court. There are many types of bankruptcies, and the most common for an individual is "Chapter 7 No Asset," which relieves the borrower of most types of debts.

bargain and sale deed a deed that conveys title, but does not necessarily carry warranties against liens or encumbrances.

base line one of the imaginary East-West lines used as a reference point when describing property with the rectangular or government survey method of property description.

bench mark a permanently marked point with a known elevation, used as a reference by surveyors to measure elevations.

beneficiary (1) one who benefits from the acts of another; (2) the lender in a deed of trust.

bequest personal property given by provision of a will.

betterment an improvement to property that increases its value.

bilateral contract a contract in which each party promises to perform an act in exchange for the other party's promise also to perform an act.

bill of sale a written instrument that transfers ownership of personal property. A bill of sale cannot be used to transfer ownership of real property, which is passed by deed.

binder an agreement, accompanied by an earnest money deposit, for the purchase of a piece of real estate to show the purchaser's good faith intent to complete a transaction.

biweekly mortgage a mortgage in which payments are made every two weeks instead of once a month. Therefore, instead of making 12 monthly payments during the year, the borrower makes the equivalent of 13 monthly payments. The extra payment reduces the principal, thereby reducing the time it takes to pay off a 30-year mortgage.

blanket mortgage a mortgage in which more than one parcel of real estate is pledged to cover a single debt.

blockbusting the illegal and discriminatory practice of inducing homeowners to sell their properties by suggesting or implying the introduction of members of a protected class into the neighborhood.

bona fide in good faith, honest.

bond evidence of personal debt secured by a mortgage or other lien on real estate.

boot money or property provided to make up a difference in value or equity between two properties in an exchange.

branch office a place of business secondary to a principal office. The branch office is a satellite office generally run by a licensed broker, for the benefit of the broker running the principal office, as well as the associate broker's convenience.

breach of contract violation of any conditions or terms in a contract without legal excuse.

broker the term *broker* can mean many things, but in terms of real estate, it is the owner-manager of a business that brings together the parties to a real estate transaction for a fee. The roles of brokers and brokers' associates are defined by state law. In the mortgage industry, broker usually refers to a company or individual that does not lend the money for the loans directly, but that brokers loans to larger lenders or investors.

brokerage the business of bringing together buyers and sellers or other participants in a real estate transaction.

broker's price opinion (BPO) a broker's opinion of value based on a competitive market analysis, rather than a certified appraisal.

building code local regulations that control construction, design, and materials used in construction that are based on health and safety regulations.

building line the distance from the front, rear, or sides of a building lot beyond which no structures may extend.

building restrictions limitations listed in zoning ordinances or deed restrictions on the size and type of improvements allowed on a property.

bundle of rights the concept that ownership of a property includes certain rights regarding the property, such as possession, enjoyment, control of use, and disposition.

buydown usually refers to a fixed-rate mortgage where the interest rate is "bought down" for a temporary period, usually one to three years. After that time and for the remainder of the term, the borrower's payment is calculated at the note rate. In order to buy down the initial rate for the temporary payment, a lump sum is paid and held in an account used to supplement the borrower's monthly payment. These funds usually come from the seller as a financial incentive to induce someone to buy their property.

buyer's broker real estate broker retained by a prospective buyer; this buyer becomes the broker's client to whom fiduciary duties are owed.

bylaws rules and regulations adopted by an association—for example, a condominium.

▶ C

cancellation clause a provision in a lease that confers on one or all parties to the lease the right to terminate the parties' obligations, should the occurrence of the condition or contingency set forth in the clause happen.

canvassing the practice of searching for prospective clients by making unsolicited phone calls and/or visiting homes door-to-door.

cap the limit on fluctuation rates regarding adjustable-rate mortgages. Limitations, or caps, may apply to how much the loan may adjust over a six-month period, an annual period, and over the life of the loan. There is also a limit on how much that payment can change each year.

capital money used to create income, or the net worth of a business as represented by the amount by which its assets exceed its liabilities.

capital expenditure the cost of a betterment to a property.

capital gains tax a tax charged on the profit gained from the sale of a capital asset.

capitalization the process of estimating the present value of an income-producing piece of property by dividing anticipated future income by a capitalization rate.

capitalization rate the rate of return a property will generate on an owner's investment.

cash flow the net income produced by an investment property, calculated by deducting operating and fixed expenses from gross income.

caveat emptor a phrase meaning "let the buyer beware."

CC&R covenants, conditions, and restrictions of a cooperative or condominium development.

certificate of discharge a document used when the security instrument is a mortgage.

certificate of eligibility a document issued by the Veterans Administration that certifies a veteran's eligibility for a VA loan.

certificate of reasonable value (CRV) once the appraisal has been performed on a property being bought with a VA loan, the Veterans Administration issues a CRV.

certificate of sale the document given to a purchaser of real estate that is sold at a tax foreclosure sale.

certificate of title a report stating an opinion on the status of a title, based on the examination of public records.

chain of title the recorded history of conveyances and encumbrances that affect the title to a parcel of land.

chattel personal property, as opposed to real property.

chattel mortgage a loan in which personal property is pledged to secure the debt.

city a large municipality governed under a charter and granted by the state.

clear title a title that is free of liens and legal questions as to ownership of a property that is a requirement for the sale of real estate; sometimes referred to as just title, good title, or free and clear.

closing the point in a real estate transaction when the purchase price is paid to the seller and the deed to the property is transferred from the seller to the buyer.

closing costs there are two kinds: (1) "non-recurring closing costs" and (2) "pre-paid items." Non-recurring closing costs are any items paid once as a result of buying the property or obtaining a loan. Pre-paid items are items that recur over time, such as property taxes and homeowners insurance. A lender makes an attempt to estimate the amount of non-recurring closing costs and pre-paid items on the good faith estimate, which is issued to the borrower within three days of receiving a home loan application.

closing date the date on which the buyer takes over the property.

closing statement a written accounting of funds received and disbursed during a real estate transaction. The buyer and seller receive separate closing statements.

cloud on the title an outstanding claim or encumbrance that can affect or impair the owner's title.

clustering the grouping of home sites within a subdivision on smaller lots than normal, with the remaining land slated for use as common areas.

codicil a supplement or addition to a will that modifies the original instrument.

coinsurance clause a clause in an insurance policy that requires the insured to pay a portion of any loss experienced.

collateral something of value hypothecated (real property) or pledged (personal property) by a borrower as security for a debt.

collection when a borrower falls behind, the lender contacts the borrower in an effort to bring the loan current. The loan goes to "collection."

color of title an instrument that gives evidence of title, but may not be legally adequate to actually convey title.

commercial property property used to produce income, such as an office building or a restaurant.

commingling the illegal act of an agent mixing a client's monies, which should be held in a separate escrow account, with the agent's personal monies; in some states, it means placing funds that are separate property in an account containing funds that are community property.

commission the fee paid to a broker for services rendered in a real estate transaction.

commitment letter a pledge in writing affirming an agreement.

common law the body of laws derived from local custom and judicial precedent.

common areas portions of a building, land, and amenities owned (or managed) by a planned unit development or condominium project's homeowners' association or a cooperative project's cooperative corporation. These areas are used by all of the unit owners, who share in the common expenses of their operation and maintenance. Common areas may include swimming pools, tennis courts, and other recreational facilities, as well as common corridors of buildings, parking areas, and lobbies.

community property a system of property ownership in which each spouse has equal interest in property acquired during the marriage; recognized in nine states.

comparable sales recent sales of similar properties in nearby areas that are used to help estimate the current market value of a property.

competent parties people who are legally qualified to enter a contract, usually meaning that they are of legal age, of sound mind, and not under the influence of drugs or other mind-altering substances.

competitive market analysis (CMA) an analysis intended to assist a seller or buyer in determining a property's range of value.

condemnation the judicial process by which the government exercises its power of eminent domain.

condominium a form of ownership in which an individual owns a specific unit in a multi-unit building and shares ownership of common areas with other unit owners.

condominium conversion changing the ownership of an existing building (usually a multi-dwelling rental unit) from single ownership to condominium ownership.

conformity an appraisal principle that asserts that property achieves its maximum value when a neighborhood is homogeneous in its use of land; the basis for zoning ordinances.

consideration something of value that induces parties to enter into a contract, such as money or services.

construction mortgage a short-term loan used to finance the building of improvements to real estate.

constructive eviction action or inaction by a landlord that renders a property uninhabitable, forcing a tenant to move out with no further liability for rent.

constructive notice notice of a fact given by making the fact part of the public record. All persons are responsible for knowing the information, whether or not they have actually seen the record.

contingency a condition that must be met before a contract is legally binding. A satisfactory home inspection report from a qualified home inspector is an example of a common type of contingency.

contract an agreement between two or more legally competent parties to do or to refrain from doing some legal act in exchange for a consideration.

contract for deed a contract for the sale of a parcel of real estate in which the buyer makes periodic payments to the seller and receives title to the property only after all, or a substantial part, of the purchase price has been paid, or regular payments have been made for one year or longer.

conventional loan a loan that is neither insured nor guaranteed by an agency of government.

conversion option an option in an adjustable-rate mortgage to convert it to a fixed-rate mortgage.

convertible ARM an adjustable-rate mortgage that allows the borrower to change the ARM to a fixed-rate mortgage at a specific time.

conveyance the transfer of title from the grantor to the grantee.

cooperative a form of property ownership in which a corporation owns a multi-unit building and stockholders of the corporation may lease and occupy individual units of the building through a proprietary lease.

corporation a legal entity with potentially perpetual existence that is created and owned by shareholders who appoint a board of directors to direct the business affairs of the corporation.

cost approach an appraisal method whereby the value of a property is calculated by estimating the cost of constructing a comparable building, subtracting depreciation, and adding land value.

counteroffer an offer submitted in response to an offer. It has the effect of overriding the original offer.

credit an agreement in which a borrower receives something of value in exchange for a promise to repay the lender.

credit history a record of an individual's repayment of debt.

cui-de-sac a dead-end street that widens at the end, creating a circular turnaround area.

curtesy the statutory or common law right of a husband to all or part of real estate owned by his deceased wife, regardless of will provisions, recognized in some states.

curtilage area of land occupied by a building, its outbuildings, and yard, either actually enclosed or considered enclosed.

► **D**

damages the amount of money recoverable by a person who has been injured by the actions of another.

datum a specific point used in surveying.

DBA the abbreviation for "doing business as."

debt an amount owed to another.

decedent a person who dies.

dedication the donation of private property by its owner to a governmental body for public use.

deed a written document that, when properly signed and delivered, conveys title to real property from the grantor to the grantee.

deed-in-lieu a foreclosure instrument used to convey title to the lender when the borrower is in default and wants to avoid foreclosure.

deed of trust a deed in which the title to property is transferred to a third party trustee to secure repayment of a loan; three-party mortgage arrangement.

deed restriction an imposed restriction for the purpose of limiting the use of land, such as the size or type of improvements to be allowed. Also called a *restrictive covenant*.

default the failure to perform a contractual duty.

defeasance clause a clause in a mortgage that renders it void where all obligations have been fulfilled.

deficiency judgment a personal claim against a borrower when mortgaged property is foreclosed and sale of the property does not produce sufficient funds to pay off the mortgage. Deficiency judgments may be prohibited in some circumstances by anti-deficiency protection.

delinquency failure to make mortgage or loan payments when payments are due.

density zoning a zoning ordinance that restricts the number of houses or dwelling units that can be built per acre in a particular area, such as a subdivision.

depreciation a loss in value due to physical deterioration, functional, or external obsolescence.

descent the transfer of property to an owner's heirs when the owner dies intestate.

devise the transfer of title to real estate by will.

devisee one who receives a bequest of real estate by will.

devisor one who grants real estate by will.

directional growth the direction toward which certain residential sections of a city are expected to grow.

discount point 1% of the loan amount charged by a lender at closing to increase a loan's effective yield and lower the fare rate to the borrower.

discount rate the rate that lenders pay for mortgage funds—a higher rate is passed on to the borrower.

dispossess to remove a tenant from property by legal process.

dominant estate (tenement) property that includes the right to use an easement on adjoining property.

dower the right of a widow in the property of her husband upon his death in non-community property states.

down payment the part of the purchase price that the buyer pays in cash and is not financed with a mortgage or loan.

dual agency an agent who represents both parties in a transaction.

due-on-sale clause a provision in a mortgage that allows the lender to demand repayment in full if the borrower sells the property that serves as security for the mortgage.

duress the use of unlawful means to force a person to act or to refrain from an action against his or her will.

▶ E

earnest money down payment made by a buyer of real estate as evidence of good faith.

easement the right of one party to use the land of another for a particular purpose, such as to lay utility lines.

easement by necessity an easement, granted by law and requiring court action that is deemed necessary for the full enjoyment of a parcel of land. An example would be an easement allowing access from land-locked property to a road.

easement by prescription a means of acquiring an easement by continued, open, and hostile use of someone else's property for a statutorily defined period of time.

easement in gross a personal right granted by an owner with no requirement that the easement holder own adjoining land.

economic life the period of time over which an improved property will generate sufficient income to justify its continued existence.

effective age an appraiser's estimate of the physical condition of a building. The actual age of a building may be different than its effective age.

emblements cultivated crops; generally considered to be personal property.

eminent domain the right of a government to take private property for public use upon payment of its fair market value. Eminent domain is the basis for condemnation proceedings.

encroachment a trespass caused when a structure, such as a wall or fence, invades another person's land or air space.

encumbrance anything that affects or limits the title to a property, such as easements, leases, mortgages, or restrictions.

equitable title the interest in a piece of real estate held by a buyer who has agreed to purchase the property, but has not yet completed the transaction; the interest of a buyer under a contract for deed.

equity the difference between the current market value of a property and the outstanding indebtedness due on it.

equity of redemption the right of a borrower to stop the foreclosure process.

erosion the gradual wearing away of land by wind, water, and other natural processes.

escalation clause a clause in a lease allowing the lessor to charge more rent based on an increase in costs; sometimes called a pass-through clause.

escheat the claim to property by the state when the owner dies intestate and no heirs can be found.

escrow the deposit of funds and/or documents with a disinterested third party for safekeeping until the terms of the escrow agreement have been met.

escrow account a trust account established to hold escrow funds for safekeeping until disbursement.

escrow analysis annual report to disclose escrow receipts, payments, and current balances.

escrow disbursements money paid from an escrow account.

estate an interest in real property. The sum total of all the real property and personal property owned by an individual.

estate for years a leasehold estate granting possession for a definite period of time.

estate tax federal tax levied on property transferred upon death.

estoppel certificate a document that certifies the outstanding amount owed on a mortgage loan, as well as the rate of interest.

et al. abbreviation for the Latin phrase *et alius,* meaning "and another."

et ux. abbreviation for Latin term *et uxor,* meaning "and wife."

et vir Latin term meaning "and husband."

eviction the lawful expulsion of an occupant from real property.

evidence of title a document that identifies ownership of property.

examination of title a review of an abstract to determine current condition of title.

exchange a transaction in which property is traded for another property, rather than sold for money or other consideration.

exclusive agency listing a contract between a property owner and one broker that only gives the broker the right to sell the property for a fee within a specified period of time but does not obligate the owner to pay the broker a fee if the owner produces his own buyer without the broker's assistance. The owner is barred only from appointing another broker within this time period.

exclusive right to sell a contract between a property owner and a broker that gives the broker the right to collect a commission regardless of who sells the property during the specified period of time of the agreement.

execution the signing of a contract.

executor/executrix a person named in a will to administer an estate. The court will appoint an administrator if no executor is named. "Executrix" is the feminine form.

executory contract a contract in which one or more of the obligations have yet to be performed.

executed contract a contract in which all obligations have been fully performed.

express contract an oral or written contract in which the terms are expressed in words.

extension agreement an agreement between mortgagor and mortgagee to extend the maturity date of the mortgage after it is due.

external obsolescence a loss in value of a property due to factors outside the property, such as a change in surrounding land use.

▶ **F**

fair housing law a term used to refer to federal and state laws prohibiting discrimination in the sale or rental of residential property.

fair market value the highest price that a buyer, willing but not compelled to buy, would pay, and the lowest a seller, willing but not compelled to sell, would accept.

Federal Housing Administration (FHA) an agency within the U.S. Department of Housing and Urban Development (HUD) that insures mortgage loans by FHA-approved lenders to make loans available to buyers with limited cash.

Federal National Mortgage Association (Fannie Mae) a privately owned corporation that buys existing government-backed and conventional mortgages.

Federal Reserve System the central banking system of the United States, which controls the monetary policy and, therefore, the money supply, interest rates, and availability of credit.

fee simple the most complete form of ownership of real estate.

FHA-insured loan a loan insured by the Federal Housing Administration.

fiduciary relationship a legal relationship with an obligation of trust, as that of agent and principal.

finder's fee a fee or commission paid to a mortgage broker for finding a mortgage loan for a prospective borrower.

first mortgage a mortgage that has priority to be satisfied over all other mortgages.

fixed-rate loan a loan with an interest rate that does not change during the entire term of the loan.

fixture an article of personal property that has been permanently attached to the real estate so as to become an integral part of the real estate.

foreclosure the legal process by which a borrower in default of a mortgage is deprived of interest in the mortgaged property. Usually, this involves a forced sale of the property at public auction, where the proceeds of the sale are applied to the mortgage debt.

forfeiture the loss of money, property, rights, or privileges due to a breach of legal obligation.

franchise in real estate, an organization that lends a standardized trade name, operating procedures, referral services, and supplies to member brokerages.

fraud a deliberate misstatement of material fact or an act or omission made with deliberate intent to deceive (active fraud) or gross disregard for the truth (constructive fraud).

freehold estate an estate of ownership in real property.

front foot a measurement of property taken by measuring the frontage of the property along the street line.

functional obsolescence a loss in value of a property due to causes within the property, such as faulty design, outdated structural style, or inadequacy to function properly.

future interest ownership interest in property that cannot be enjoyed until the occurrence of some event; sometimes referred to as a household or equitable interest.

▶ **G**

general agent an agent who is authorized to act for and obligate a principal in a specific range of matters, as specified by their mutual agreement.

general lien a claim on all property, real and personal, owned by a debtor.

general warranty deed an instrument in which the grantor guarantees the grantee that the title being conveyed is good and free of other claims or encumbrances.

government backed mortgage a mortgage that is insured by the Federal Housing Administration (FHA) or guaranteed by the Department of Veterans Affairs (VA) or the Rural Housing Service (RHS). Mortgages that are not government loans are identified as conventional loans.

Government National Mortgage Association (Ginnie Mae) a government-owned corporation within the U.S. Department of Housing and Urban Development (HUD). Ginnie Mae manages and liquidates government-backed loans and assists HUD in special lending projects.

government survey system a method of land description in which meridians (lines of longitude) and base lines (lines of latitude) are used to divide land into townships and sections.

graduated lease a lease that calls for periodic, stated changes in rent during the term of the lease.

grant the transfer of title to real property by deed.

grant deed a deed that includes three warranties: (1) that the owner has the right to convey title to the property, (2) that there are no encumbrances other than those noted specifically in the deed, and (3) that the owner will convey any future interest that he or she may acquire in the property.

grantee one who receives title to real property.

grantor one who conveys title to real property; the present owner.

gross income the total income received from a property before deducting expenses.

gross income multiplier a rough method of estimating the market value of an income property by multiplying its gross annual rent by a multiplier discovered by dividing the sales price of comparable properties by their annual gross rent.

gross lease a lease in which a tenant pays only a fixed amount for rental and the landlord pays all operating expenses and taxes.

gross rent multiplier similar to *gross income multiplier*, except that it looks at the relationship between sales price and monthly gross rent.

ground lease a lease of land only, on which a tenant already owns a building or will construct improvements.

guaranteed sale plan an agreement between a broker and a seller that the broker will buy the seller's property if it does not sell within a specified period of time.

guardian one who is legally responsible for the care of another person's rights and/or property.

► **H**

habendum **clause** the clause in a deed, beginning with the words "to have and to hold," that defines or limits the exact interest in the estate granted by the deed.

hamlet a small village.

heir one who is legally entitled to receive property when the owner dies intestate.

highest and best use the legally permitted use of a parcel of land that will yield the greatest return to the owner in terms of money or amenities.

holdover tenancy a tenancy where a lessee retains possession of the property after the lease has expired, and the landlord, by continuing to accept rent, agrees to the tenant's continued occupancy.

holographic will a will that is entirely handwritten, dated, and signed by the testator.

home equity conversion mortgage (HECM) often called a reverse-annuity mortgage; instead of making payments to a lender, the lender makes payments to you. It enables older homeowners to convert the equity they have in their homes into cash, usually in the form of monthly payments. Unlike traditional home equity loans, a borrower does not qualify on the basis of income but on the value of his or her home. In addition, the loan does not have to be repaid until the borrower no longer occupies the property.

home equity line of credit a mortgage loan that allows the borrower to obtain cash drawn against the equity of his or her home, up to a pre-determined amount.

home inspection a thorough inspection by a professional that evaluates the structural and mechanical condition of a property. A satisfactory home inspection is often included as a contingency by the purchaser.

homeowner's insurance an insurance policy specifically designed to protect residential property owners against financial loss from common risks such as fire, theft, and liability.

homeowner's warranty an insurance policy that protects purchasers of newly constructed or pre-owned homes against certain structural and mechanical defects.

homestead the parcel of land and improvements legally qualifying as the owner's principal residence.

HUD an acronym for the Department of Housing and Urban Development, a federal agency that enforces federal fair housing laws and oversees agencies such as FHA and GNMA.

► **I**

implied contract a contract where the agreement of the parties is created by their conduct.

improvement human-made addition to real estate.

income capitalization approach a method of estimating the value of income-producing property by dividing its expected annual net operating income of the property by a capitalization rate.

income property real estate developed or improved to produce income.

incorporeal right Intangible, non-possessory rights in real estate, such as an easement or right of way.

independent contractor one who is retained by another to perform a certain task and is not subject to the control and direction of the hiring person with regard to the end result of the task. Individual contractors receive a fee for their services but pay their own expenses and taxes and receive no employee benefits.

index a number used to compute the interest rate for an adjustable-rate mortgage (ARM). The index is a published number or percentage, such as the average yield on Treasury bills. A margin is added to the index to determine the interest rate to be charged on the ARM. This interest rate is subject to any caps that are associated with the mortgage.

industrial property buildings and land used for the manufacture and distribution of goods, such as a factory.

inflation an increase in the amount of money or credit available in relation to the amount of goods or services available, which causes an increase in the general price level of goods and services.

initial interest rate the beginning interest rate of the mortgage at the time of closing. This rate changes for an adjustable-rate mortgage (ARM).

installment the regular, periodic payment that a borrower agrees to make to a lender, usually related to a loan.

installment contract see *contract for deed.*

installment loan borrowed money that is repaid in periodic payments, known as installments.

installment sale a transaction in which the sales price is paid to the seller in two or more installments over more than one calendar year.

insurance a contract that provides indemnification from specific losses in exchange for a periodic payment. The individual contract is known as an insurance policy, and the periodic payment is known as an insurance premium.

insurance binder a document that states that temporary insurance is in effect until a permanent insurance policy is issued.

insured mortgage a mortgage that is protected by the Federal Housing Administration (FHA) or by private mortgage insurance (PMI). If the borrower defaults on the loan, the insurer must pay the lender the insured amount.

interest (1) a fee charged by a lender for the use of the money loaned; (2) a share of ownership in real estate.

interest accrual rate the percentage rate at which interest accrues on the mortgage.

interest rate the rent or rate charged to use funds belonging to another.

interest rate buydown plan an arrangement where the property seller (or any other party) deposits money to an account so that it can be released each month to reduce the mortgagor's monthly payments during the early years of a mortgage. During the specified period, the mortgagor's effective interest rate is "bought down" below the actual interest rate.

interest rate ceiling the maximum interest rate that may be charged for an adjustable-rate mortgage (ARM), as specified in the mortgage note.

interest rate floor the minimum interest rate for an adjustable-rate mortgage (ARM), as specified in the mortgage note.

interim financing a short-term loan made during the building phase of a project; also known as a construction loan.

intestate to die without having authored a valid will.

invalid not legally binding or enforceable.

investment property a property not occupied by the owner.

► **J**

joint tenancy co-ownership that gives each tenant equal interest and equal rights in the property, including the right of survivorship.

joint venture an agreement between two or more parties to engage in a specific business enterprise.

judgment a decision rendered by court determining the rights and obligations of parties to an action or lawsuit.

judgment lien a lien on the property of a debtor resulting from a court judgment.

judicial foreclosure a proceeding that is handled as a civil lawsuit and conducted through court; used in some states.

jumbo loan a loan that exceeds Fannie Mae's mortgage amount limits. Also called a *nonconforming loan*.

junior mortgage any mortgage that is inferior to a first lien and that will be satisfied only after the first mortgage; also called a secondary mortgage.

► **L**

laches a doctrine used by a court to bar the assertion of a legal claim or right, based on the failure to assert the claim in a timely manner.

land the earth from its surface to its center, and the air space above it.

landlocked property surrounded on all sides by property belonging to another.

lease a contract between a landlord and a tenant wherein the landlord grants the tenant possession and use of the property for a specified period of time and for a consideration.

leased fee the landlord's interest in a parcel of leased property.

lease option a financing option that allows homebuyers to lease a home with an option to buy. Each month's rent payment may consist of rent, plus an additional amount that can be applied toward the down payment on an already specified price.

leasehold a tenant's right to occupy a parcel of real estate for the term of a lease.

legal description a description of a parcel of real estate specific and complete enough for an independent surveyor to locate and identify it.

lessee the one who receives that right to use and occupy the property during the term of the leasehold estate.

lessor the owner of the property who grants the right of possession to the lessee.

leverage the use of borrowed funds to purchase an asset.

levy to assess or collect a tax.

license (1) a revocable authorization to perform a particular act on another's property; (2) authorization granted by a state to act as a real estate broker or salesperson.

lien a legal claim against a property to secure payment of a financial obligation.

life estate a freehold estate in real property limited in duration to the lifetime of the holder of the life estate or another specified person.

life tenant one who holds a life estate.

liquidity the ability to convert an asset into cash.

lis pendens a Latin phrase meaning "suit pending"; a public notice that a lawsuit has been filed that may affect the title to a particular piece of property.

listing agreement a contract between the owner and a licensed real estate broker where the broker is employed to sell real estate on the owner's terms within a given time, for which service the owner agrees to pay the broker an agreed-upon fee.

listing broker a broker who contracts with a property owner to sell or lease the described property; the listing agreement typically may provide for the broker to make property available through a multiple listing system.

littoral rights landowner's claim to use water in large, navigable lakes and oceans adjacent to property; ownership rights to land-bordering bodies of water up to the high-water mark.

loan a sum of borrowed money, or principal, that is generally repaid with interest.

loan officer or lender, serves several functions and has various responsibilities, such as soliciting loans; a loan officer both represents the lending institution and represents the borrower to the lending institution.

lock-in an agreement in which the lender guarantees a specified interest rate for a certain amount of time.

lock-in period the time period during which the lender has guaranteed an interest rate to a borrower.

lot and block description a method of describing a particular property by referring to a lot and block number within a subdivision recorded in the public record.

▶ **M**

management agreement a contract between the owner of an income property and a firm or individual who agrees to manage the property.

margin the difference between the interest rate and the index on an adjustable-rate mortgage. The margin remains stable over the life of the loan, while the index fluctuates.

market data approach a method of estimating the value of a property by comparing it to similar properties recently sold and making monetary adjustments for the differences between the subject property and the comparable property.

market value the amount that a seller may expect to obtain for merchandise, services, or securities in the open market.

marketable title title to property that is free from encumbrances and reasonable doubts and that a court would compel a buyer to accept.

mechanic's lien a statutory lien created to secure payment for those who supply labor or materials for the construction of an improvement to land.

metes and bounds a method of describing a parcel of land using direction and distance.

mill one-tenth of one cent; used by some states to express or calculate property tax rates.

minor a person who has not attained the legal age of majority.

misrepresentation a misstatement of fact, either deliberate or unintentional.

modification the act of changing any of the terms of the mortgage.

money judgment a court order to settle a claim with a monetary payment, rather than specific performance.

month-to-month tenancy tenancy in which the tenant rents for only one month at a time.

monument a fixed, visible marker used to establish boundaries for a survey.

mortgage a written instrument that pledges property to secure payment of a debt obligation as evidenced by a promissory note. When duly recorded in the public record, a mortgage creates a lien against the title to a property.

mortgage banker an entity that originates, funds, and services loans to be sold into the secondary money market.

mortgage broker an entity that, for a fee, brings borrowers together with lenders.

mortgage lien an encumbrance created by recording a mortgage.

mortgagee the lender who benefits from the mortgage.

mortgagor the borrower who pledges the property as collateral.

multi-dwelling units properties that provide separate housing units for more than one family that secure only a single mortgage. Apartment buildings are also considered multi-dwelling units.

multiple listing system (MLS—also multiple listing service) the method of marketing a property listing to all participants in the MLS.

mutual rescission an agreement by all parties to a contract to release one another from the obligations of the contract.

▶ **N**

negative amortization occurs when an adjustable-rate mortgage is allowed to fluctuate independently of a required minimum payment. A gradual increase in mortgage debt happens when the monthly payment is not large enough to cover the entire principal and interest due. The amount of the shortfall is added to the remaining balance to create negative amortization.

net income the income produced by a property, calculated by deducting operating expenses from gross income.

net lease a lease that requires the tenant to pay maintenance and operating expenses, as well as rent.

net listing a listing in which the broker's fee is established as anything above a specified amount to be received by the seller from the sale of the property.

net worth the value of all of a person's assets.

no cash-out refinance a refinance transaction in which the new mortgage amount is limited to the sum of the remaining balance of the existing first mortgage.

nonconforming use a use of land that is permitted to continue, or grandfathered, even after a zoning ordinance is passed that prohibits the use.

non-liquid asset an asset that cannot easily be converted into cash.

notarize to attest or certify by a notary public.

notary public a person who is authorized to administer oaths and take acknowledgments.

note a written instrument acknowledging a debt, with a promise to repay, including an outline of the terms of repayment.

note rate the interest rate on a promissory note.

notice of default a formal written notice to a borrower that a default has occurred on a loan and that legal action may be taken.

novation the substitution of a new contract for an existing one; the new contract must reference the first and indicate that the first is being replaced and no longer has any force and effect.

▶ O

obligee person on whose favor an obligation is entered.

obligor person who is bound to another by an obligation.

obsolescence a loss in the value of a property due to functional or external factors.

offer to propose as payment; bid on property.

offer and acceptance two of the necessary elements for the creation of a contract.

open-end mortgage a loan containing a clause that allows the mortgagor to borrow additional funds from the lender, up to a specified amount, without rewriting the mortgage.

open listing a listing contract given to one or more brokers in which a commission is paid only to the broker who procures a sale. If the owner sells the house without the assistance of one of the brokers, no commission is due.

opinion of title an opinion, usually given by an attorney, regarding the status of a title to property.

option an agreement that gives a prospective buyer the right to purchase a seller's property within a specified period of time for a specified price.

optionee one who receives or holds an option.

optionor one who grants an option; the property owner.

ordinance a municipal regulation.

original principal balance the total amount of principal owed on a loan before any payments are made; the amount borrowed.

origination fee the amount charged by a lender to cover the cost of assembling the loan package and originating the loan.

owner financing a real estate transaction in which the property seller provides all or part of the financing.

ownership the exclusive right to use, possess, control, and dispose of property.

▶ P

package mortgage a mortgage that pledges both real and personal property as collateral to secure repayment of a loan.

parcel a lot or specific portion of a large tract of real estate.

participation mortgage a type of mortgage in which the lender receives a certain percentage of the income or resale proceeds from a property, as well as interest on the loan.

partition the division of property held by co-owners into individual shares.

partnership an agreement between two parties to conduct business for profit. In a partnership, property is owned by the partnership, not the individual partners, so partners cannot sell their interest in the property without the consent of the other partners.

party wall a common wall used to separate two adjoining properties.

payee one who receives payment from another.

payor one who makes payment to another.

percentage lease a lease in which the rental rate is based on a percentage of the tenant's gross sales. This type of lease is most often used for retail space.

periodic estate tenancy that automatically renews itself until either the landlord or tenant gives notice to terminate it.

personal property (hereditaments) all items that are not permanently attached to real estate; also known as chattels.

physical deterioration a loss in the value of a property due to impairment of its physical condition.

PITI principal, interest, taxes, and insurance—components of a regular mortgage payment.

planned unit development (PUD) a type of zoning that provides for residential and commercial uses within a specified area.

plat a map of subdivided land showing the boundaries of individual parcels or lots.

plat book a group of maps located in the public record showing the division of land into subdivisions, blocks, and individual parcels or lots.

plat number a number that identifies a parcel of real estate for which a plat has been recorded in the public record.

PMI private mortgage insurance.

point a point is one percent of the loan.

point of beginning the starting point for a survey using the "metes and bounds" method of description.

police power the right of the government to enact laws, ordinances, and regulations to protect the public health, safety, welfare, and morals.

power of attorney a legal document that authorizes someone to act on another's behalf. A power of attorney can grant complete authority or can be limited to certain acts and/or certain periods of time.

pre-approval condition where a borrower has completed a loan application and provided debt, income, and savings documentation that an underwriter has reviewed and approved. A pre-approval is usually done at a certain loan amount, making assumptions about what the interest rate will actually be at the time the loan is actually made, as well as estimates for the amount that will be paid for property taxes, insurance, and so on.

prepayment amount paid to reduce the outstanding principal balance of a loan before the due date.

prepayment penalty a fee charged to a borrower by a lender for paying off a debt before the term of the loan expires.

prequalification a lender's opinion on the ability of a borrower to qualify for a loan, based on furnished information regarding debt, income, and available capital for down payment, closing costs, and prepaids. Prequalification is less formal than pre-approval.

prescription a method of acquiring an easement to property by prolonged, unauthorized use.

primary mortgage market the financial market in which loans are originated, funded, and serviced.

prime rate the short-term interest rate that banks charge to their preferred customers. Changes in prime rate are used as the indexes in some adjustable-rate mortgages, such as home equity lines of credit.

principal (1) one who authorizes another to act on his or her behalf, (2) one of the contracting parties to a transaction, (3) the amount of money borrowed in a loan, separate from the interest charged on it.

principal meridian one of the 36 longitudinal lines used in the rectangular survey system method of land description.

probate the judicial procedure of proving the validity of a will.

procuring cause the action that brings about the desired result. For example, if a broker takes actions that result in a sale, the broker is the procuring cause of the sale.

promissory note details the terms of the loan and is the debt instrument.

property management the operating of an income property for another.

property tax a tax levied by the government on property, real or personal.

prorate to divide ongoing property costs such as taxes or maintenance fees proportionately between buyer and seller at closing.

pur autre vie a phrase meaning "for the life of another." In a life estate *pur autre vie,* the term of the estate is measured by the life of a person other than the person who holds the life estate.

purchase agreement a written contract signed by the buyer and seller stating the terms and conditions under which a property will be sold.

purchase money mortgage a mortgage given by a buyer to a seller to secure repayment of any loan used to pay part or all of the purchase price.

▶ **Q**

qualifying ratios calculations to determine whether a borrower can qualify for a mortgage. There are two ratios. The "top" ratio is a calculation of the borrower's monthly housing costs (principle, taxes, insurance, mortgage insurance, homeowner's association fees) as a percentage of monthly income. The "bottom" ratio includes housing costs as well as all other monthly debt.

quitclaim deed a conveyance where the grantor transfers without warranty or obligations whatever interest or title he/she may have.

▶ **R**

range an area of land six miles wide, numbered East or West from a principal meridian in the rectangular survey system.

ready, willing, and able one who is able to pay the asking price for a property and is prepared to complete the transaction.

real estate land, the earth below it, the air above it, and anything permanently attached to it.

real estate agent a real estate broker who has been appointed to market a property for and represent the property owner (listing agent), or a broker who has been appointed to represent the interest of the buyer (buyer's agent).

real estate board an organization whose members are primarily comprised of real estate sales agents, brokers, and administrators.

real estate broker a licensed person, association, partnership, or corporation who negotiates real estate transactions for others for a fee.

Real Estate Settlement Procedures Act (RESPA) a consumer protection law that requires lenders to give borrowers advance notice of closing costs and prohibits certain abusive practices against buyers using federally related loans to purchase their homes.

real property the rights of ownership to land and its improvements.

REALTOR® a registered trademark for use by members of the National Association of REALTORS® and affiliated state and local associations.

recording entering documents, such as deeds and mortgages, into the public record to give constructive notice.

rectangular survey system a method of land description based on principal meridians (lines of longitude) and base lines (lines of latitude). Also called the *government survey system*.

redemption period the statutory period of time during which an owner can reclaim foreclosed property by paying the debt owed plus court costs and other charges established by statute.

redlining the illegal practice of lending institutions refusing to provide certain financial services, such as mortgage loans, to property owners in certain areas.

refinance transaction the process of paying off one loan with the proceeds from a new loan using the same property as security or collateral.

Regulation Z a Federal Reserve regulation that implements the federal Truth-in-Lending Act.

release clause a clause in a mortgage that releases a portion of the property upon payment of a portion of the loan.

remainder estate a future interest in an estate that takes effect upon the termination of a life estate.

remaining balance in a mortgage, the amount of principal that has not yet been repaid.

remaining term the original amortization term minus the number of payments that have been applied to it.

rent a periodic payment paid by a lessee to a landlord for the use and possession of leased property.

replacement cost the estimated current cost to replace an asset similar or equivalent to the one being appraised.

reproduction cost the cost of building an exact duplicate of a building at current prices.

rescission canceling or terminating a contract by mutual consent or by the action of one party on default by the other party.

restriction (restrict covenant) a limitation on the way a property can be used.

reversion the return of interest or title to the grantor of a life estate.

reverse annuity mortgage when a homeowner receives monthly checks or a lump sum with no repayment until property is sold, usually an agreement between mortgagor and elderly homeowners.

revision a revised or new version, as in a contract.

right of egress (or ingress) the right to enter or leave designated premises.

right of first refusal the right of a person to have the first opportunity to purchase property before it is offered to anyone else.

right of redemption the statutory right to reclaim ownership of property after a foreclosure sale.

right of survivorship in joint tenancy, the right of survivors to acquire the interest of a deceased joint tenant.

riparian rights the rights of a landowner whose property is adjacent to a flowing waterway, such as a river, to access and use the water.

► S

safety clause a contract provision that provides a time period following expiration of a listing agreement, during which the agent will be compensated if there is a transaction with a buyer who was initially introduced to the property by the agent.

sale-leaseback a transaction where the owner sells improved property and, as part of the same transaction, signs a long-term lease to remain in possession of its premises, thus becoming the tenant of the new owner.

sales contract a contract between a buyer and a seller outlining the terms of the sale.

salesperson one who is licensed to sell real estate in a given territory.

salvage value the value of a property at the end of its economic life.

satisfaction an instrument acknowledging that a debt has been paid in full.

second mortgage a mortgage that is in less than first lien position; see *junior mortgage*.

section as used in the rectangular survey system, an area of land measuring one square mile, or 640 acres.

secured loan a loan that is backed by property or collateral.

security property that is offered as collateral for a loan.

selling broker the broker who secures a buyer for a listed property; the selling broker may be the listing agent, a sub-agent, or a buyer's agent.

separate property property owned individually by a spouse, as opposed to community property.

servient tenement a property on which an easement or right-of-way for an adjacent (dominant) property passes.

setback the amount of space between the lot line and the building line, usually established by a local zoning ordinance or restrictive covenants; see *deed restrictions*.

settlement statement (HUD-1) the form used to itemize all costs related to closing of a residential transaction covered by RESPA regulations.

severalty the ownership of a property by only one legal entity.

special assessment a tax levied against only the specific properties that will benefit from a public improvement, such as a street or sewer; an assessment by a homeowners' association for a capital improvement to the common areas for which no budgeted funds are available.

special warranty deed a deed in which the grantor guarantees the title only against the defects that may have occurred during the grantor's ownership and not against any defects that occurred prior to that time.

specific lien a lien, such as a mortgage, that attaches to one defined parcel of real estate.

specific performance a legal action in which a court compels a defaulted party to a contract to perform according to the terms of the contract, rather than awarding damages.

standard payment calculation the method used to calculate the monthly payment required to repay the remaining balance of a mortgage in equal installments over the remaining term of the mortgage at the current interest rate.

Statute of Frauds the state law that requires certain contracts to be in writing to be enforceable.

Statute of Limitations the state law that requires that certain actions be brought to court within a specified period of time.

statutory lien a lien imposed on property by statute, such as a tax lien.

steering the illegal practice of directing prospective homebuyers to or away from particular areas.

straight-line depreciation a method of computing depreciation by decreasing value by an equal amount each year during the useful life of the property.

subdivision a tract of land divided into lots as defined in a publicly recorded plat that complies with state and local regulations.

sublet the act of a lessee transferring part or all of his or her lease to a third party while maintaining responsibility for all duties and obligations of the lease contract.

subordinate to voluntarily accept a lower priority lien position than that to which one would normally be entitled.

substitution the principle in appraising that a buyer will be willing to pay no more for the property being appraised than the cost of purchasing an equally desirable property.

subrogation the substitution of one party into another's legal role as the creditor for a particular debt.

suit for possession a lawsuit filed by a landlord to evict a tenant who has violated the terms of the lease or retained possession of the property after the lease expired.

suit for specific performance a lawsuit filed for the purpose of compelling a party to perform particular acts to settle a dispute, rather than pay monetary damages.

survey a map that shows the exact legal boundaries of a property, the location of easements, encroachments, improvements, rights of way, and other physical features.

syndicate a group formed by a syndicator to combine funds for real estate investment.

▶ T

tax deed in some states, an instrument given to the purchaser at the time of sale.

tax lien a charge against a property created by law or statute. Tax liens take priority over all other types of liens.

tax rate the rate applied to the assessed value of a property to determine the property taxes.

tax sale the court-ordered sale of a property after the owner fails to pay *ad valorem* taxes owed on the property.

tenancy at sufferance the tenancy of a party who unlawfully retains possession of a landlord's property after the term of the lease has expired.

tenancy at will an indefinite tenancy that can be terminated by either the landlord or the tenant at any time by giving notice to the other party one rental period in advance of the desired termination date.

tenancy by the entirety ownership by a married couple of property acquired during the marriage with right of survivorship; not recognized by community property states.

tenancy in common a form of co-ownership in which two or more persons hold an undivided interest in property without the right of survivorship.

tenant one who holds or possesses the right of occupancy title.

tenement the space that may be occupied by a tenant under the terms of a lease.

testate to die having created a valid will directing the testator's desires with regard to the disposition of the estate.

"time is of the essence" a phrase in a contract that requires strict adherence to the dates listed in the contract as deadlines for the performance of specific acts.

timesharing undivided ownership of real estate for only an allotted portion of a year.

title a legal document that demonstrates a person's right to, or ownership of, a property. **Note:** Title is *not* an instrument. The instrument, such as a deed, gives evidence of title or ownership.

title insurance an insurance policy that protects the holder from defects in a title, subject to the exceptions noted in the policy.

title search a check of public records to ensure that the seller is the legal owner of the property and that there are no liens or other outstanding claims.

Torrens System a system of registering titles to land with a public authority, who is usually called a registrar.

township a division of land, measuring 36 square miles, in the government survey system.

trade fixtures an item of personal property installed by a commercial tenant and removable upon expiration of the lease.

transfer tax a state or municipal tax payable when the conveyancing instrument is recorded.

trust an arrangement in which title to property is transferred from a grantor to a trustee, who holds title but not the right of possession for a third party, the beneficiary.

trustee a person who holds title to property for another person designated as the beneficiary.

Truth-in-Lending Law also known as Regulation Z; requires lenders to make full disclosure regarding the terms of a loan.

▶ **U**

underwriting the process of evaluating a loan application to determine the risk involved for the lender.

undivided interest the interest of co-owners to use an entire property despite the fractional interest owned.

unilateral contract a one-sided contract in which one party is obligated to perform a particular act completely, before the other party has any obligation to perform.

unsecured loan a loan that is not backed by collateral or security.

useful life the period of time a property is expected to have economic utility.

usury the practice of charging interest at a rate higher than that allowed by law.

▶ V

VA-guaranteed loan a mortgage loan made to a qualified veteran that is guaranteed by the Department of Veterans Affairs.

valid contract an agreement that is legally enforceable and binding on all parties.

valuation estimated worth.

variance permission obtained from zoning authorities to build a structure that is not in complete compliance with current zoning laws. A variance does not permit a non-conforming use of a property.

vendee a buyer.

vendor a seller; the property owner.

village an incorporated minor municipality usually larger than a hamlet and smaller than a town.

void contract a contract that is not legally enforceable; the absence of a valid contract.

voidable contract a contract that appears to be valid but is subject to cancellation by one or both of the parties.

▶ W

waiver the surrender of a known right or claim.

warranty deed a deed in which the grantor fully warrants a good clear title to the property.

waste the improper use of a property by a party with the right to possession, such as the holder of a life estate.

will a written document that directs the distribution of a deceased person's property, real and personal.

wraparound mortgage a mortgage that includes the remaining balance on an existing first mortgage plus an additional amount. Full payments on both mortgages are made to the wraparound mortgagee who then forwards the payments on the first mortgage to the first mortgagee.

writ of execution a court order to the sheriff or other officer to sell the property of a debtor to satisfy a previously rendered judgment.

▶ Z

zone an area reserved by authorities for specific use that is subject to certain restrictions.

zoning ordinance the exercise of regulating and controlling the use of a property in a municipality.

► Massachusetts Real Estate Sales Exam II

1. Tenancy by the entirety is a special form of ownership available only to
   a. sole owners.
   b. corporations.
   c. married couples.
   d. limited partners.

2. The holder of a life estate may do all of the following EXCEPT
   a. pay the property taxes and special assessments.
   b. maintain the property.
   c. mortgage the life interest.
   d. direct the disposition of the property at the end of the measuring life.

3. In the market or sales data approach to appraisal, the sales prices of similar, recently sold properties are
   a. assessed.
   b. analyzed.
   c. adjusted.
   d. added.

4. Which of the following is the simplest form of ownership?
   a. severalty
   b. joint tenancy
   c. community property
   d. tenants in common

5. The formula for determining the value of investment property is
   a. net operating income ÷ capitalization rate = value.
   b. potential gross income ÷ capitalization rate = value.
   c. effective gross income × capitalization rate = value.
   d. cost of replacing the property × capitalization rate = value.

6. The cost approach is best suited for estimating the value of
   a. a large tract of land.
   b. the income generated by a commercial property.
   c. a historic building.
   d. a condominium apartment.

7. A specific tract of land is called
   a. an acre.
   b. a lot.
   c. a parcel.
   d. a subdivision.

8. Riparian rights are
   a. an owner's rights in land bordering a river or stream.
   b. the right of an owner to sue a tenant.
   c. the government's ability to take over land.
   d. the rights of purchasers to sue for specific performance.

9. Before a property owner can have a septic tank installed, he or she must have the soil tested to determine how much wastewater the soil can absorb by ordering a(n)
   a. percolation test.
   b. pest inspection.
   c. field investigation.
   d. home inspection.

10. Remediation and testing for asbestos can only be done by contractors who have been specifically trained, and are approved by either
   a. the local municipality or the county.
   b. the federal or state government.
   c. the Department of Health or the EPA.
   d. the EPA or the Commonwealth of Massachusetts.

11. While the objective in the cost approach generally is to estimate the value of both land and improvements, the land typically is appraised using the
   a. income approach.
   b. gross rent multiplier approach.
   c. market data approach.
   d. option approach.

12. The economic characteristics of land that affect the value include
   a. construction and labor costs.
   b. proximity to land fills.
   c. relative scarcity, improvements, and area preference.
   d. eminent domain.

13. A salesperson may be hired by his or her broker as a(n)
   a. part-time employee.
   b. independent contractor.
   c. full-time employee.
   d. all of the above

14. A subagency relationship cannot be created without
   a. the principal's consent.
   b. a written contract.
   c. the buyer's permission.
   d. approval of the agent's broker.

15. Expense adjustments that are prorated on the closing statement appear as
   a. debits only.
   b. debits and credits.
   c. abstract of title.
   d. encroachments.

16. Which of the following would NOT be considered a freehold estate?
   a. fee simple estate
   b. life estate
   c. estate for the years
   d. defeasance fee estate

17. The formal judicial proceedings to prove the validity of a deed is
   a. courtesy.
   b. probate.
   c. life tenant.
   d. chattel.

18. An owner of real estate has which of the following ownership rights?
   a. air rights
   b. surface rights
   c. subsurface rights
   d. all of the above

19. A real estate gift by a will would be
   a. a devise.
   b. an acquisition.
   c. a prescription.
   d. a succession.

20. The process of applying all three appraisal approaches on the same property to determine value is called
   a. summary.
   b. comparison.
   c. reconciliation.
   d. assessment.

21. If a house had no closets in the bedrooms, this would be an example of what type of depreciation?
   a. physical
   c. functional
   b. economic
   d. obsolescence

22. What would MOST affect the value of real estate?
   a. the appraisal
   b. the location
   c. the book value
   d. the age of the building

23. If you owned unit number nine in a condominium complex, what would you own?
   a. the tennis courts and health club
   b. the hallways in the building
   c. an equal share of each unit in the complex
   d. the air space within unit number nine

24. A husband and wife own a multi-family building jointly in which they do not live. If they sell the building, their capital gain exclusion would be
   a. zero.
   b. $250,000.
   c. $500,000.
   d. $100,000.

25. An addition to a will that could transfer real property and personal property would be
   a. a bequest.
   b. a gift.
   c. a codicil.
   d. an agreement of sale.

26. The purpose of metes and bounds boundaries is
   a. meridians.
   b. to allow a surveyor to walk the boundaries.
   c. ranges.
   d. a bearing system.

27. In an FHA mortgage, if the appraised value is less than the selling price, the borrower must
   a. pay the difference in cash.
   b. cancel the loan.
   c. apply for another loan.
   d. obtain a second loan.

28. A junior mortgage can be obtained from all of the following EXCEPT
   a. the seller.
   b. the buyer's aunt.
   c. another bank.
   d. Fannie Mae.

29. Which would be true in a foreclosure sale?
   a. The owner would retain title to the property.
   b. The mortgagor has a six-month right of redemption.
   c. If there is a balance of sale proceeds after the debts have been paid, the mortgagor is entitled to them.
   d. The owner can pay points to avoid the foreclosure sale.

30. The earnest money deposit in the settlement statement is
   a. not shown.
   b. debited to the buyer.
   c. credited to the seller.
   d. credited to the buyer.

31. A year that starts on October 1 and concludes on September 30 of the following year would
   a. not be possible.
   b. be a calendar year.
   c. be an accelerated year.
   d. be a fiscal year.

32. What must happen at the closing of a real estate transaction?
   a. The buyer and seller must sign the deed.
   b. The deed must be executed and delivered by the grantor.
   c. The deed must be recorded.
   d. The broker must be present.

33. If Mr. and Mrs. Braun, the sellers, signed a Purchase and Sales Agreement with Mr. and Mrs. Jones, and then for no apparent reason, refused to go through with the sale, the buyer(s) could sue for
   a. adverse possession.
   b. specific performance.
   c. adverse easement.
   d. dower and courtesy.

34. When a principal gives an agent the right to act on the principal's behalf, this creates
   a. an agency.
   b. a fiduciary.
   c. an obligation of good faith and loyalty.
   d. all of the above

35. The effort that brings about the producing of a buyer for a listed property is
   a. the procuring cause.
   b. a market analysis.
   c. hypothecation.
   d. cooperation.

36. Seller Hall tells the broker that he wants to net out a net price of $225,000 and the broker can retain any amount over that as his commission. In Massachusetts, that would be
   a. an exclusive listing.
   b. illegal.
   c. advantageous to the seller.
   d. advantageous to the agent.

37. Miss Morgan bought a parcel of land for $115,000. She built a 36' by 24' home on it at a cost of $200 per square foot. What was the total cost of the land and the building?
   a. $172,800
   b. $205,000
   c. $287,800
   d. $305,000

38. Miss Morgan then sold the property described in question 37 for a 25% profit. She paid a broker a 6% commission. How much did she net from the sale?
   a. $405,000
   b. $359,750
   c. $338,165
   d. $287,800

39. What is the law that prohibits telephone solicitation to any household number illegal unless one has express written permission?
a. Rice-Evans Do Not Call Law
b. Do Not Call Registry
c. ADA Law
d. Truth-in-Lending Law

40. What is the name of the regulation to assist consumers so that they can readily compare the various credit terms available to them?
a. Regulation Z
b. Regulation 21E
c. Regulation 1031
d. none of the above

41. An asphalt company gives a property owner an estimated cost of $15.00 per cubic foot to install a driveway that is 40 feet long by 20 feet wide with a height of 3 inches of asphalt over the driveway. What would be the cost to install the driveway?
a. $1,200
b. $1,500
c. $3,000
d. $18,000

42. In order to practice real estate in Massachusetts, all salespersons must
a. be affiliated with a broker.
b. join the Multiple Listing Service.
c. become a REALTOR®.
d. obtain an appraiser's license.

43. A property owner's right to sell, lease, encumber, use, enjoy, and exclude would be described as
a. a fee simple.
b. a bundle of rights.
c. a devise.
d. littoral.

44. Lessee Belanger rented a building for the purpose of operating a health club and installed a running track for members of the club. This track would be considered
a. a fixture.
b. real property.
c. an easement.
d. a trade fixture.

45. Arlene and Jack Smith inherited their home from his parents by a will. This would be an example of
a. escheat.
b. devise.
c. demise.
d. life estate.

46. Jesse, John's tenant, was arrested. John wants to end the tenancy. What can John do?
a. He can immediately remove Jesse's personal belongings.
b. He can change the locks.
c. He can stop providing services.
d. He can serve Jesse with a 30-Day Notice to Quit.

47. You wish to fill in your rectangular swimming pool with concrete. The pool size is 50 feet long, 25 feet wide, and 8 feet deep. You get an estimate of $45 per cubic yard for concrete. What would be the cost to fill in the pool?
a. $45,000
b. $27,195.13
c. $20,000
d. $16,667.67

48. If a married man willed all of his real estate to his sister and nothing to his wife, upon his death what rights would his wife have?
   a. none
   b. courtesy
   c. dower
   d. license

49. You are trying to determine the value of a three-family house for purchase. What factors would you need to determine the property value?
   a. net income and capitalization rates
   b. gross income
   c. property assessment
   d. the mortgage payments

50. A junior mortgage would be an example of
   a. a secondary mortgage market.
   b. secondary financing.
   c. a reverse mortgage.
   d. a FHA mortgage

51. If a seller has to pay a prepayment penalty in the first three years of the mortgage, this would be an example of
   a. an open-end mortgage.
   b. an open/closed mortgage.
   c. a closed/open mortgage.
   d. a moratorium.

52. Alan bought his land with an agreement that he could not stable a horse on the property. This would be
   a. a restrictive covenant.
   b. discriminatory.
   c. unfair.
   d. a dominant estate.

53. Broker Borden has a hiring contract with seller Carl. Buyer Grace then hires broker Borden to be her buyer-agent. Buyer Grace now wants to buy seller Carl's property. What can broker Borden do?
   a. represent each party independently
   b. represent both parties as a dual agent
   c. Broker Borden is not able to represent either party.
   d. only collect a commission from the seller

54. Agent B has a listing and shows it to Buyer Z. Buyer Z does not like the property because it does not have a garage. Agent B gives Buyer Z several business cards and tells Buyer not to view or buy any property without Agent B. Buyer Z goes to an open house hosted by Agent C and buys the property directly from Agent C. Agent B
   a. is entitled to a commission.
   b. is a buyer's agent.
   c. does not have an agency relationship with Buyer Z.
   d. is a subagent.

55. In Massachusetts, a seller's description of property
   a. must be given at the first meeting.
   b. must be prepared by the broker.
   c. must be presented at the closing.
   d. is not required.

56. A seller tells the agent that there is a crack in the foundation, but the insulation is covering it. The agent
   a. does not have to tell the buyer.
   b. must inform the seller it has to be repaired before listing the property.
   c. must inform the buyer, even if the buyer does not ask about the foundation.
   d. does not have any responsibility concerning this issue.

57. Broker Smith knows that the real estate taxes on a property are $5,200. He knows that if he states that amount, the buyers will not buy the property; so he states that the taxes are $2,500. This would be a violation of what Massachusetts general law?
   a. Chapter 93A
   b. Chapter 21E
   c. Tristam's Landing
   d. Taft-Hartly Law

58. Seller Jones sells property to Buyer Mulligan. The transfer deed tax is $1,368. Who owes the tax?
   a. the buyer
   b. the seller
   c. both **a** and **b**
   d. the mortgagor

59. If you lived in a common law state and you married a person who owned his or her property in severalty, you
   a. would not have any ownership rights.
   b. would become a 50% co-owner automatically.
   c. would become a grantor.
   d. would be entitled to $\frac{1}{3}$ of the ownership.

60. A buyer and seller have a Purchase and Sales Agreement to close on the sale by the fifteenth day of the next month. What would be the most important factor of those listed below?
   a. the earnest money
   b. the assessed value of the property
   c. notarizing the Purchase and Sales Agreement
   d. Time is of the essence.

61. Wear and tear on a property would be an example of what type of obsolescence?
   a. economic
   b. functional
   c. physical
   d. scarcity

62. Effective gross income would be
   a. annual gross rents less an amount for vacancy and collection costs.
   b. gross income less the debt service.
   c. gross income less the operating expenses.
   d. the building's cash flow.

63. A runner ran the Boston Marathon, which is 26.2 miles, in four hours. What was the length of the course in feet?
   a. 138,336 feet
   b. 43,560 feet
   c. 137,800 feet
   d. 3,800,400 feet

64. The Massachusetts Mandatory Licensee-Consumer Relationship Disclosure replaces what form?
   a. Sellers Disclosure form
   b. Lead Paint Disclosure form
   c. UFFI form
   d. the Agency Disclosure form

65. The office policy for your office is to do a two-call listing presentation. When must disclosure of agency be given?
   a. at the first meeting
   b. at the signing of the listing agreement
   c. at the time of the offer
   d. at the time of the closing

66. In order to do subagency in Massachusetts, you must obtain permission from the
   a. Board of Registration.
   b. buyer.
   c. seller.
   d. none of the above

67. A facilitator has which of the following duties?
   a. to be honest
   b. to account for funds
   c. both **a** and **b**
   d. The facilitator has no duties.

68. You are a landlord and have a one-year lease with tenant Miller. You have just received a 15% real estate tax increase. When can you increase the tenant's rent?
   a. immediately
   b. after giving a 30-day written notice
   c. at the end of the lease period
   d. never

69. Your apartment lease is for three years. Two years into the tenancy, the building is sold and the new owners want you to vacate. What are your rights?
   a. You can remain until the lease ends.
   b. You can sublet your apartment.
   c. You have no rights.
   d. You can stop paying the rent.

70. A Chevrolet dealer has a ground lease with the city of Newton. If the Chevrolet dealer wants to have the right to transfer all of its rights to another party, this would be an example of a/an
   a. sub-lease.
   b. assignment.
   c. escheat.
   d. termination.

71. If a branch of your neighbor's pear tree extends over your property, this would be called a(n)
   a. testator.
   b. encroachment.
   c. riparian.
   d. littoral.

72. Property owner Davis inherited property from his mother in a life estate and then immediately sold the property to buyer Jones. If property owner Davis dies, who owns the property?
   a. the grantee
   b. the executor
   c. the remainderman
   d. no one

73. If a person owned an investment property and then sold it, how could that person defer the capital gain taxes?
   a. by completing a 1031 exchange
   b. The taxes cannot be deferred.
   c. The person must wait until reaching age 55 before selling.
   d. A real estate agent must be hired.

74. To comply with the Massachusetts Mandatory Licensee-Consumer Relationship Disclosure, a broker principal should
   a. take continuing education classes.
   b. become a facilitator.
   c. develop an office policy for the associates to follow.
   d. become a REALTOR®.

75. A buyer enters into an exclusive buyer agency contract with broker Borden and then buys a property with broker Carl without broker Borden being involved in the sale. Who owes broker Borden a commission?
a. Broker Carl
b. the buyer
c. the seller
d. Broker Borden is not entitled to a commission.

76. A bank's closing attorney is responsible to
a. establish the commissions for the agents.
b. provide the 6D Certificate.
c. prepare the Purchase and Sales Agreement.
d. prepare the HUD-1 Uniform Settlement Statement form.

77. You are a licensed salesperson, and you have an attorney acquaintance who wants to start a realty brokerage company and hire you. Which of the following is true?
a. You can start the company with your license.
b. The attorney can immediately start the company.
c. The attorney has to take the broker's test.
d. The attorney can obtain a broker's license by applying for it.

78. If a borrower has private mortgage insurance on his loan and wants to eliminate it, the current loan balance would have to be less than what percent of the original loan balance?
a. 60%
b. 75%
c. 80%
d. 95%

79. An elderly couple hired a maid to assist them and then willed their property to the maid. Thirty years later, the maid died without leaving a will or having any known family heirs. The government could acquire the property through
a. escheat.
b. a disclosure act.
c. testate.
d. tenancy.

80. A mortgage that incorporates existing mortgages and is subordinate to them is known as
a. a take-over mortgage.
b. a secondary mortgage market.
c. a wraparound mortgage.
d. a primary mortgage.

81. A Massachusetts broker has been hired by a Colorado developer to sell his unimproved lots, sight unseen, in Massachusetts. The broker must comply with
a. the dual agency laws.
b. the designated agency laws.
c. the Interstate Land Sales Full Disclosure Act.
d. the Installment Land Sales Contract Act.

82. At the closing, the mortgagee would have to sign which of the following documents?
a. the promissory note
b. the mortgage deed
c. the deed
d. none of the above

83. At the closing, who would be responsible for calculating the proration of expenses between the parties?
a. the salesperson
b. the broker
c. the closing attorney
d. the buyer's attorney

84. Why would a property owner want to file for the Homestead Exemption?
   a. to protect the property against claims of mechanic's liens
   b. to protect the property against a mortgage lien
   c. to protect the property against riparian rights
   d. to protect the property against an appurtenance

85. In Massachusetts, a landlord must do which of the following if the last month's rent is held for MORE than one year?
   a. return it
   b. pay interest on it
   c. apply it to damages to the property
   d. deposit it in an escrow account

86. A landlord who owns a two-family house collects $1,200 in rent from each tenant on the first day of the month. On the twelfth of the month, the landlord sells the property. The adjustment would be
   a. an amount of $960 would be due to the buyer.
   b. an amount of $1,400 would be due to the seller.
   c. an amount of $1,440 would be due to the buyer.
   d. an amount of $1,520 would be due to the seller.

87. The role of the appraiser is to
   a. analyze the value of the property.
   b. qualify the buyer for the loan.
   c. both **a** and **b**
   d. neither **a** nor **b**

88. An investor asks your advice about the best way to take title to an investment property. What would you advise?
   a. by single proprietorship
   b. by corporation
   c. by a real estate trust
   d. You would refer the investor to an attorney.

89. You are associated with Ace Realty and are terminating the association in order to become associated with Plus Realty. What actions have to be taken?
   a. You must notify the Board of your new obligation.
   b. Ace Realty must notify the Board.
   c. Plus Realty must notify the Board.
   d. all of the above

90. If a tenant moves into an apartment and replaces an old light with a new ceiling fan, the ceiling fan would be considered to be
   a. real property.
   b. personal property.
   c. a trade fixture.
   d. littoral property.

91. If an investor was using factors of annual gross income and average selling prices of properties in a community, this would be an example of
   a. capitalization.
   b. gross rent multiplier.
   c. comparison.
   d. substitution.

92. If an investment property was purchased for $300,000, the annual depreciation was $3,000, and the owner has owned the property for 12 years, then the book value of the property would be
a. $300,000.
b. $270,000.
c. $264,000.
d. $36,000.

93. One of the disadvantages of buying an investment property is
a. lack of liquidity.
b. appreciation.
c. revocation.
d. blockbusting.

94. A broker principal deposits the earnest money from a buyer into the office business account in order that the rent can be paid. This would be considered to be
a. a business expense.
b. commingling of funds.
c. legal.
d. a personal expense.

95. To obtain a license in Massachusetts, a person can be
a. a resident of the Commonwealth.
b. a non-resident of the Commonwealth.
c. Both **a** and **b** are correct.
d. Neither **a** nor **b** are correct.

96. In Massachusetts, in order for a real estate salesperson to become a real estate broker, the person must
a. work as a salesperson for two years.
b. obtain a license by applying for it.
c. become a REALTOR®.
d. be actively associated with a broker for a minimum of 25 hours per week for one year.

97. A minor signed a two-year lease for an apartment. This would be an example of
a. a valid contract.
b. a voided contract.
c. a voidable contract.
d. consummation.

98. The owner of a health food store in a mall wants you to sell his business. What type of license would you need?
a. None is required.
b. a real estate salesperson's license
c. a real estate broker's license
d. a commercial real estate license

99. What provides the basis for an accurate appraisal?
a. assessment value
b. the appraiser's knowledge
c. the listing information
d. the cooperation of the home inspector

100. A buyer of investment property would be most interested in what appraisal method?
a. cost
b. comparison
c. income
d. accelerated

101. Most appraisals will require the use of
   a. one approach.
   b. more than one approach.
   c. the plat.
   d. city planning.

102. The city or town board that surveys the social and economic needs of the community is
   a. the Board of Appeals.
   b. the Board of Governors.
   c. the Board of Health.
   d. the Planning Board.

103. What gives municipal government the right to regulate and control the use of land for the protection of public health, safety, and general welfare of its citizens?
   a. environmental protection laws
   b. a master plan
   c. police power
   d. Board of Registration

104. A gas station owner owns a station in an area that had no zoning, but now has been zoned as residential. The gas station owner can continue to operate his business because of
   a. nonconforming use.
   b. variance.
   c. cluster zoning.
   d. urban development.

105. A woman willed her estate as follows: 63% to her husband, 10% to her son, 12% to her daughter, and the remainder to her college. If the college received $30,000, how much did her daughter receive?
   a. $10,000
   b. $15,000
   c. $20,000
   d. $24,000

106. A lease would be an estate
   a. that expires on a certain date.
   b. that has the landlord's consent.
   c. that has novation.
   d. that is intestate.

107. Leading prospective home buyers to or away from certain areas would be
   a. redlining.
   b. steering.
   c. legal.
   d. a violation of RESPA.

108. A person buys a property for $500,000 with a 10% down payment and pays 2 points for a better rate. The amount of the points would be
   a. $10,000.
   b. $9,000.
   c. $5,000.
   d. $4,500.

109. The Federal Housing Administration (FHA)
   a. lends monies to banks.
   b. buys mortgages from banks.
   c. lends money for the purchase of homes to qualified individuals.
   d. sets the Federal Discount Rate.

110. If a home is 44 feet long and is being built on a lot which has a 50-foot setback on each side, what frontage must that lot have?
   a. 1,232 square feet
   b. 44 feet
   c. 94 feet
   d. 150 feet

▶ Answers

1. **c.** Tenancy by the entirety, available in most non-community property states, is automatically assumed when a married couple purchases real estate together, unless they specify some other form of ownership. Tenancy by the entirety means that on the death of the spouse, the survivor becomes the owner of the property.

2. **d.** Within the terms of the life estate, the holder's interest ends at the death of the person (typically, the holder) against whose life the life estate is measured.

3. **c.** Sales prices of comparable properties are adjusted to match the specifications of the subject property.

4. **a.** Severalty is the simplest because there is only one person involved. All other forms involve multiple owners.

5. **a.** Net operating income is divided by the appropriate capitalization rate to arrive at the value of the property.

6. **c.** The cost approach is preferable when appraising unique properties.

7. **c.** A parcel has definite boundaries and is a specific tract of land.

8. **a.** Riparian rights are an owner's rights in land bordering a body of water.

9. **a.** A percolation test is required prior to installing a septic tank; the septic tank must also be large enough to accommodate the number of occupants that will be residing in the home.

10. **d.** Since asbestos, if disturbed, has the potential to pose severe health risks, great care must be taken to protect individuals at or nearby the affected area. The Environmental Protection Agency (EPA) or the State both provide an intensive training program for individuals whose job it is to remove the asbestos.

11. **c.** Land is appraised by comparing the subject property to recent sales of comparable parcels of land.

12. **c.** In addition to relative scarcity, improvements, and area preference, the economic characteristics of land include permanence of investment.

13. **d.** A licensed sales agent is required by law to be supervised by his or her broker, and may be hired as an employee, full time or part time, or as an independent contractor.

14. **a.** Subagents are those upon whom the power of an agent has been conferred by the listing agent, but can only be created with the principal's consent.

15. **b.** Entries for expenses are shown as debits and credits to the appropriate parties.

16. **c.** An estate for the years is a non-freehold estate. The others are all freehold estates.

17. **b.** Probate is the judicial procedure to prove the validity of a deed.

18. **d.** All of the choices are rights of ownership.

19. **a.** Devise is when ownership is transferred by means of a will.

20. **c.** Reconciliation is the process of applying all three methods.

21. **b.** Since most homes have closets in the bedrooms, this is an example of functional loss of value.

22. **b.** The location of the property is the most important feature of real estate.

23. **d.** Air space is the only area of ownership. All of the other choices are common areas.

24. **a.** There are no exclusions for capital gains in non-owner occupied buildings.

25. **c.** The codicil is the addition to the will that could transfer real and personal property.

26. b. This allows the surveyor to identify the length and boundaries of the property.

27. a. The buyer must pay the difference in cash. He may utilize secondary financing to accomplish this.

28. d. Fannie Mae does not lend money. It is part of the secondary mortgage market.

29. c. The mortgagor would be entitled to any equity.

30. d. An earnest money deposit would be a credit to the buyer.

31. d. The fiscal year is any 12-month period.

32. b. The deed must be signed and delivered by the grantor. Recording is not mandatory.

33. b. If the sellers refuse to sell, the buyers can sue for specific performance.

34. d. An agency relationship occurs when the principal hires the agent and the agent must perform with good faith and loyalty.

35. a. Procuring cause is the effort in which the agents produce the buyer for the listed property.

36. b. This would be a net listing, which is illegal in Massachusetts.

37. c. The cost of the building: 36' × 24' = 864 square feet × $200 = $172,800 + $115,000 (the cost of the land).

38. c. $287,800 (cost of the building) × 1.25% = $359,750 − broker's commission of $21,585 = $338,165.

39. b. The Do Not Call registry is the legislation that requires permission to make telephone solicitation.

40. a. Regulation Z of the Truth-in-Lending Law requires that a meaningful disclosure must be given to the borrower regarding the cost of obtaining credit.

41. c. 40' × 20' × .25 ($\frac{3}{12}$") = 200 cubic feet × $15 per cubic foot = $3,000.

42. a. To practice real estate, a salesperson must be affiliated with a broker.

43. b. A bundle of legal rights gives the property owner the legal rights of ownership.

44. d. It is a trade fixture because it is used in the business and can be removed.

45. b. Devise is a transfer of real property by means of a will.

46. d. The landlord must serve the tenant with a Notice to Quit. The other actions are illegal.

47. d. 50 × 25 × 8 = 10,000 cubic feet ÷ 27 cubic feet = 370.37 cubic yards × $45 per cubic yard = $16,666.67.

48. c. Dower is the widow's interest in the husband's property.

49. a. Net income and capitalization rates would be required to determine the value.

50. b. The junior mortgage is secondary financing.

51. c. A prepayment penalty would have to be paid if the loan was paid off within the first three years.

52. a. A restrictive covenant restricts the use and occupancy of real estate.

53. b. The broker can represent both parties as a dual agent provided consent is given by both parties.

54. c. Agent B does not have an agency relationship with Buyer Z.

55. d. The Commonwealth of Massachusetts does not require the seller's description of property.

56. c. The agent must inform the buyer; *caveat emptor* does not apply.

57. a. Chapter 93A protects the consumer from misrepresentation.

58. b. The revenue tax is the responsibility of the seller.

59. b. In this situation, you would automatically become a 50% co-owner.

60. d. Time is of the essence; if the property is to close by the fifteenth of the month, then it must be accomplished by this date.

61. c. Wear and tear would be physical obsolescence.

62. a. Effective gross income is gross rents less an amount for vacancy and collection expenses.

63. a. There are 5,280 feet in a mile × 26.2 miles = 138,336 feet.

64. d. It replaces the Agency Disclosure form.

65. a. Disclosure must be given at the first meeting.

66. c. You must obtain permission from the seller to practice subagency.

67. c. The facilitator has the duties of honesty and accountability for the funds.

68. c. A lease is a specific contract. You would have to wait until the end of the lease period.

69. a. You have the right to remain, as the lease is binding on the new owner.

70. b. Assignment is the transfer of the entire remaining terms of the lease.

71. b. Encroachment is when the property of one party intrudes onto another's property.

72. c. The remainder person would own it, not the buyer.

73. a. This person can do a 1031 tax-deferred exchange by buying a like-kind property.

74. c. An office policy should be developed so that the agents have guidelines to follow in order to practice real estate.

75. b. The buyer would owe broker Borden the commission because the buyer had signed an exclusive buyer agency contract.

76. d. The attorney is responsible for preparing the HUD-1 Uniform Settlement Statement form.

77. d. The attorney can just apply for the license without taking the test.

78. c. The loan-to-value ratio would have to be below 80%.

79. a. Escheat is the power of the government to take title of the property of a person who dies intestate.

80. c. A wraparound mortgage incorporates existing mortgages and becomes subordinate to them.

81. c. The broker must comply with the Interstate Land Sales Full Disclosure Act.

82. d. The mortgagee is the lender and would not be required to sign any of these documents.

83. c. The closing attorney is responsible for pro-rating the expenses between the parties.

84. a. To protect the property against claims of mechanic's liens, the Homestead Exemption should be filed.

85. b. The landlord must pay interest on it.

86. c. Rent collected in advance $1,200 × 2 = $2,400; $2,400 ÷ 30 days = $80 per day. If the closing is on the twelfth, the seller is entitled to 12 days worth of rent and the buyer is entitled to 18 days. The adjustment of 18 days × $80 = $1,440 due to the buyer.

87. a. The role of the appraiser is to analyze the value of the property.

88. d. Real estate agents cannot give legal advice.

89. d. Sales agents and brokers must notify the Board of Registration of Real Estate Brokers and Salespersons of these types of changes.

90. a. When the ceiling fan becomes affixed, it becomes real property.

91. b. The gross rent multiplier would be the method utilizing these factors.

92. c. Book value is the cost less the cumulative depreciation; $300,000 − $36,000 ($3,000 × 12) − $264,000.

93. a. Lack of liquidity means having to sell the property in order to obtain cash.

94. b. A broker cannot commingle funds. Earnest money must be deposited into an escrow account.

95. c. A person can be either a resident or a non-resident.

96. d. A person must work at least 25 hours per week for one year to become a broker.

97. c. This is a voidable contract. The minor could cancel the contract.

98. a. A license is not required when selling a business.

99. b. The appraiser's knowledge provides the basis for an accurate appraisal.

100. c. The buyer would be most interested in the income approach.

101. b. Appraisals will require the use of more than one approach.

102. d. The Planning Board surveys the needs of the community.

103. c. Police power gives the municipality the power to regulate for the protection of citizens.

104. a. A new zoning law will not affect the use of any building that had been used before the adoption of the new law.

105. d. The college received 15% of the total; 63 + 10 + 12 donated to the family equals 85%; 100% − 85% = 15% to the college. College contribution of $30,000 ÷ 15% = a total value of $200,000. The daughter received 12% of that, or $24,000.

106. a. A lease has a specific ending date.

107. b. You cannot steer a person into or away from specific neighborhoods.

108. b. Points are based on the mortgage amount; $500,000 − $50,000 (10% down payment) gives a mortgage amount of $450,000 × 2% = $9,000.

109. c. The FHA lends money to qualified individuals.

110. d. The house size equals 44 feet plus the set back requirement of 50 feet on each side, which gives a total measurement of 144 feet. The frontage would need to be greater than 144 feet.

Scoring

Again, evaluate how you did on this practice exam by finding the number of questions you got right, disregarding, for the moment, the ones you got wrong or skipped. If you achieved a score of at least 77 questions correct, you will most likely pass the Massachusetts Real Estate Sales Exam.

If you did not score as well as you would like, ask yourself the following: Did I run out of time before I could answer all of the questions? Did I go back and change my answers from right to wrong? Did I get flustered and sit staring at a difficult question for what seemed like hours? If you had any of these problems, be sure to go over the LearningExpress Test Preparation System in Chapter 2 to review how best to avoid them.

You probably have seen improvement from your first practice exam score and this one; but if you didn't improve as much as you would like, following are some options:

If you scored below the passing score on each section, you should seriously consider whether you are ready for the exam at this time. A good idea would be to take some brush-up courses in the areas you feel less sure of. If you don't have time for a course, you might try private tutoring.

If you scored close to the minimum passing score, you need to work as hard as you can to improve your skills. Go back to your real estate license course textbooks to review. Improve your math skills by reading the LearningExpress book, *Practical Math Success in 20 Minutes a Day*. Also, reread and pay close attention to the information in Chapter 4, Massachusetts Real Estate Refresher Course; Chapter 5, Real Estate Math Review; and Chapter 6, Real Estate Glossary. It might be helpful, as well, to ask friends and family to make up mock test questions and quiz you on them.

Now, revise your study schedule according to the time you have left, emphasizing those parts that gave you the most trouble this time. Use the following table to see where you need more work, so that you can concentrate your preparation efforts. After working more on the subject areas that give you problems, take the third practice exam in Chapter 8 to see how much you have improved.

EXAM II FOR REVIEW

Test II Subject Area	Question Numbers (Questions 1–110)
Real Estate Principles and Practices	1, 2, 4, 7, 8, 10, 16, 17, 18, 19, 23, 25, 25, 45, 48, 52, 59, 71, 72, 79, 81, 84, 87, 88, 93, 102, 103, 104,107
Property Valuation/Appraisal	3, 5, 6, 11, 12, 20, 21, 22, 49, 61, 62, 73, 91, 99, 100, 101
Financing	27, 28, 29, 40, 50, 51, 78, 80, 82, 83, 108, 109
Contacts/Agency Relationship	33, 34, 35, 55, 57, 66, 97, 98
Law, Definition, and Nature of Agency Relationships, Type of Agencies, and Agents	13, 14, 36, 42, 53, 54, 60, 75, 96
Settlement/Transfer of Property	9, 15, 30, 31, 42, 76, 78, 86, 106
Business Practices	24, 39, 56, 64, 65, 67, 74, 77, 89, 94, 95
Property Management	43, 44, 46, 68, 69, 70, 85, 90
Real Estate Math	37, 38, 41, 47, 63, 92, 105, 110

Massachusetts Real Estate Sales Exam III

CHAPTER SUMMARY

This is the third of four practice tests in this book. Use this test to identify which types of questions are still giving you problems.

YOU ARE NOW more familiar with the content and format of the Massachusetts Real Estate Sales Exam, and most likely you feel more confident than you did at first. However, your practice test-taking experience will help you most if you create a situation as close as possible to the real one.

For this exam, try to simulate real testing conditions. Find a quiet place where you will not be disturbed. Make sure you have two sharpened pencils and a good eraser. You should have plenty of time to answer all of the questions when you take the real exam, but you will want to practice working quickly without rushing. Be sure to leave enough time to complete the test in one sitting. Remember you will have four hours for the actual exam. Use a timer or a stopwatch and see if you can work through all the test questions in the allotted time.

As before, the answer sheet you should use is on the next page. Following the exam, you will find the answer key and explanations. These explanations, along with the table at the end of this chapter, will help you see where you need further study.

► Massachusetts Real Estate Sales Exam III Answer Sheet

1.	ⓐ	ⓑ	ⓒ	ⓓ	38.	ⓐ	ⓑ	ⓒ	ⓓ	75.	ⓐ	ⓑ	ⓒ	ⓓ
2.	ⓐ	ⓑ	ⓒ	ⓓ	39.	ⓐ	ⓑ	ⓒ	ⓓ	76.	ⓐ	ⓑ	ⓒ	ⓓ
3.	ⓐ	ⓑ	ⓒ	ⓓ	40.	ⓐ	ⓑ	ⓒ	ⓓ	77.	ⓐ	ⓑ	ⓒ	ⓓ
4.	ⓐ	ⓑ	ⓒ	ⓓ	41.	ⓐ	ⓑ	ⓒ	ⓓ	78.	ⓐ	ⓑ	ⓒ	ⓓ
5.	ⓐ	ⓑ	ⓒ	ⓓ	42.	ⓐ	ⓑ	ⓒ	ⓓ	79.	ⓐ	ⓑ	ⓒ	ⓓ
6.	ⓐ	ⓑ	ⓒ	ⓓ	43.	ⓐ	ⓑ	ⓒ	ⓓ	80.	ⓐ	ⓑ	ⓒ	ⓓ
7.	ⓐ	ⓑ	ⓒ	ⓓ	44.	ⓐ	ⓑ	ⓒ	ⓓ	81.	ⓐ	ⓑ	ⓒ	ⓓ
8.	ⓐ	ⓑ	ⓒ	ⓓ	45.	ⓐ	ⓑ	ⓒ	ⓓ	82.	ⓐ	ⓑ	ⓒ	ⓓ
9.	ⓐ	ⓑ	ⓒ	ⓓ	46.	ⓐ	ⓑ	ⓒ	ⓓ	83.	ⓐ	ⓑ	ⓒ	ⓓ
10.	ⓐ	ⓑ	ⓒ	ⓓ	47.	ⓐ	ⓑ	ⓒ	ⓓ	84.	ⓐ	ⓑ	ⓒ	ⓓ
11.	ⓐ	ⓑ	ⓒ	ⓓ	48.	ⓐ	ⓑ	ⓒ	ⓓ	85.	ⓐ	ⓑ	ⓒ	ⓓ
12.	ⓐ	ⓑ	ⓒ	ⓓ	49.	ⓐ	ⓑ	ⓒ	ⓓ	86.	ⓐ	ⓑ	ⓒ	ⓓ
13.	ⓐ	ⓑ	ⓒ	ⓓ	50.	ⓐ	ⓑ	ⓒ	ⓓ	87.	ⓐ	ⓑ	ⓒ	ⓓ
14.	ⓐ	ⓑ	ⓒ	ⓓ	51.	ⓐ	ⓑ	ⓒ	ⓓ	88.	ⓐ	ⓑ	ⓒ	ⓓ
15.	ⓐ	ⓑ	ⓒ	ⓓ	52.	ⓐ	ⓑ	ⓒ	ⓓ	89.	ⓐ	ⓑ	ⓒ	ⓓ
16.	ⓐ	ⓑ	ⓒ	ⓓ	53.	ⓐ	ⓑ	ⓒ	ⓓ	90.	ⓐ	ⓑ	ⓒ	ⓓ
17.	ⓐ	ⓑ	ⓒ	ⓓ	54.	ⓐ	ⓑ	ⓒ	ⓓ	91.	ⓐ	ⓑ	ⓒ	ⓓ
18.	ⓐ	ⓑ	ⓒ	ⓓ	55.	ⓐ	ⓑ	ⓒ	ⓓ	92.	ⓐ	ⓑ	ⓒ	ⓓ
19.	ⓐ	ⓑ	ⓒ	ⓓ	56.	ⓐ	ⓑ	ⓒ	ⓓ	93.	ⓐ	ⓑ	ⓒ	ⓓ
20.	ⓐ	ⓑ	ⓒ	ⓓ	57.	ⓐ	ⓑ	ⓒ	ⓓ	94.	ⓐ	ⓑ	ⓒ	ⓓ
21.	ⓐ	ⓑ	ⓒ	ⓓ	58.	ⓐ	ⓑ	ⓒ	ⓓ	95.	ⓐ	ⓑ	ⓒ	ⓓ
22.	ⓐ	ⓑ	ⓒ	ⓓ	59.	ⓐ	ⓑ	ⓒ	ⓓ	96.	ⓐ	ⓑ	ⓒ	ⓓ
23.	ⓐ	ⓑ	ⓒ	ⓓ	60.	ⓐ	ⓑ	ⓒ	ⓓ	97.	ⓐ	ⓑ	ⓒ	ⓓ
24.	ⓐ	ⓑ	ⓒ	ⓓ	61.	ⓐ	ⓑ	ⓒ	ⓓ	98.	ⓐ	ⓑ	ⓒ	ⓓ
25.	ⓐ	ⓑ	ⓒ	ⓓ	62.	ⓐ	ⓑ	ⓒ	ⓓ	99.	ⓐ	ⓑ	ⓒ	ⓓ
26.	ⓐ	ⓑ	ⓒ	ⓓ	63.	ⓐ	ⓑ	ⓒ	ⓓ	100.	ⓐ	ⓑ	ⓒ	ⓓ
27.	ⓐ	ⓑ	ⓒ	ⓓ	64.	ⓐ	ⓑ	ⓒ	ⓓ	101.	ⓐ	ⓑ	ⓒ	ⓓ
28.	ⓐ	ⓑ	ⓒ	ⓓ	65.	ⓐ	ⓑ	ⓒ	ⓓ	102.	ⓐ	ⓑ	ⓒ	ⓓ
29.	ⓐ	ⓑ	ⓒ	ⓓ	66.	ⓐ	ⓑ	ⓒ	ⓓ	103.	ⓐ	ⓑ	ⓒ	ⓓ
30.	ⓐ	ⓑ	ⓒ	ⓓ	67.	ⓐ	ⓑ	ⓒ	ⓓ	104.	ⓐ	ⓑ	ⓒ	ⓓ
31.	ⓐ	ⓑ	ⓒ	ⓓ	68.	ⓐ	ⓑ	ⓒ	ⓓ	105.	ⓐ	ⓑ	ⓒ	ⓓ
32.	ⓐ	ⓑ	ⓒ	ⓓ	69.	ⓐ	ⓑ	ⓒ	ⓓ	106.	ⓐ	ⓑ	ⓒ	ⓓ
33.	ⓐ	ⓑ	ⓒ	ⓓ	70.	ⓐ	ⓑ	ⓒ	ⓓ	107.	ⓐ	ⓑ	ⓒ	ⓓ
34.	ⓐ	ⓑ	ⓒ	ⓓ	71.	ⓐ	ⓑ	ⓒ	ⓓ	108.	ⓐ	ⓑ	ⓒ	ⓓ
35.	ⓐ	ⓑ	ⓒ	ⓓ	72.	ⓐ	ⓑ	ⓒ	ⓓ	109.	ⓐ	ⓑ	ⓒ	ⓓ
36.	ⓐ	ⓑ	ⓒ	ⓓ	73.	ⓐ	ⓑ	ⓒ	ⓓ	110.	ⓐ	ⓑ	ⓒ	ⓓ
37.	ⓐ	ⓑ	ⓒ	ⓓ	74.	ⓐ	ⓑ	ⓒ	ⓓ					

► Massachusetts Real Estate Sales Exam III

1. An acre contains approximately
   a. 5,270 square yards.
   b. 40,000 square feet.
   c. 43,560 square feet.
   d. 42,560 square feet.

2. The local town tax rate is $16.50 per $1,000. A property has a tax assessment of $935,980. How much is the annual real estate tax?
   a. $14,443.67
   b. $24,443.67
   c. $18,998.02
   d. $15,443.67

3. The use of a Massachusetts Mandatory Licensee-Consumer Relationship Disclosure form must be presented
   a. when the broker-salesperson has reasonable control of a customer.
   b. when a buyer is prepared to submit a written offer.
   c. at the first meeting to discuss a specific property.
   d. upon the first contact with any client.

4. An individual who chooses to hire a real estate agent to represent his or her best interests is called
   a. a buyer.
   b. a subagent.
   c. a principal.
   d. a fiduciary.

5. The four powers of government that can affect property valuation do NOT include which of the following?
   a. police power
   b. reconciliation
   c. eminent domain
   d. escheat

6. In order to renew a real estate license, Massachusetts requires that each agent
   a. complete a minimum of 15 hours of continuing education courses per year.
   b. complete a minimum of 12 hours of broker continuing education courses every two years.
   c. complete a minimum of 15 hours of broker continuing education courses per year, and pass an exam.
   d. complete two transactions, 20 hours of broker continuing education courses every two years, and pass an exam.

7. Which of the following is an advantage of a biweekly payment plan?
   a. The borrower pays less per month in return for a longer term.
   b. It is equivalent to 12 monthly payments each year.
   c. There are lower interest rates.
   d. The loan is paid off earlier than scheduled.

8. The act of one person transferring his property to a new owner is called
   a. ownership.
   b. alienation.
   c. subordination.
   d. deeding.

9. Massachusetts protects consumers on real estate matters through
   a. 93A.
   b. 21E.
   c. Title V.
   d. Title IX.

10. A real estate agent is working with a couple from China in Massachusetts for a new home. The couple is very traditional and wants to be sure that the new home has the right "feel." The real estate agent realizes that he should focus on
   a. Chinese superstitions.
   b. avoiding houses next to cemeteries.
   c. Feng Shui.
   d. the Art of Plebo.

11. One of the three major roles of the property manager is to
   a. free the owner from the details of operations.
   b. create revenue for the property manager.
   c. evict nuisance tenants.
   d. choose parties that can be a tenant.

12. Real estate license laws were enacted to
   a. be able to track prospective and existing licensees.
   b. set standards and promote professionalism.
   c. stop consumers from collecting referral fees.
   d. become a source of revenue for the state government.

13. If a consumer declines to sign a disclosure form, then
   a. the agent has completed his or her obligations.
   b. the agent cannot work on the assignment or with the consumer.
   c. the agent is still required to complete the licensee section of the form and provide a license number.
   d. the consumer has basically agreed to agency.

14. At minimum, an appraiser must hold which of the following to conduct valuation services for most bank financing?
   a. appraisal license
   b. appraisal certification
   c. appraisal license trainee
   d. appraisal generalization

15. The U.S. Supreme Court in 1968 reaffirmed a law passed in 1866 that prohibits discrimination based on color known as
   a. Title IX.
   b. the Civil Rights Act.
   c. the Anti-discriminatory Act.
   d. the Civil Protection Rights.

16. John Doe had his property taken by eminent domain and transferred his property to the state for a highway upgrade. This type of transfer is known to be
   a. an act of dedication.
   b. involuntary transfer.
   c. an act for the public domain.
   d. partitioning of land.

17. A couple purchased a house as a principle residence in the amount of $200,000. Six years later, they sold it for $653,499. Their personal federal effective income tax bracket is 33%. What is the federal income tax owed on the capital gain profit?

   a. $0

   b. $215,654.67

   c. $149,654.67

   d. $98,024.85

18. A legally enforceable agreement is called

   a. a non-binding agreement.

   b. a contract.

   c. an offer.

   d. a voluntary act.

19. A commingling of funds refers to

   a. the funds gathered at the closing table.

   b. mixing deposit monies with a broker's funds.

   c. co-brokering with another broker.

   d. obtaining interest on funds deposited at a bank.

20. Which of the following describes the function of mortgage bankers?

   a. They use depositor's money to make mortgage loans.

   b. They are intermediaries who bring borrowers and other lenders together.

   c. They make mortgage loans and sell them on the secondary market.

   d. They often keep loans in their own portfolios.

21. The appraisal is an unbiased

   a. estimate of value.

   b. professional opinion.

   c. written opinion.

   d. market opinion.

22. A resident manager is defined as

   a. a manager employed by an outside management firm.

   b. a new property manager training to be a full-time manager.

   c. a part-time manager.

   d. a manager hired by the owner who lives in the building.

23. A seller's agent is an agent who represents

   a. the seller on a client basis and the buyer as a customer.

   b. the seller as a client and the buyer as a client.

   c. the seller as a customer and the buyer as a client.

   d. the seller as a customer and the buyer as a customer.

24. A buyer gives an owner a $5,000 payment and a written agreement stating that on July 1 of the following year, the buyer can purchase the property for $150,000 cash or the owner may keep the money. This transaction is known as

   a. a lease with an option to purchase.

   b. a purchase contract with a delayed settlement.

   c. an option agreement.

   d. a limited partnership.

25. The basis for legal contracts in Massachusetts is old English Law known as

   a. the King's Act.

   b. the Act of England.

   c. the Statute of Frauds.

   d. the Statute of Law.

26. A client owns a 20,000-square-foot office building fully leased with tenants generating a $52,000 net income. The client wants to sell the building but will face huge capital gains income tax. The agent might suggest that the client
   a. wait until new tax laws are passed.
   b. consider an installment sale.
   c. consider a 1031 exchange.
   d. sell as part of the new 42B LLC program.

27. As it relates to residential real estate, the Federal Fair Housing Act of 1968 makes it illegal to discriminate based on
   a. sex, religion, health, and age.
   b. race, color, age, and health.
   c. sex, race, color, and religion.
   d. race, color, religion, sex, or national origin.

28. The U.S. government initiated its own regulations on the appraisal process which is noted as
   a. FIRREA.
   b. USPAP.
   c. MAI.
   d. TLC.

29. Depreciation on investment real estate is $27\frac{1}{2}$ years on the building value only. Assuming an investor purchased an investment property for $750,000 with an 80/20 ratio of building to land, what is the annual depreciation?
   a. $21,818.18
   b. $20,625
   c. $41,250
   d. $5,454.55

30. The function of the Federal Housing Administration (FHA) is to
   a. make loans.
   b. insure loans.
   c. guarantee loans.
   d. buy loans.

31. On April 1, 1983, Massachusetts passed a state hazardous waste regulation known as
   a. MGL Ch. 21E.
   b. Title V.
   c. MGL Ch. 63B.
   d. MGL Ch. 49C.

32. A real estate agent has six legally required duties that include all EXCEPT
   a. obedience to carry out all lawful instructions of his or her client.
   b. accountability to protect and account for all money.
   c. disclosure of all information on real estate.
   d. loyalty to act in the best interest of the client.

33. A false statement made about a property by an agent is called
   a. an opinion by right.
   b. duress.
   c. reality.
   d. misrepresentation.

34. A closing takes place
   a. when a Purchase and Sales Agreement has been signed.
   b. as the final step in the transfer of title.
   c. when the real estate agent decides.
   d. when a willing buyer meets a willing seller.

35. The area of a building is commonly measured by
a. length × width = square feet.
b. length × width × height = cubic feet.
c. using square yards.
d. obtaining the square meters.

36. A homeowner has AIDS and lists his house for sale with a real estate agent. During a showing, a prospective buyer asks the agent if there were any health issues he should know about concerning the property. Should the agent disclose that the owner has AIDS and has lived in the house?
a. Yes, disclosure is a requirement to real estate brokerage licenses and 93A.
b. No, the law states that the buyer should conduct his own due diligence.
c. No, the real estate agent works for the seller and not the buyer.
d. No, it is against Massachusetts law to address the question.

37. A property management firm usually makes its revenues by
a. gaining an equity position in the buildings it manages.
b. having tenants pay a fee for leasing space.
c. being paid a percent of the collected gross revenues.
d. being paid a percent of added net income.

38. The definition of "highest and best use" does NOT include
a. legally permitted.
b. financially feasible.
c. physically possible.
d. assumes a reasonable value.

39. A 50,000-square-foot industrial building has an annual income of $250,000 on a triple net basis. What is the annual rent per square foot (psf)?
a. Not enough information is available.
b. $5.00 psf, annually
c. $2.50 psf, monthly
d. $0.20 psf, annually

40. John Doe, real estate agent, has an exclusive agreement to represent a buyer. The buyer is interested in a house that is also listed by John Doe exclusively. This type of agency is called
a. designated agency.
b. dual agency.
c. twin agency.
d. facilitator agency.

41. A buyer's agent
a. represents both sellers and buyers on the same property.
b. represents a buyer-client in a real estate transaction.
c. represents the seller but works with the buyer.
d. works with the buyer but is a subagent of the seller.

42. A letter of commitment is issued by the lender and contains
a. the amount of the loan, the loan interest rate, and repayment options.
b. different options for financing a residential home.
c. the loan-to-value ratio, debt-coverage ratio, and debt-to-cost ratio.
d. the credit report, net operating income, and commission fee.

43. Contracts have possible legal status that includes all EXCEPT
a. valid.
b. executed.
c. void.
d. voidable.

44. To ensure a new buyer that no other party will make a claim of ownership on a newly purchased property, the buyer will obtain
a. environmental warranty insurance.
b. liens.
c. title insurance.
d. liability insurance.

45. A real estate agent is aware that a murder had taken place at one time in a house that he recently listed. Is he required to disclose that information to prospective buyers?
a. No, the agent represents the seller and it could hurt the value of the house.
b. Yes, full disclosure of information on real estate is a requirement.
c. No, not unless there is a specific inquiry by the buyer.
d. Yes, the Fair Housing Act requires full disclosure.

46. Dual agency, under Massachusetts's regulations, is allowed when
a. the agent has disclosed the dual agency prior to a closing.
b. the agent is not required to disclose the agency under MA regulations.
c. both the seller and buyer have been disclosed and both have given informed written consent.
d. both buyer and seller have been disclosed prior to the signing of a P & S agreement.

47. One of the key components to a monthly report is
a. gross receipts.
b. real estate tax collections.
c. net operating income.
d. total operating expenses.

48. The many functions of a property manager DO NOT include
a. collecting rents.
b. keeping records and lease abstracts.
c. providing property maintenance.
d. finding a loan for the property.

49. The term *comps* refers to
a. operating expense ratios.
b. recent, nearby sales comparable to the subject property.
c. complimentary information.
d. reproduction cost.

50. Loan-to-value ratio is a breakdown between
a. the former owner's mortgage and the new loan value.
b. the building value minus the land and depreciation.
c. the ratio of the amount of the loan to the total value of the real estate.
d. the loan amount and the land value amount.

51. A real estate broker sells a building for $569,888 with a 5.25% commission fee. What is the amount of the commission fee?
a. $19,219.21
b. $108,550.09
c. $299,191.20
d. $29,919.12

52. A buyer contacts a real estate agent to help the him or her find a home. The agent at the first meeting must
   a. explain how the agent is paid for his or her services.
   b. disclose possible material defects a building might have.
   c. qualify the buyer for a mortgage.
   d. submit a MA Mandatory Licensee Consumer Relationship Disclosure form.

53. When an agent represents both the seller and buyer without their knowledge, then
   a. the agent has undisclosed dual agency which is illegal.
   b. the agent has undisclosed dual agency and that is legal in Massachusetts.
   c. the agent is a designated agent and can act on behalf of both parties.
   d. the agent is then required to use a subagent.

54. Some contracts may require performance by one party and are known as
   a. unilateral.
   b. vicelateral.
   c. monolateral.
   d. sololateral.

55. A required state certificate by a lender on a conveyance of a house would include
   a. a smoke detector certificate.
   b. mold certification.
   c. radon certification.
   d. clean air certification.

56. A real estate agent is driving around a neighborhood and sees a sign on the front yard of a house that says FSBO with a telephone number. What does FSBO mean?
   a. Real estate brokers are not allowed to call the number.
   b. The house is for sale but only to buyers directly.
   c. for sale by owner
   d. for sale by offers

57. At the first meeting with a buyer and agent, the buyer explains that he only wants help from the agent to identify possible homes to purchase. The agent has no other clients and asks the buyer for exclusive representation, but the buyer says no. Therefore,
   a. the agent cannot do so. He must be a buyer or seller representative.
   b. the agent could act as a facilitator and remain neutral in representation.
   c. the agent could act as a designated agent.
   d. the agent could do so only if he is a salesperson and not a broker.

58. An in-house agent, with written consent, can be appointed by a principal broker to represent a buyer or seller and then becomes
   a. a facilitator.
   b. a designated agent.
   c. a dual agent.
   d. designated dual agency.

59. When a real estate agent represents both the seller and buyer in a transaction then the agent is acting as a
   a. designated agent.
   b. subagent.
   c. dual agent.
   d. facilitator.

60. Joanna Murphy has a lease and pays rent of $1,000 monthly, which includes her utilities, water, insurance, taxes, and repairs. This type of lease is known as a
   a. net lease.
   b. percent lease.
   c. ground lease.
   d. gross lease.

61. An owner of a building wants to net $500,000 and has told a real estate broker that he can charge any commission he wants over the $500,000. The building eventually sells for $565,233. Calculate the broker's commission.
   a. $65,233
   b. He can't charge any commission.
   c. $28,261.65
   d. It is an average fee of 5%.

62. An agent that acts as a facilitator must do all EXCEPT which of the following
   a. keep information from either party confidential.
   b. present each property honestly and accurately.
   c. disclose known material defects.
   d. account for funds.

63. The discipline of appraisal recognizes three types of properties which includes
   a. real estate.
   b. real deeds.
   c. real title.
   d. real interests.

64. A lease, as a contract, is an example of a
   a. duocontract.
   b. bilateral contract.
   c. systematic contract.
   d. regulatory contract.

65. The appraisal process became regulated and licensed by the U.S. government in 1989 after the failure of the Savings and Loans and the passing of a bill known as
   a. Title IX.
   b. FIRREA.
   c. USP.
   d. MAI.

66. During 2005, Massachusetts debated the final wording for a new bill to require what kind of new certification at the conveyance of a building sale?
   a. hard-wired smoke detectors
   b. carbon monoxide detectors
   c. underground septic radon fields
   d. methane vent detectors

67. To reduce the liability of risk management, a property manager would buy
   a. a life insurance policy.
   b. a liability insurance policy.
   c. car insurance.
   d. an annuity.

68. A broker sells a building for $973,455 and earned a fee of $34,070.93. What is the commission fee percent?
   a. 5.5%
   b. 6.0%
   c. 2.6%
   d. 3.5%

69. An agent in a firm represents a buyer while another agent in the same firm represents a seller. The buyer has an interest to buy the seller's building. Does the firm have a conflict?
 a. No, as long as the two agents represent the two parties separately.
 b. Yes, the firm is now representing two parties in the same transaction.
 c. No, the firm does not represent the buyer or seller; it is the individual agents.
 d. Yes, both the brokers represent all parties.

70. When an agent becomes a facilitator, the agent can later convert to
 a. an open agency.
 b. any agency with written consent.
 c. The agent cannot change roles even with written consent.
 d. designated agency.

71. Origination fees are also known as
 a. loan fees.
 b. application fees.
 c. broker's fees.
 d. finder's fees.

72. An agent who assists a buyer and seller in completing an agreement but does not represent either party is known as a(n)
 a. subagent.
 b. facilitator.
 c. open agent.
 d. dual agent.

73. A seller receives net sales proceeds of $456,888 after $22,888 of transactional fees and a broker's fee of $30,624. How much was the original selling price of the building and the commission fee percent?
 a. $510,400 and 6%
 b. $510,400 and 4%
 c. $487,512 and 8%
 d. $479,776 and 3.6%

74. Two agents work in the same firm. One agent represents a buyer, while the other agent represents the seller. The buyer wants to buy a house from the seller. Both parties have been disclosed that a dual agency exists. Both the buyer and seller are upset and do not agree to dual agency. What can the firm do?
 a. The firm can ask to be a designated agent.
 b. The firm has to decline representation of either party.
 c. The firm has to call another firm to represent one of the parties.
 d. The firm does not need to do anything.

75. The board that administers the rules and regulations for real estate brokers and salespeople is called the
 a. Massachusetts Board of Registration of Real Estate Brokers and Salespersons.
 b. Massachusetts Licensing Board of Real Estate Professionals.
 c. Massachusetts Association of REALTORS®.
 d. Massachusetts Board of Real Estate Brokers.

76. A tenant makes a verbal agreement to rent space from a landlord on a 30-day basis and pay separately for trash removal. After the first month, the tenant stops paying for trash removal and the landlord argues that they have an agreement. Is the agreement enforceable?

    a. Yes, the agreement was made prior to occupancy.

    b. Yes, and the landlord has grounds to evict.

    c. No, verbal agreements are not enforceable.

    d. No, because it is in violation of the King's Act.

77. A municipal lien certificate is

    a. a certificate removing the loan.

    b. a certificate that all local taxes have been paid in full.

    c. a certificate that a lien survey is complete.

    d. a certificate that the title is good and marketable.

78. A property manager is allowed to lease vacant space and collect a commission fee only if

    a. he has a real estate license.

    b. he has an attorney.

    c. the owner is present during negotiations.

    d. he has been contracted as the building's property management firm.

79. When defining real estate, an appraiser recognizes that it is physical, tangible, and

    a. has appurtenances.

    b. immobile.

    c. has rights.

    d. has interests.

80. S&Ls were the cause of the debacle of the 1980s in the banking industry. What does S&L stand for?

    a. standby and loans.

    b. security and loans.

    c. savings and loans.

    d. standard and loan index.

81. A property lot dimensions are 200' frontage, 150' sidelines, and 200' rear lot line. How many square feet is the property?

    a. 700 square feet

    b. 30,000 square feet

    c. 60,000 square feet

    d. 120,000 square feet

82. Once a real estate firm becomes a designated agent, do all the agents in the firm work either for the buyer or for the seller?

    a. Yes, that is correct in all cases once a written disclosure has been signed.

    b. No, only the principal broker is the designated agent.

    c. No, only the original agents for the buyer and seller are the designated agent.

    d. No one can be a designated agent.

83. John Doe, a software engineer, has a neighbor who wants to sell his house. John calls his friend, Rob, a broker, in order to refer the house as a listing. John expects a 10% referral fee. Rob is able to sell the house after three months and thanks John for the friendly referral. John sends a bill to Rob for a 10% referral fee but Rob refuses to pay it. Can John Doe sue Rob for the fee?
  a. Yes, as long as the referral fee was discussed and agreed to prior to the listing.
  b. Yes, as long as Rob has a real estate broker's license, he can pay John.
  c. No, both parties need to hold a real estate broker's license.
  d. No, the neighbor has to agree to allow John to collect a referral fee.

84. When a tenant has an option to buy a building, this type of property rights is referred to as
  a. an option.
  b. real property.
  c. real estate.
  d. benefits.

85. In the sale of real estate, a seller is obligated to convey
  a. an environmentally clean site.
  b. a title that is good and marketable.
  c. personal property.
  d. leased fee title.

86. Independent contractors, prior to being hired for services by property management companies, must provide
  a. proof they have separate worker's compensation.
  b. proof they are insured and bonded.
  c. proof they have a broker's license in case of leasing situations.
  d. a completed of a W-2 form.

87. A house may have a UST that is a disclosure requirement by a selling broker. What is a UST?
  a. UFFI Standard Trust
  b. underground storage tank
  c. uniform standard tank
  d. uniform insulation toxics

88. Mortgage brokers are helpful to borrowers as they
  a. originate and issue loans for home buyers.
  b. locate borrowers, find lenders, and process applications.
  c. review credit reports and issue mortgages.
  d. are non-profit organizations that exist as a service for first-time home buyers.

89. A buyer is planning to purchase a house for $425,000 with a 20% down payment. The bank will give a loan for the balance at 7% interest only during the first five years. What is the monthly payment?
  a. $2,827.54
  b. $2,380
  c. $2,262.03
  d. $1,983.33

90. Designated agency must be obtained prior to
  a. the signing of the P & S Agreement.
  b. the closing.
  c. the first meeting with the buyer.
  d. an Offer to Purchase.

91. Bill Smith, a licensed real estate broker, showed a prospective buyer a number of buildings. They never actually went into the buildings. Months later, Bill finds out that his buyer went ahead and bought one of these buildings though another broker. Bill makes a claim for a commission fee. Is Bill entitled to any commission fee of any kind?
   a. Yes, if Bill had not exposed the buildings to the buyer, the buyer would not have known about the properties.
   b. Yes, both Bill and the other broker have claims to a commission, as they are both a procuring cause.
   c. No, Bill was not a procuring cause.
   d. No, the other broker was never made aware that Bill showed these buildings and cannot be liable.

92. Once an agent has a written seller's agency agreement, it would legally terminate if
   a. the agent does not sell the house in a month.
   b. the agent went insane.
   c. the seller will not spend money on advertising.
   d. a buyer does not offer the asking price.

93. John Smith and Rob Doe each own separate real estate brokerage firms but are good friends. One day, they start talking about competition and decide to use the same fee schedule. Is this allowed?
   a. Yes, they both agreed in an open and free market.
   b. No, it is in violation of the Sherman Anti-trust Act.
   c. Yes, they could always change the agreement.
   d. No, pricing should never be a major negotiating item.

94. Rich Smith met a real estate broker for dinner to discuss making an offer on a building. During dinner, Rich had too many glasses of wine. Before Rich went home, he drafted an offer to purchase the building for the real estate broker to present to the seller. If the seller accepts the offer, is the offer invalid?
   a. No, because Rich is an adult over the age of 18 years.
   b. No, because Rich is not mentally ill.
   c. No, but it is voidable by Rich because he was incompetent.
   d. Yes, because Rich was clearly intoxicated.

95. When a mortgage is involved, an engineering survey is required by
   a. the lender.
   b. the broker.
   c. the seller.
   d. the FHA.

96. A real estate agent is required by Massachusetts law to notify all prospective buyers about
   a. the dangers of lead paint.
   b. UFFI location.
   c. the requirement of radon testing.
   d. a seller with credit problems.

97. A property manager would carry casualty insurance for
   a. loss of rent due.
   b. an increase in any construction costs.
   c. plate glass breakage.
   d. injury to workers.

98. An appraisal report must be presented
   a. in writing.
   b. verbally.
   c. It depends on the client.
   d. in detail with all the supporting information.

99. Once a buyer's agency agreement has terminated, the agent can
  a. switch allegiance to a seller on a building that the buyer had interest.
  b. reveal confidential information once the client is no longer a client.
  c. become a broker for the seller with written consent of the original buyer.
  d. reveal material information if the party promises to keep the information confidential.

100. John Doe, real estate broker, wants to list a building for sale. But he wants to be paid a commission even if the seller finds a buyer. Therefore, the type of brokerage agreement that John Doe should seek is
  a. an open listing.
  b. an exclusive right to sell.
  c. an exclusive agency.
  d. a dual agreement.

101. There are three main types of mortgages that do NOT include which of the following?
  a. conventional mortgage
  b. FHA mortgage
  c. FIRREA mortgage
  d. privately backed mortgage

102. A buyer plans to give a 33% down payment on a house purchase. The house is being purchased for $321,788. What is the down payment?
  a. $64,357.60
  b. $257,430.40
  c. $106,190.04
  d. $215,597.96

103. A consumer needs to leave Massachusetts immediately for a West Coast job relocation. He wants his house appraised and sold as quickly as possible because he needs the money. An appraiser is engaged to determine current market value but determines a lower value. Why?
  a. The client did not upgrade his landscaping.
  b. The client did not pay the appraiser adequate fees.
  c. The broker asked the appraiser to low-ball the value.
  d. The client is under duress.

104. A seller gives John Doe, real estate broker, a written letter authorizing him to sell his building. But the seller has also indicated that he has given other real estate brokers in the area authorization to sell the property. This type of agency is called
  a. a non-conforming agency.
  b. an exclusive agency.
  c. an open agency.
  d. a procuring agency.

105. A seller wants to sell his house and net $300,000 after real estate commissions. The seller doesn't care what the agent charges for a commission as long as he nets $300,000. This type of compensation is known as
  a. a net commission fee and is illegal.
  b. a net commission fee and is frequently conducted with the seller's approval only.
  c. a premium commission fee and is common.
  d. a sandwich commission fee and is rare.

106. A deposit is given with an offer because
   a. it is the only means to possibly bind an offer.
   b. the seller cannot accept offers without consideration.
   c. it indicates to a seller that the buyer is serious.
   d. it takes the property off the market.

107. At the closing, if the broker held the escrow funds, then he should
   a. write a check from the general funds and bring it to the closing.
   b. keep any amount that is due to the broker's commission invoice and bring the difference.
   c. have a check written from a separate escrow account.
   d. place a lien on the property until his fee is paid.

108. A residential buyer, after the acceptance of an offer, can have a property professionally inspected for the presence of lead paint within
   a. five days of the offer's acceptance.
   b. ten days of the offer's acceptance.
   c. fifteen days of the offer's acceptance.
   d. thirty days of the offer's acceptance.

109. A listing agent is another name for
   a. an agent representing a buyer interested in houses.
   b. an agent representing a seller with property to sell.
   c. an agent representing a seller who may someday own property to sell.
   d. an agent that works for a broker.

110. A real estate listing is
   a. a list of properties.
   b. an employment contract or agreement with a real estate broker and seller.
   c. an employment contract with a principal broker and a new salesperson.
   d. a license issued by the Massachusetts Registration Board of Real Estate.

► Answers

1. **c.** 43,560 square feet comprises an acre.
2. **d.** $935,980 \div \$1,000 = \$935.98 \times \$16.50 = \$15,443.67$
3. **c.** Massachusetts requires disclosure at the first actual meeting with a buyer or seller to discuss a specific property.
4. **c.** A principal is the individual who has employed the services of a real estate agent to represent his or her best interests.
5. **b.** The fourth power is taxation.
6. **b.** Massachusetts requires all brokers and sales agents to complete 12 hours of state-approved courses offered at an approved school every two years.
7. **d.** Biweekly plans involve 26 half payments per year, the equivalent of 13 full payments. The extra payment entirely goes to reduce principal, shortening the remaining term.
8. **b.** Alienation is the act of transferring or conveying ownership of real estate.
9. **a.** Consumer Protection Act Chapter 93A regulates disclosures on behalf of a real estate agent to either party and regulates the practice of fair trade.
10. **c.** Massachusetts real estate agents have recognized that international customs and traditions are influencing international buyers. Feng Shui is the Chinese art of placement of items in a house.
11. **a.** The three roles include: to free up the owner from the specifics of operating a building; to increase the net operating income; and to protect the interests of the owner.
12. **b.** Real estate license laws were developed in order to protect the public and promote high standards of professionalism and competence.
13. **c.** In Massachusetts, the form has a check-off box for the agent stating that the consumer refused to sign the form. The agent then completes the licensee section of the form and provides a license number. The agent wants proof that the consumer was offered the disclosure form.
14. **a.** At minimum, an appraiser must hold an appraisal license, although many banks prefer certification.
15. **b.** The Civil Rights Act was passed in 1866 to give every citizen in the United States without regard to color, the right to inherit, purchase, lease, sell, hold, and convey real and personal property.
16. **b.** There are two types of transfer: voluntary and involuntary. When property is being transferred without consent, it is involuntary.
17. **a.** When a couple owns a house as a principal residence for 24 months or longer, the first $500,000 of profit is tax exempt.
18. **b.** A contract is a legally enforceable agreement more often between two or more parties.
19. **b.** Commingling of funds is prohibited and pertains to mixing deposit monies with a broker's funds.
20. **c.** Mortgage bankers are in the business of originating, selling, and servicing loans.
21. **b.** The U.S. government changed the definition from "estimate of value" as people thought it was "perfect science." It is an unbiased, professional opinion.
22. **d.** A resident manager differs from a building manager in that the resident manager lives in the building that he manages.
23. **a.** The seller is the client. The buyer is a customer, but the agent does not represent the buyer's interests.

24. **c.** An option contract is when a buyer purchases the right to buy a property at fixed terms within a defined period of time. If the option is not executed, the owner gets to keep the deposit.

25. **c.** The Statute of Frauds is the foundation for our system that says if an agreement is to be enforceable, it must be in writing and must be signed by both parties.

26. **c.** IRS Code 1031 tax-deferred exchange is an excellent alternative for an investor to sell income real estate and not trigger income taxes on the transfer.

27. **d.** The Federal Fair Housing Act of 1968 prohibits discrimination in residential real estate based on race, color, religion, sex, or national origin.

28. **b.** USPAP stands for Uniform Standards of Professional Appraisal Practice.

29. **a.** The property has a value of $750,000 × .80 = $600,000. $600,000 ÷ 27.5 years = $21,818.18.

30. **b.** The FHA does not lend any money. The FHA administers an insurance program that allows home buyers to borrow almost the full purchase price with a low down payment.

31. **a.** Massachusetts General Law Chapter 21 E is also known as the SuperLien Act and can be placed as a priority lien on real estate for the presence of hazardous waste.

32. **c.** The agent must disclose information and material property defects as required by law to the buyer but not necessarily volunteer all information.

33. **d.** Misrepresentation is any false statement by an agent on real estate whether knowingly or unknowingly.

34. **b.** A closing is the final step of the selling or transfer process. It occurs when all the adjustments, financing, and documentations are finalized and the title is ready for conveyance.

35. **a.** In Massachusetts, area is commonly measured by length × width = square footage.

36. **d.** In Massachusetts, it is illegal for an agent to address questions on HIV status of any former or current occupant of a residence.

37. **c.** A property management firm is usually paid a percent of all collected receipts for the building. The percent is negotiable but can vary between 3–6% depending on the size and complexity of the project.

38. **d.** The correct answer is, assumes a reasonable value, because the definition of "highest and best use" is that it "produces the greatest net value over all alternative uses."

39. **b.** $250,000 ÷ 50,000 square foot = $5.00 per square foot, annually.

40. **b.** Dual agency is when an agent or firm represents both the buyer and seller in the same property transaction.

41. **b.** When an agent has a written agreement to represent the best interests of the buyer then the agent is a buyer's agent.

42. **a.** A letter of commitment for a loan is issued by a lender after a review of the credit report of the borrower and an analysis of the real estate asset. The letter contains the amount of the loan, the loan interest rate, and the repayment options.

43. **b.** The fourth legal status is unenforceable.

44. **c.** Title insurance is issued and underwritten by a reputable national title insurance company.

45. **c.** There is no duty for a seller's agent to disclose such information unless a buyer or buyer's agent inquires specifically.

46. c. Both the seller and buyer must be disclosed of the dual agency immediately and prior to the signing of any Offer to Purchase. Dual agency can only be granted if both parties agree with written consent.

47. c. The net operating income is gross receipts minus total operating expenses, and provides an owner with the true cash flow before mortgage and taxes.

48. d. The property manager provides many functions including hiring personnel, keeping the property insured, and maintaining records.

49. b. *Comps* is short for comparables meaning other like-kind property sales in the neighborhood that could assist in establishing the market value of the subject property.

50. c. The ratio is the breakdown of the loan amount to the total real estate value and the amount of equity required.

51. d. $569,888 \times 0.0525 = $29,919.12

52. d. Every agent must submit a MA Mandatory Licensee-Consumer Relationship Disclosure form no later than the first personal meeting.

53. a. Without full disclosure and written permission from both parties, the representation is illegal.

54. a. A contract requiring the act of one person can be known as a unilateral contract.

55. a. Massachusetts law requires that smoke detectors are inspected and certified by the local fire department prior to the transfer of the house.

56. c. FSBO stands for "for sale by owner." A broker may still call the number for information, but the seller is not required to pay a commission fee.

57. b. The agent, with written consent on the MA Mandatory Licensee-Consumer Relationship Disclosure form, could act as a facilitator and remain neutral in representation.

58. b. Massachusetts has approved this new agency known as designated agent during 2005. Appointments are made within the same firm when the firm has contracts to represent a buyer and seller of the same property.

59. c. Dual agency is allowed in Massachusetts as long as the agent has disclosed to both parties that a conflict exists and the agent has obtained written consent from both the buyer and seller to act as a dual agent.

60. d. A gross lease is a lease in which the rent includes all the operating expenses to a tenant.

61. b. Charging a net commission is illegal. The broker must agree to a fee schedule in advance and charge a fee as a percent of the gross selling price.

62. a. There is no duty to keep information received by either party confidential as a facilitator.

63. b. The three types of properties include real estate, real property, and personal property.

64. b. A lease is an example of a bilateral contract in which the contract binds two parties equally.

65. b. FIRREA stands for Financial Institution's Reform, Recovery, and Enforcement Act of 1989 or the "Bail Out Bill" that established new regulations to become an appraiser and develop an appraisal report.

66. b. In 2005 a bill passed requiring residential and commercial real estate properties to install carbon monoxide detectors and have certificates upon property transfer.

67. b. A building liability insurance policy would off-set risk for a property owner.

68. d. $34,070.93 \div $973,455 = 3.5\%

69. b. Yes, the firm has contracts representing the buyer's and seller's best interests.

70. b. A buyer or seller can eventually decide to engage the agent to represent its best interests and engage the agent as its buyer's agent or seller's agent.

71. a. The origination fee is the loan fee or sometimes is referred to as the discount fee.

72. a. A facilitator works with buyers and sellers in reaching an agreement but has no fiduciary responsibility to either party.

73. a. $456,888 + $22,888 + $30,624 = $510,400; $30,624 ÷ $510,624 = 6%

74. a. A real estate firm can obtain written consent from both parties to have a designated agent, the principal broker. Then, two individuals in the firm would be appointed to work with the buyer and the seller separately.

75. a. The Massachusetts Board of Registration of Real Estate Brokers and Salespersons serves this function.

76. c. Agreements are enforceable if in writing and executed by both parties as stated in the Statute of Frauds. Verbal agreements are not enforceable.

77. b. Towns issue a certificate that a specific property has no outstanding liens or balances for any taxes or charges owed by the owner to the town. As part of a closing, the certificate is required as part of the title search.

78. a. To collect any commission fee requires a real estate license.

79. b. The definition is that real estate is physical, tangible, and immobile.

80. c. S&L is short for Savings and Loans, which are local savings banks that issue loans on real estate.

81. b. Square feet is measured by length × width. The lot is a rectangle of 150' × 200'. Therefore, 150' × 200' = 30,000 square feet.

82. b. No, only one person, the principal broker, can be the designated agent.

83. c. John Doe does not have a real estate broker's license and by law cannot collect any commission of any kind.

84. b. Real property includes rights, interests, and benefits that are inherent with real estate.

85. b. A seller is conveying title that is good and marketable. However, a buyer should determine if the seller has clear title prior to the purchase of the property.

86. a. Independent contractors are not employees of property management firms. They may be specialists such as plumbers or manual laborers. In all cases, however, employers must provide worker's compensation insurance for employees unless they are independent contractors.

87. b. UST stands for underground storage tanks, which are primarily used for storing heating oil for a house. Full disclosure is required by a listing agent.

88. b. A mortgage broker does not issue loans but does locate borrowers and lenders as an intermediary. They do charge a loan fee.

89. d. First calculate the loan balance by multiplying $425,000 × .20 = $85,000; $425,000 − $85,000 = $340,000. The loan is $340,000 × 0.07 = $23,800 per year divided by 12 months = $1,983.33.

90. d. An agent always needs consent prior to an Offer to Purchase.

91. c. Assuming that Bill does not have an exclusive arrangement with the buyer, Bill was not a procuring cause. Procuring cause is a person who is setting in motion and is involved in a chain of events from which the sale of a transaction is consummated.

92. b. There are many ways that agency agreements can be terminated. One option is upon death or insanity of the agent or client principal.

93. b. No, the Federal Trade Commission forbids brokers from discussing their commission fee schedules and collaborating to agree to one schedule for the market. Commission fees are open to negotiations and should be listed in writing in a brokerage agreement.

94. c. A person who is intoxicated does not have legal competency. The offer is voidable but only by Rich, since only the person with the disability can void a contract.

95. a. The lender will always ask for some type of registered engineering survey. However, it is a good practice for buyers always to ask for a registered survey.

96. a. Agents are required to notify all prospective purchasers and tenants about the dangers of lead paint.

97. c. Casualty insurance can cover many issues such as plate glass breakage, theft, a broken furnace, etc.

98. c. The client dictates how the appraisal will be delivered. It could be verbal, such as court testimony services, or may be in writing.

99. c. An agent cannot switch allegiance to a seller and become a subagent or direct broker of the seller without informed, written consent of the original buyer/client.

100. b. An exclusive right to sell gives the broker the only right to sell the property and to always collect a commission fee in accordance with his listing agreement, no matter who finds the buyer.

101. c. The three main types of mortgages include conventional, privately backed mortgages, and government-backed mortgages such as FHA, VA, etc.

102. c. $321,788 × .33 = $106,190.04

103. d. The client has time constraints and duress. The appraiser has determined that current market value cannot be obtained.

104. c. An open agency is when a broker has authorization to sell a building but not the sole authorization. The seller does have a right to market the property himself or through other brokers and only pay a commission to the procuring cause broker.

105. a. An agent must have a disclosed set fee percentage. The agent cannot add the fee to the price. The seller pays the fee to the agent for services provided based upon the transaction.

106. a. The deposit is also known as earnest money to bind an offer to purchase if both parties execute the offer.

107. c. All escrow funds must be held in a separate escrow accounting checkbook. Co-mingling of funds is not allowed except for monies to pay local bank fees or to maintain a minimum balance for the escrow account.

108. b. The buyer has ten days from the acceptance of an offer to have a professional inspection for the presence of lead paint at the buyer's expense.

109. b. A listing agent is an agent representing actual property for sale and the seller is the actual client.

110. b. It is an agreement or contract detailing the description of the property, terms and conditions of commission payment, and length of the marketing. It is a marketing agreement between a real estate agent and seller. In Massachusetts, a listing agreement is not required to be in writing but it is enforceable if in writing.

Scoring

Again, evaluate how you did on this practice exam by finding the number of questions you got right, disregarding, for the moment, the ones you got wrong or skipped. If you achieve a score of at least 77 questions correct, you will most likely pass the Massachusetts Real Estate Sales Exam.

If you did not score as well as you would like, ask yourself the following: Did I run out of time before I could answer all of the questions? Did I go back and change my answers from right to wrong? Did I get flustered and sit staring at a difficult question for what seemed like hours? If you had any of these problems, be sure to go over the LearningExpress Test Preparation System in Chapter 2 to review how best to avoid them.

You probably have seen improvement from your first two practice exam scores and this one; but if you didn't improve as much as you would like, following are some options:

If you scored below the passing score on each section, you should seriously consider whether you are ready for the exam at this time. A good idea would be to take some brush-up courses in the areas you feel less sure of. If you don't have time for a course, you might try private tutoring.

If you scored close to the minimum passing score, you need to work as hard as you can to improve your skills. Go back to your real estate license course textbooks to review. Strengthen your math skills by using the LearningExpress book, *Practical Math Success in 20 Minutes a Day.* Also, reread and pay close attention to the information in Chapter 4, Massachusetts Real Estate Refresher Course; Chapter 5, Real Estate Math Review; and Chapter 6, Real Estate Glossary. It might be helpful, as well, to ask friends and family to make up mock test questions and quiz you on them.

Now, revise your study schedule according to the time you have left, emphasizing those parts that gave you the most trouble this time. Use the following table to see where you need more work, so that you can concentrate your preparation efforts. After working more on the subject areas that give you problems, take the fourth practice exam in Chapter 9 to see how much you have improved.

EXAM III FOR REVIEW

Test III Subject Area	Question Numbers (Questions 1–110)
Real Estate Principles and Practices	1, 6, 12, 19, 24, 31, 35, 40, 46, 52, 57, 62, 69, 74, 82, 90, 92, 99, 105, 109
Property Valuation/Appraisal	5, 14, 21, 28, 38, 49, 60, 63, 65, 79, 84, 98, 103
Financing	7, 20, 30, 42, 50, 71, 80, 88, 101
Contacts/Agency Relationship	4, 18, 25, 33, 43, 54, 64, 76, 94, 106
Law, Definition, and Nature of Agency Relationships, Type of Agencies and Agents	3, 13, 23, 32, 41, 53, 58, 59, 70, 73, 75, 83, 91, 93, 100, 104, 110
Settlement/Transfer of Property	8, 16, 26, 34, 44, 55, 66, 77, 85, 95, 107
Business Practices	9, 10, 15, 27, 36, 45, 56, 87, 96, 108
Property Management	11, 22, 37, 47, 48, 67, 78, 86, 97
Real Estate Math	2, 17, 29, 39, 51, 61, 68, 73, 81, 89, 102

Massachusetts Real Estate Sales Exam IV

CHAPTER SUMMARY

This is the last of the four practice tests in this book based on the Massachusetts Real Estate Sales Exam. Using all of the experience and strategies that you gained from the other three exams, take this exam to see how far you have come.

THIS IS THE last practice exam in this book, but it is not designed to be any harder than the other three. It is simply another representation of what you might expect on the real test. Just as when you take the real test, there should not be anything here that surprises you. In fact, you probably already know what is in a lot of it! That will be the case with the real test, too.

For this exam, pull together all the tips you have been practicing since the first practice exam. Give yourself the time and the space to work. Since you won't be taking the real test in your living room, you might take this one in an unfamiliar location such as a library. Make sure you have plenty of time to complete the exam in one sitting. In addition, use what you have learned from reading the answer explanations on previous practice tests. Remember the types of questions that caused problems for you in the past, and when you are unsure, try to consider how those answers were explained.

After you have taken this written exam, you should try the computer-based test using the CD-ROM found at the back of this book. That way, you will be familiar with taking exams on computer.

Once again, use the answer explanations at the end of the exam to understand questions you may have missed.

▶ Massachusetts Real Estate Sales Exam IV Answer Sheet

1.	ⓐ	ⓑ	ⓒ	ⓓ	38.	ⓐ	ⓑ	ⓒ	ⓓ	75.	ⓐ	ⓑ	ⓒ	ⓓ
2.	ⓐ	ⓑ	ⓒ	ⓓ	39.	ⓐ	ⓑ	ⓒ	ⓓ	76.	ⓐ	ⓑ	ⓒ	ⓓ
3.	ⓐ	ⓑ	ⓒ	ⓓ	40.	ⓐ	ⓑ	ⓒ	ⓓ	77.	ⓐ	ⓑ	ⓒ	ⓓ
4.	ⓐ	ⓑ	ⓒ	ⓓ	41.	ⓐ	ⓑ	ⓒ	ⓓ	78.	ⓐ	ⓑ	ⓒ	ⓓ
5.	ⓐ	ⓑ	ⓒ	ⓓ	42.	ⓐ	ⓑ	ⓒ	ⓓ	79.	ⓐ	ⓑ	ⓒ	ⓓ
6.	ⓐ	ⓑ	ⓒ	ⓓ	43.	ⓐ	ⓑ	ⓒ	ⓓ	80.	ⓐ	ⓑ	ⓒ	ⓓ
7.	ⓐ	ⓑ	ⓒ	ⓓ	44.	ⓐ	ⓑ	ⓒ	ⓓ	81.	ⓐ	ⓑ	ⓒ	ⓓ
8.	ⓐ	ⓑ	ⓒ	ⓓ	45.	ⓐ	ⓑ	ⓒ	ⓓ	82.	ⓐ	ⓑ	ⓒ	ⓓ
9.	ⓐ	ⓑ	ⓒ	ⓓ	46.	ⓐ	ⓑ	ⓒ	ⓓ	83.	ⓐ	ⓑ	ⓒ	ⓓ
10.	ⓐ	ⓑ	ⓒ	ⓓ	47.	ⓐ	ⓑ	ⓒ	ⓓ	84.	ⓐ	ⓑ	ⓒ	ⓓ
11.	ⓐ	ⓑ	ⓒ	ⓓ	48.	ⓐ	ⓑ	ⓒ	ⓓ	85.	ⓐ	ⓑ	ⓒ	ⓓ
12.	ⓐ	ⓑ	ⓒ	ⓓ	49.	ⓐ	ⓑ	ⓒ	ⓓ	86.	ⓐ	ⓑ	ⓒ	ⓓ
13.	ⓐ	ⓑ	ⓒ	ⓓ	50.	ⓐ	ⓑ	ⓒ	ⓓ	87.	ⓐ	ⓑ	ⓒ	ⓓ
14.	ⓐ	ⓑ	ⓒ	ⓓ	51.	ⓐ	ⓑ	ⓒ	ⓓ	88.	ⓐ	ⓑ	ⓒ	ⓓ
15.	ⓐ	ⓑ	ⓒ	ⓓ	52.	ⓐ	ⓑ	ⓒ	ⓓ	89.	ⓐ	ⓑ	ⓒ	ⓓ
16.	ⓐ	ⓑ	ⓒ	ⓓ	53.	ⓐ	ⓑ	ⓒ	ⓓ	90.	ⓐ	ⓑ	ⓒ	ⓓ
17.	ⓐ	ⓑ	ⓒ	ⓓ	54.	ⓐ	ⓑ	ⓒ	ⓓ	91.	ⓐ	ⓑ	ⓒ	ⓓ
18.	ⓐ	ⓑ	ⓒ	ⓓ	55.	ⓐ	ⓑ	ⓒ	ⓓ	92.	ⓐ	ⓑ	ⓒ	ⓓ
19.	ⓐ	ⓑ	ⓒ	ⓓ	56.	ⓐ	ⓑ	ⓒ	ⓓ	93.	ⓐ	ⓑ	ⓒ	ⓓ
20.	ⓐ	ⓑ	ⓒ	ⓓ	57.	ⓐ	ⓑ	ⓒ	ⓓ	94.	ⓐ	ⓑ	ⓒ	ⓓ
21.	ⓐ	ⓑ	ⓒ	ⓓ	58.	ⓐ	ⓑ	ⓒ	ⓓ	95.	ⓐ	ⓑ	ⓒ	ⓓ
22.	ⓐ	ⓑ	ⓒ	ⓓ	59.	ⓐ	ⓑ	ⓒ	ⓓ	96.	ⓐ	ⓑ	ⓒ	ⓓ
23.	ⓐ	ⓑ	ⓒ	ⓓ	60.	ⓐ	ⓑ	ⓒ	ⓓ	97.	ⓐ	ⓑ	ⓒ	ⓓ
24.	ⓐ	ⓑ	ⓒ	ⓓ	61.	ⓐ	ⓑ	ⓒ	ⓓ	98.	ⓐ	ⓑ	ⓒ	ⓓ
25.	ⓐ	ⓑ	ⓒ	ⓓ	62.	ⓐ	ⓑ	ⓒ	ⓓ	99.	ⓐ	ⓑ	ⓒ	ⓓ
26.	ⓐ	ⓑ	ⓒ	ⓓ	63.	ⓐ	ⓑ	ⓒ	ⓓ	100.	ⓐ	ⓑ	ⓒ	ⓓ
27.	ⓐ	ⓑ	ⓒ	ⓓ	64.	ⓐ	ⓑ	ⓒ	ⓓ	101.	ⓐ	ⓑ	ⓒ	ⓓ
28.	ⓐ	ⓑ	ⓒ	ⓓ	65.	ⓐ	ⓑ	ⓒ	ⓓ	102.	ⓐ	ⓑ	ⓒ	ⓓ
29.	ⓐ	ⓑ	ⓒ	ⓓ	66.	ⓐ	ⓑ	ⓒ	ⓓ	103.	ⓐ	ⓑ	ⓒ	ⓓ
30.	ⓐ	ⓑ	ⓒ	ⓓ	67.	ⓐ	ⓑ	ⓒ	ⓓ	104.	ⓐ	ⓑ	ⓒ	ⓓ
31.	ⓐ	ⓑ	ⓒ	ⓓ	68.	ⓐ	ⓑ	ⓒ	ⓓ	105.	ⓐ	ⓑ	ⓒ	ⓓ
32.	ⓐ	ⓑ	ⓒ	ⓓ	69.	ⓐ	ⓑ	ⓒ	ⓓ	106.	ⓐ	ⓑ	ⓒ	ⓓ
33.	ⓐ	ⓑ	ⓒ	ⓓ	70.	ⓐ	ⓑ	ⓒ	ⓓ	107.	ⓐ	ⓑ	ⓒ	ⓓ
34.	ⓐ	ⓑ	ⓒ	ⓓ	71.	ⓐ	ⓑ	ⓒ	ⓓ	108.	ⓐ	ⓑ	ⓒ	ⓓ
35.	ⓐ	ⓑ	ⓒ	ⓓ	72.	ⓐ	ⓑ	ⓒ	ⓓ	109.	ⓐ	ⓑ	ⓒ	ⓓ
36.	ⓐ	ⓑ	ⓒ	ⓓ	73.	ⓐ	ⓑ	ⓒ	ⓓ	110.	ⓐ	ⓑ	ⓒ	ⓓ
37.	ⓐ	ⓑ	ⓒ	ⓓ	74.	ⓐ	ⓑ	ⓒ	ⓓ					

▶ Massachusetts Real Estate Sales Exam IV

1. A property is assessed at $824,566. The real estate tax rate in town is $15.66 per $1,000 of assessed value. What are the annual real estate taxes?
   a. $12,912.70
   b. $824.57
   c. $52,654.28
   d. $129,127.04

2. The Veterans Administration will guarantee, for the most part, a loan of what percent?
   a. 40%
   b. 55%
   c. 60%
   d. 80%

3. In order to be hired, a property manager while under contract must
   a. be a licensed real estate broker.
   b. be a certified property manager.
   c. be licensed as a property manager.
   d. have a clear understanding of leases and agreements.

4. All are true about an appraisal EXCEPT which of the following?
   a. It is the impartial third party who prepares the appraisal.
   b. The appraiser's fee is contingent on the valuation.
   c. An appraisal is an unbiased professional opinion.
   d. An appraisal may be in writing or delivered verbally.

5. A real estate agent at the first personal meeting with a buyer to discuss a specific property must present
   a. a listing agreement.
   b. a Mandatory Specific Form on the details of the property.
   c. a Massachusetts Mandatory Licensee-Consumer Relationship Disclosure form.
   d. a Mandatory Commission schedule.

6. During showings of a property, on the topic of UFFI in Massachusetts, the broker is required to
   a. disclose.
   b. provide the buyer with a Lead Paint Notification and Tenant Certification form.
   c. MA brokers are not required to disclose this information.
   d. not answer any questions on the topic.

7. A listing agent finds a buyer who makes an offer to purchase contingent on a home inspection. The offer is accepted, and the buyer has one week for the home inspection. The buyer asks the agent for a good home inspector. The agent should
   a. give a list of a minimum of three local home inspectors as required by law.
   b. not offer any names, but at the signing of the offer direct the buyer to the state's home inspection website list and offer a brochure from consumer affairs.
   c. direct the buyer to the town's building inspector for possible names.
   d. offer a minimum of five names as required from the state's website of home inspectors.

8. John Doe, a real estate agent, heard at a cocktail party that a building in the neighborhood was for sale. The next day, he brings a buyer who makes an offer and eventually a sale was consummated. John Doe sent a commission invoice to the seller, and the seller refused to pay the commission. Does the seller have grounds not to pay?

a. No, the seller is unrealistic.

b. No, the seller should pay because he took the buyer's offer.

c. Yes, the broker was never hired in writing from the seller.

d. Yes, the broker was not the procuring cause.

9. In the Theory of Distribution, one of the four factors of production is

a. building.

b. socialization.

c. redistribution.

d. labor.

10. Rob Lehigh, real estate agent, represents a seller on a house listing. A buyer calls to meet with Rob. Upon the first meeting, Rob presents the MA Mandatory Licensee-Consumer Relationship Disclosure form, but the buyer declines to sign the form. What now?

a. Rob cannot work with the buyer.

b. Rob must have the consumer contact his own legal counsel.

c. Rob can check off a box that the consumer has declined to sign and state the reasons.

d. Rob must have the buyer contract with an outside competitor for representation.

11. A buyer's agent is working exclusively with a buyer and finds a house. He makes an offer and has one week for a home inspection. The buyer asks his buyer's agent for recommendations for home inspectors.

a. The agent should direct the buyer to the state website of home inspectors.

b. The agent can make recommendations of home inspectors.

c. The agent should have the buyer contact his attorney for recommendations.

d. The agent should contact the seller's agent for recommendations.

12. A material defect is a defect that can materially

a. hurt the public health.

b. impede on the sale of real estate.

c. influence a buyer's decision to buy or not to buy a particular property.

d. hurt the value of real estate that the seller should not disclose.

13. In Massachusetts, who pays the deed tax stamps?

a. the broker

b. the buyer

c. the seller

d. the lender

14. A buyer asks his agent to draft an Offer to Purchase. If the Offer to Purchase is accepted, then the buyer use his attorney for negotiations during the Purchase and Sales Agreement. To protect the buyer, the agent should include which of the following in the Offer?

a. a deadline of one day

b. a disclaimer that the offer is non-binding

c. a contingency that the offer is based on a satisfactory P & S Agreement

d. that the offer is based on financing

15. A real estate broker in Massachusetts is required to hold a real estate bond in the amount of
   a. $25,000.
   b. $10,000.
   c. $5,000.
   d. $1,000.

16. Single-family residential appraisals are reported on a form known as
   a. USPAP forms.
   b. URAR forms.
   c. a Banking and Capital form.
   d. a Truth-in-Lending form.

17. If a tenant agrees with a property manager to lease an apartment on a thirty-day basis, then this type of lease is known as
   a. tenant in common.
   b. tenant at will.
   c. tenant in sufferance.
   d. leased fee interest.

18. A seller discloses to a real estate agent that he has an old oil tank under his house unused since he converted to gas twenty years ago. The seller asks that the tank's existence not be discussed with buyers.
   a. The real estate agent must comply under agency law and fiduciary duties.
   b. The real estate agent, upon being privy of the tank's existence, must disclose the information to prospective buyers.
   c. The real estate should ask for indemnification in his listing agreement so that he can maintain the information as confidential.
   d. The real estate agent should obtain the state's mandatory confidentiality form on hazardous material and have the seller give the broker permission to maintain the information as confidential.

19. An apparent title defect is also known as
   a. a malicious fraud.
   b. streamlining.
   c. a cloud.
   d. a gray aberration.

20. If a home buyer wants to know from the listing agent if the previous owner of a house had HIV, the agent should
   a. answer the question honestly and accurately.
   b. not address the question of HIV status of any former or current occupants.
   c. direct the buyer to the town's Board of Health.
   d. arrange a meeting with the owner and prospective buyer.

21. Upon the death of a sole proprietor real estate broker, the spouse may practice brokerage if that spouse
   a. completes the brokerage course and exam.
   b. works for another broker's firm without a license.
   c. files for a temporary license valid for one year.
   d. files for a temporary license valid for one year and then renews.

22. A property is sold for $570,300 and the real estate commission is 4.5%. The listing broker owes 50% to a cooperating broker. The cooperating broker owes 20% of the collected commission to his real estate salesperson. How much did the salesperson receive?
   a. $25,663.50
   b. $12,831.75
   c. $2,566.35
   d. $10,265.40

23. Upon the sale of a building for $400,000, the buyer was able to secure a loan for $320,000. To help finance the entire amount, the seller issued a second loan in the amount of $80,000. This seller's loan is known as
   a. a buydown mortgage.
   b. an equity sharing mortgage.
   c. a graduated payment mortgage.
   d. a deferred purchase money mortgage.

24. A listing agent has an exclusive agreement to represent a building. During the marketing of the building, some potential buyers had interest. One night, the building burned down in a thunderstorm. The agent believes that he could have completed the transaction and is still due a fee. Is the agent correct?
   a. Under MA law, if the agent can prove there was *bona fide* interest, then a fee is due.
   b. The impossibility of performance is grounds for an agency termination.
   c. If there is building insurance, then the sale negotiations must continue.
   d. The seller only owes 25% of the fee under MA law.

25. A listing broker finds a buyer who submits an offer to the seller. The seller agrees to the offer and signs a Purchase and Sales Contract with a closing to occur in 14 days. On the day prior to the closing, the seller changes his mind and takes the property off the market. The agent believes his fee is still due. Is the agent correct?
   a. A brokerage fee is due only if the property title is transferred.
   b. As long as the agent had a buyer that was ready, willing, and able, then a fee is due.
   c. The agent might want a fee but no fee is due.
   d. Without monetary consideration from the buyer, there is no deal.

26. All appraisal reports must be
   a. in writing.
   b. in conformance with USPAP.
   c. delivered on a URAR form.
   d. verbally presented.

27. A real estate license is valid for
   a. three years.
   b. two years.
   c. one year.
   d. five years.

28. John Doe came from another country into the U.S. He is illiterate in the English language. The law in Massachusetts states
   a. that John cannot own real estate.
   b. that John is not prohibited from buying or selling his own real estate.
   c. that John is required to hire a state licensed real estate broker.
   d. that John is incompetent and is not allowed to buy real estate.

29. In the northeastern United States, the primary method to describe real estate on a deed is
   a. the U.S. rectangular survey system.
   b. the Torrens System.
   c. a Sheriff's Deed System.
   d. the Metes and Bounds System.

30. A real estate client is defined as
   a. a person who empowers another to act as his agent.
   b. a person interested in buying real estate.
   c. a person interested in selling real estate.
   d. a person who signs a Mandatory Disclosure form.

31. John Smith owns an apartment building with a gross annual income of $56,700. The annual operating expenses are $15,600. Rob Doe, a buyer, is willing to purchase the apartment building on an 8.5% capitalization rate. How much is he willing to pay?
a. $481,950
b. $349,350
c. $483,529
d. $132,600

32. A listing agent receives two offers on his listing. One offer states that "time is of the essence," while the other offer does not include this provision. Is there a difference?
a. There is no difference as all offers are "time is of the essence."
b. Yes, "time is of the essence" means all parties must meet the performance deadlines.
c. "Time is of the essence" means move quickly.
d. The offer without the language is a stronger offer.

33. A real estate agent must keep records of escrow account deposits and withdrawals for
a. five years.
b. three years.
c. ten years.
d. fifteen years.

34. A legal status of a contract might be all of the following EXCEPT
a. void.
b. voidable.
c. valid.
d. arm's length.

35. During building maintenance, all tenant complaints should be responded by property management
a. within 24 hours.
b. within 48 hours.
c. as soon as possible.
d. within three days.

36. The Federal Reserve Bank administers the Federal Truth-in-Lending Law, which is also known as
a. Title V.
b. Regulation Z.
c. MGL Ch. 140C.
d. Freddie Mac.

37. An agent lists a house for sale built in 1965. What environmental concern might the agent have as a disclosure requirement?
a. mold bacteria
b. a sewer line to the house
c. lead paint
d. radon

38. In Massachusetts, a real estate salesperson may hold escrow accounts if
a. they carry escrow insurance.
b. they hold a Massachusetts real estate license.
c. They are never allowed to hold escrow accounts.
d. they deposit checks within three hours from submission.

39. A self-contained appraisal report has
a. all detailed research gathered by the appraiser.
b. all the relevant summary information by the appraiser.
c. restrictions in terms of who is authorized to read the report.
d. limited information but is still in compliance with USPAP standards.

40. John Weston hires a real estate agent to sell his house. To increase the exposure of the property, the real estate agent has sent information to outside brokers. Does the broker have to pay a commission to the outside brokers?

  a. No, the listing broker can advertise that he will split his fees, or a separate agreement can made with the outside broker.

  b. Yes, once the listing broker advertises to outside brokers, then vicarious compensation is automatic.

  c. Yes, otherwise it would be misleading and fraudulent.

  d. No, the law prohibits compensation to dual agents.

41. A person that dies without a will is said to have died

  a. intestate.

  b. testator.

  c. codicil.

  d. prescriptive.

42. In Massachusetts, a salesperson can automatically become self-employed under what circumstances?

  a. never

  b. after working full time for one year

  c. after working full time for two years

  d. if he or she works with a broker

43. An out-of-town buyer has interest in buying a house that has been vacant for five years. The house has had no interested parties and yet the house seems to be in good condition. There were town rumors that a murder took place in that house and that it is stigmatized. Should the listing agent disclose the rumor?

  a. No, not under any conditions.

  b. Not unless the buyer specifically inquires.

  c. Yes, full disclosure is an agent's responsibility.

  d. Yes, unless the murder was actually a suicide.

44. Which advertised phrase might trigger further lending disclosures?

  a. The interest rate is 5.4% per annum.

  b. We have 95% financing available.

  c. Financing terms available include 5% APR with 30-year amortization.

  d. We have fixed and adjustable rates.

45. A real estate agent listed a house and was told by the seller that it had a leaky roof. A prospective buyer asked about any physical defects. The real estate broker, to protect his seller, answered none that he was aware of and the buyer decided to therefore make an offer. The broker's comments are known as

  a. misrepresentation.

  b. fiduciary responsibility.

  c. an expression of opinion.

  d. acting under duress.

46. In Massachusetts, to be a real estate agent a person must be at least

  a. 21 years old.

  b. 18 years old.

  c. 25 years old.

  d. 16 years old.

47. An agent is driving around the neighborhood prospecting for homes and sees a few signs that state FSBO. What is FSBO?
a. first to stop is the best offer
b. for sale to the best offer
c. The homeowner is a seller and a buyer.
d. for sale by owner

48. If a client asks a real estate agent if they should use an attorney on a very simple transaction that may cost more in legal fees than the transaction itself, a real estate agent in this case can
a. advise that an attorney is not always necessary.
b. advise that the client has an option not to use an attorney.
c. never advise against the use of an attorney.
d. offer advice that is not wasteful with the client's funds.

49. A listing agent is contacted by an agent representing a buyer wanting detailed information about the building for sale. The listing agent does not want to share that information and states that they will not co-broke the fees. The outside agent argues that a listing broker must cooperate. Which is true below?
a. There is no requirement to offer information by state regulation unless the agent advertised differently.
b. The outside agent has a claim. The listing agent must give information so the buyer can make a decision.
c. The outside agent should call the homeowner himself and get the information.
d. Agents must split their fees by law.

50. RESPA was passed in what year?
a. 1980
b. 1988
c. 1974
d. 1965

51. Net operating income divided by the capitalization rate equals
a. the debt service.
b. the property value.
c. the annual interest rate.
d. the annual percentage rate.

52. A listing agreement is an example of a
a. bilateral contract.
b. unilateral contract.
c. voidable contract.
d. descriptive contract.

53. A person that receives title to real estate is known as the
a. grantor.
b. grantee.
c. titletor.
d. recipient.

54. A buyer's broker has the legal duty to represent the best interests of his buyer. Therefore, who pays the buyer-broker's commission fee?
a. The buyer has to compensate the agent upon the completion of a transaction.
b. The seller always compensates the agent.
c. Compensation is based on the terms negotiated in the agreement.
d. The seller is now required to compensate the agent.

55. A person who advertises that he is a real estate broker but in fact does not have a license can be fined as much as
  a. $25,000.
  b. $10,000.
  c. $1,000.
  d. $500.

56. To *cooperate* means to *compensate*, and all real estate agents are required to cooperate in real estate transactions to increase the marketability of a property for a consumer.
  a. That is true, the law wants to increase market exposure.
  b. MA law does not require any agent to split fees or cooperate with information.
  c. The NAR requires compensation sharing as well as Massachusetts.
  d. To cooperate is to vicariously offer compensation.

57. If an investment property has a net operating income of $135,678 and the investor's capitalization rate is 8.55%, then what is the potential value of the property?
  a. $1,160,047
  b. $1,586,877
  c. $1,443,277
  d. $1,045,998

58. A listing agent meets a potential buyer who also has interest in another neighborhood. To influence the buyer, the agent stated that he knows for a fact that a sex offender lives in the competing neighborhood. And, in fact, the information is true. Is this legitimate?
  a. Yes, the information helped the buyer make a knowledgeable decision.
  b. No, statute imposes criminal penalties for misuse of information provided to an inquirer.
  c. Yes, as long as the information is honest and accurate.
  d. No, the listing agent does not represent the buyer.

59. When a lender allows a borrower to control and use pledged real estate, this action is known as
  a. mortgaging.
  b. titling.
  c. hypothecation.
  d. retention.

60. A person who has received official notice that he has passed the state real estate exam must pay the state fee within
  a. 10 days.
  b. 20 days.
  c. 30 days.
  d. 45 days.

61. An Offer to Purchase was submitted to a seller by a buyer. The buyer's broker inserted the words "Time is of the Essence." If the seller signs this offer, then what commitment is the seller making?

a. The seller isn't making any commitment. The offer is not a purchase contract.

b. The seller and buyer are agreeing to perform and meet any time requirements stipulated in the offer.

c. None. "Time is of the essence" stipulates how long the offer is valid.

d. The seller is agreeing to pay the broker on a certain date.

62. Joe Smith has been parking his car on his neighbor's land for years. One day, Joe filed a claim for title of ownership due to Adverse Possession. How long would he have had to be continuously using the neighbor's land?

a. 15 years

b. 20 years

c. 21 years

d. 7 years

63. The book value of real estate is

a. the actual value on the effective date of the appraisal.

b. the depreciated cost basis.

c. the insured value.

d. the taxable value.

64. A real estate broker waited too long to renew his real estate license and take the mandatory 12 hours of real estate continuing education. How long after the license expires, does the broker have to renew during a grace period?

a. six months

b. sixty days

c. one year

d. thirty days

65. In Massachusetts, real estate is commonly transferred using a

a. quitclaim deed.

b. fee simple deed.

c. bargain and sale deed.

d. grant deed.

66. For a real estate salesperson to become a real estate broker, the salesperson must first work under the guidance of a real estate broker for

a. two years.

b. one year.

c. three years.

d. 2.5 years.

67. According to state regulations, agency disclosure forms must be held by the real estate broker in record for what time period?

a. for five years

b. for three years

c. for the life of the client

d. for one year

68. How many acres are contained in a parcel that is 121 feet wide and 240 yards deep?

a. 1

b. $1\frac{1}{2}$

c. 2

d. $2\frac{1}{2}$

69. If a real estate salesperson wants to become a real estate broker and has already terminated employment with a broker after one year, the salesperson must obtain the license within
a. one year.
b. two years.
c. six months.
d. three years.

70. A father owns a house in Boston and decides to retire to Cape Cod. His son wants to buy the house but has limited financial resources, so the father gives the son a very favorable price. This is an example of
a. ratification.
b. an arm's length transaction.
c. a non–arm's length transaction.
d. undue influence.

71. Rita Morgan has $86,576 remaining on her 8.5% mortgage. Her monthly payment is set at $852.56 for principal and interest (she pays her own taxes and insurance). How much of her next payment will go to reduce the principal?
a. $116.76
b. $239.31
c. $613.25
d. $735.80

72. State regulations require that an agent hold copies of escrow checks for
a. three years.
b. five years.
c. ten years.
d. seven years.

73. If John Doe pays his debt in full on a house loan, then the lender will give title back to John Doe. This action is called
a. titling.
b. defeasance.
c. hypothecation.
d. collateral.

74. An inactive, licensed agent may collect
a. a commission fee.
b. a referral fee.
c. and engage in brokerage activities.
d. a co-brokerage fee.

75. The MA Contract Law Statute of Limitations for keeping real estate contracts is
a. three years.
b. five years.
c. seven years.
d. six years.

76. In order for a contract to be legally enforceable, it must include
a. a deposit.
b. the name of the real estate broker.
c. consideration.
d. the name of the lender.

77. In Massachusetts, a married couple may apply (after title transfer) for homestead protection an estate for what amount?
a. $250,000
b. $500,000
c. $150,000
d. $175,000

78. In order for a broker to offer out-of-state interest in land for sale, he must first
   a. register his brokerage firm in the state of the land location.
   b. have the owner register the property with the Board.
   c. have the owner comply as a licensed broker in Massachusetts.
   d. offer the land to residents in the state the property is located.

79. A pledge of property to secure repayment of debt is called
   a. collateral.
   b. mortgage.
   c. loan.
   d. hypothecation.

80. Supply and demand in an appraisal can affect
   a. the taxable value.
   b. the cost basis.
   c. the market value.
   d. the book value.

81. A real estate salesperson in Massachusetts cannot solely perform which of the following activities?
   a. show real estate for lease or purchase
   b. market real estate for sale
   c. complete the negotiations of an agreement that results in a sale
   d. list the physical characteristics of property

82. Zoning ordinances typically regulate the
   a. number of occupants allowed for each building.
   b. permitted uses of each parcel of land.
   c. maximum rent that may be charged.
   d. adherence to fair housing laws.

83. The Board of Registration of Real Estate Brokers and Salespersons consists of
   a. five members.
   b. three members.
   c. seven members.
   d. six members.

84. Agents are prohibited from interfering with another agent's
   a. prior clients.
   b. customers.
   c. exclusive listing agreements.
   d. agents.

85. The Band of Investment Approach is defined as
   a. cap rate divided by debt service equals value.
   b. value minus debt service equals NOI.
   c. NOI divided by cap rate equals value.
   d. gross rent minus gross operating expenses equals net income.

86. Real Estate is defined as
   a. land, structures, and appurtenances.
   b. rights, interests, and benefits.
   c. land only.
   d. land, structures, and any equipment.

87. Foreclosure allows a lender to
   a. provide defeasance.
   b. terminate a borrower's interest in property.
   c. take immediate title to real estate.
   d. recapture the mortgage.

88. A buyer makes an offer to the seller to buy his building. The seller likes the entire offer but makes some very minor changes, signs it, and delivers the offer to the buyer. The seller has just
   a. signed a binding contract.
   b. made a counteroffer.
   c. signed a novation contract.
   d. accepted the buyer's offer.

89. Real property is defined as
   a. land, structures, and appurtenances.
   b. rights, interests, and benefits.
   c. being tangible but immobile.
   d. equipment, personal property, and real estate.

90. John Doe is a property manager for an office building and has a vacant office. To market the space, John starts advertising in the classified section of the local newspaper. In the advertising, John should
   a. state the rental amount.
   b. list information that is accurate.
   c. give a free month's rent.
   d. give a bonus to outside brokers for tenants.

91. Massachusetts administers a state Truth-in-Lending Law that is also known as
   a. MGL Ch. 21E.
   b. MGL Ch. 140C.
   c. VA 23.
   d. Regulation Z.

92. The Board of Registration of Real Estate Brokers and Salespersons must have three members that are actively engaged in real estate with at least
   a. five years of experience.
   b. ten years of experience.
   c. fifteen years of experience.
   d. seven years of experience.

93. Real property has inherent rights of ownership that are known as
   a. procuring causes.
   b. a bundle of legal rights.
   c. police power and rights.
   d. bundle of sticks.

94. The following classified ad was printed in the Sunday newspaper by a listing broker. "For sale, Colonial House, approx. 2,000 sf, asking $250,000 located in Daleville, Massachusetts. Call Rob at 617-123-4567." What is legally missing from this ad?
   a. the age of the house
   b. Rob's full name
   c. identifying that Rob is a broker
   d. identifying that Rob is a broker and the firm's name

95. The government has four powers that can affect ownership, which include
   a. enforcement.
   b. escheat.
   c. sales tax.
   d. emblements.

96. A major purchaser of home loans would be the
   a. Federal National Mortgage Association.
   b. Federal Reserve Bank.
   c. Federal Deposit Insurance Corporation.
   d. National Association of REALTORS®.

97. The U.S. government authorized a survey system to develop a legal description of real estate known as
   a. metes and bounds.
   b. perimeter survey.
   c. rectangular survey.
   d. congressional survey.

98. Massachusetts Title V regulations applies only to
   a. residential real estate with an on-site disposal system.
   b. commercial real estate.
   c. all real estate on municipal sewerage systems.
   d. any real estate with an on-site disposal system.

99. There are three types of depreciation including
   a. proximate deterioration.
   b. economic deterioration.
   c. absolute deterioration.
   d. inverted deterioration.

100. As part of the original purchase, a new owner agrees to a required number of monthly payments to the former owner. All the payments have now been made and the former owner is conveying title to the new owner. This transaction is known as
   a. a lease with an option to purchase.
   b. an installment agreement.
   c. a sales agreement with a delayed settlement.
   d. a wraparound contract.

101. A person may void a contract EXCEPT due to which of the following reasons?
   a. The person is intoxicated.
   b. The person is a minor.
   c. The person is illiterate.
   d. The person is not an attorney.

102. A buyer makes an offer to buy a building for $500,000 with a $50,000 deposit and a closing in 30 days. The seller accepts the offer. The last week before the closing, the buyer changes his mind and defaults on the purchase. The seller at this point can do all of the following EXCEPT
   a. keep the deposit as liquidated damages.
   b. sue for non-performance.
   c. sue the lender for the buyer's non-performance.
   d. declare forfeiture.

103. A buyer and seller agreed on a price for an office building. They entered into a binding purchase and sales contract. A few days prior to the closing, the seller died in an accident. The Purchase and Sales Agreement at this point
   a. remains enforceable.
   b. becomes invalid.
   c. is a unilateral contract.
   d. becomes an intestate contract.

104. A fully executed contract is defined as
   a. a contract signed by either the buyer or seller.
   b. a contract that is signed by the buyer and delivered to the seller.
   c. a contract signed by both the buyer and seller.
   d. a contract signed by the buyer and broker.

105. Records should be kept by a property manager for an owner both monthly and
   a. daily.
   b. annually.
   c. seasonally.
   d. quarterly.

106. An office building has rents that total $25,456 per month. The annual operating expenses total $211,923. The annual debt service equals $23,444. What is the annual net operating income?
- **a.** $305,472
- **b.** $93,549
- **c.** $70,105
- **d.** $186,467

107. Under Massachusetts Title V regulations, the owner must
- **a.** disclose if they have underground oil tanks.
- **b.** have brokers disclose if the property contains hazardous waste.
- **c.** conduct an assessment of its on-site disposal system for a transfer of title.
- **d.** conduct a wetlands delineation.

108. A U.S. Rectangular Survey consists of
- **a.** 640 acres.
- **b.** 520 acres.
- **c.** 1,150 acres.
- **d.** 2,355 acres.

109. The three traditional approaches used by appraisers in valuation include
- **a.** sales, income, and cost approaches.
- **b.** comparables, residual, and highest/best use approach.
- **c.** highest/best use, reconciliation, and fee approach.
- **d.** contributory, adjustment, and valuation approach.

110. Massachusetts has passed new agency regulations with an effective date of the statutes as of
- **a.** April 8, 2005.
- **b.** July 1, 2005.
- **c.** January 1, 2005.
- **d.** May 19, 2004.

▶ Answers

1. a. $824,566 ÷ $1,000 = $824.57 × $15.66 = $12,912.70

2. c. The VA will guarantee 60% of a loan amount not to exceed a total guarantee of $36,000.

3. d. There are no licensing requirements to be a property manager unless he or she receives a commission fee for leasing space in the building. Then, a real estate broker's license is required.

4. b. It is illegal to have a fee contingent on the final value. An appraiser must be unbiased and paid a pre-negotiated set fee irrespective of the final value.

5. c. Massachusetts requires residential brokers to present a Massachusetts Mandatory Licensee-Consumer Relationship Disclosure form to a consumer so that the consumer can make informed decisions. However, it is not a contract.

6. c. Massachusetts was the last state to do away with broker disclosure on UFFI.

7. b. The seller's agent cannot make any recommendations as it is perceived as a conflict. MA requires agents to distribute a home inspection brochure to a buyer and direct them to the state home inspection website.

8. c. Yes, a real estate broker cannot be paid unless they are specifically hired, bring a buyer that is ready, willing, and able, and is also the procuring cause of the sale.

9. d. The four factors include: land, labor, capital, and management. Property value is at the highest if these factors are balanced.

10. c. The Massachusetts Mandatory Licensee-Consumer Relationship Disclosure form has a separate box that can be checked off that the consumer declined to sign and state any reasons given.

11. b. The buyer's agent only can make recommendations of home inspectors for his own buyer-client.

12. c. A material defect is a defect that is material information to a buyer in order to make a knowledgeable real estate purchase decision.

13. c. The seller is always required to pay the deed tax.

14. b. In 1998, a Massachusetts law case, *McCarthy v. Tobin*, stated that offers themselves could be binding unless there was disclaimer language that the offer was not to be binding.

15. c. $5,000 is the required minimum bond amount.

16. b. URAR is a Uniform Residential Appraisal Report and is required by various agencies and organizations.

17. b. A thirty-day tenant is a tenant at will. The landlord or tenant can provide thirty-day notice at any time to vacate.

18. b. Despite the seller's wishes to keep the information confidential, the real estate agent must disclose the information to all prospective buyers that he is privy that an underground tank may exist.

19. c. A title that may have a title defect of some kind is also called a "cloud" on the title. The defect is removed so that the buyer can prove that they do in fact own the property.

20. b. It is illegal in Massachusetts to address any questions about the HIV status of owners or former owners.

21. c. Upon the death of a sole proprietor broker, a spouse or any other appointed person may file for a temporary license good for one year, file a bond, and pay a prescribed fee. The temporary license cannot be renewed.

22. **c.** The property sold for $570,300 \times .045 =$ $25,663.50. The cooperating broker received 50% of the $25,663.50 or $12,831.75. The cooperating fee of $12,831.75 \times .20 =$ $2,566.35.

23. **d.** A property sold with a second mortgage taken by the owner is a deferred purchase money mortgage. Sometimes the interest due is paid monthly or deferred as well.

24. **b.** Termination of agency relationships can be due to a number of factors accepted by MA law. One of the factors is impossibility of performance such as destruction of the property.

25. **b.** Under MA's Tristram's Landing case study, a judge ruled that the seller would be liable for non-performance. If the buyer was ready, willing, and able and the seller rescinds the deal, then the agent has earned his fee as long as the agent was engaged by the owner to sell the property.

26. **b.** Appraisal reports may be in writing or verbal but must always be in conformance with Uniform Standards of Professional Appraisal Practice.

27. **b.** The license is valid for two years, and it expires on the agent's birthday.

28. **b.** A person who is incompetent due to illiteracy is not prohibited from buying or selling his own real estate.

29. **d.** Metes and bounds are primarily used in the northeast as developed in England by land surveyors. Metes and bounds use markers and radius degrees to describe the boundaries of land.

30. **a.** A client is a person who gives a real estate agent the authority to act as an agent to a seller or buyer. A customer generally refers to a person without representation involved in a transaction.

31. **c.** $56,700 - 15,600 = 41,100 \div 0.085 = 483,529$

32. **b.** "Time is of the essence" means that all parties must abide to any deadlines or be liable for non-performance.

33. **b.** These records must be kept for three years.

34. **d.** A contract is void, voidable, valid, or unenforceable.

35. **c.** There are no set legal requirements for response time. Each complaint dictates what is a reasonable timeframe.

36. **b.** The Federal Reserve Bank set up Regulation Z to implement the law on Truth-in-Lending.

37. **c.** Lead paint was used until Federal Laws prohibited it in 1977. Agents in Massachusetts must inform prospective buyers about the dangers of lead paint and a buyer's ten-day right to a lead paint inspection. Massachusetts requires the use of a lead paint disclosure form.

38. **c.** Real estate salespersons can never hold escrow accounts and must turn all deposit checks to their employing real estate broker immediately.

39. **a.** A self-contained appraisal report is lengthy and contains all the information and research gathered by the appraiser to reach his conclusion of value.

40. **a.** Laws do not mandate compensation or the amount. Advertising a property's availability is appropriate. Compensation is another matter. If the broker advertises that he will co-broke, then he must do so.

41. **a.** A person who dies intestate is a person who has died without a will and the person's property is then distributed to his or her heirs as according to state law.

42. **a.** A salesperson can never become self-employed. He or she must work for a broker for two years, take the broker's courses, and pass the state exam. Then, he or she can become self-employed as a broker.

43. **b.** There is no duty to a seller's agent unless the buyer or buyer's agent has a specific inquiry.

44. **b.** Further disclosure would need to include the loan amount, the cash amount of down payment, the terms of repayment, and the annual percentage rate.

45. **a.** The broker concealed the roof leak with a false statement from the seller, which would be material information to the buyer's decision. Concealment is known as misrepresentation.

46. **b.** A person must be at least 18 years old.

47. **d.** Many homeowners want to market their own properties, and it is easier to the use the acronym FSBO than "for sale by owner." But the owner may not compensate an agent for bringing a buyer. That must be discussed up front by the agent.

48. **c.** A real estate salesperson or broker can never advise against the use of an attorney.

49. **a.** Agents continually confuse the term *cooperate*. To cooperate is to offer information as requested by another agent. However, an agent may decide to offer a property to buyers directly and not include outside agents.

50. **c.** RESPA stands for the Real Estate Settlement Procedures Act that requires all settlement charges be itemized to buyers and sellers of 1- to 4-unit family residences and was passed in 1974.

51. **b.** This formula provides investors a tool to determining a value of an income-producing property.

52. **b.** A listing agreement does not commit that a broker has to find a buyer. But it does commit that a seller has to pay a commission fee if a buyer is found. It is a unilateral contract.

53. **b.** The person receiving the title, typically the buyer, is known as the grantee, while the person giving the title, typically the seller, is known as the grantor.

54. **c.** Compensation to a buyer's broker could be from the seller or buyer. The fiduciary interests always remains with the client, the buyer. But the compensation is negotiable in terms of who is actually paying the buyer's broker.

55. **d.** The maximum fine is up to $500.

56. **b.** There is no state regulation to share professional fees or information. If the agent decides to do so, then it is a business decision in any fashion.

57. **b.** $135,678 \div 0.0855 = \$1,586,877$

58. **b.** Statute prohibits misuse of information provided to an inquirer. The buyer never inquired, and the use of the information was to hurt the value of the competition.

59. **c.** Hypothecation is when a lender allows a borrower to possess pledged real estate for use.

60. **c.** The fee must be paid withing thirty days.

61. **b.** "Time is of the essence" binds both parties to perform any duties in the offer based on certain dates and times or else they could be liable for non-performance.

62. **b.** A person can claim title to another person's property if they have continually used that neighbor's property for twenty years in Massachusetts without notice from an owner prohibiting the use.

63. **b.** Book value is the depreciated cost basis. For accounting and tax purposes, the book value is used by corporations.

64. **c.** All real estate agents have a one-year grace period after license expiration to renew and reactivate the license.

65. **a.** Quitclaim deeds are commonly used in Massachusetts and are often used on property that may have had some type of "cloud." When a seller gives a quitclaim deed, the deed comes with no guarantees or warranties of the title.

66. **b.** A salesperson must work for a real estate broker for at least one year.

67. **b.** The forms must be held for three years.

68. **c.** 240 yards × 3 feet = 720 feet
121 feet × 720 feet = 87,120 square feet
87,120 square feet ÷ 43,560 square feet = 2 acres

69. **b.** The deadline is two years.

70. **c.** Because the seller and buyer are related and the price was favorable to the buyer due to the relationship, this transaction is not an arm's length transaction.

71. **b.** A year's interest on the present debt would be $7,358.96 ($86,576 × 0.085). A month's interest is $613.25 ($7,358.96 ÷ 12). The principal portion of her payment is $239.31 ($852.56 − 613.25).

72. **a.** They must be held for three years.

73. **b.** Defeasance clauses are used in a mortgage that states that the lender will return title to the borrower once the debt or loan has been paid in full.

74. **b.** An inactive agent can only collect a referral fee.

75. **d.** The statute of limitations is six years.

76. **c.** Consideration is a necessary element of a contract, which confers benefit or the other party; in this case, the agreed price that the buyer is willing to pay the seller.

77. **b.** Homestead protection is available at $500,000 for married couples and $250,000 for single owners.

78. **b.** A broker offering real property for sale in Massachusetts of any out-of-state land development must first have the owner register the property with the Board of Registration of Real Estate.

79. **b.** A mortgage is a pledge of property that allows property to be used as collateral in the event that the borrower does not properly repay the real estate debt.

80. **c.** Market value is affected by supply and demand of the market place, which includes the number of buyers and sellers at the time of the appraisal.

81. **c.** A real estate salesperson can perform all the same duties as a broker except complete any agreement of any kind that could result in the sale, lease, or exchange of any real estate.

82. **b.** Typical permitted uses such as residential, commercial, industrial, multi-family, or office will appear within certain zones.

83. **a.** There are five members.

84. **c.** It is unlawful for an agent to negotiate the sale, lease, or exchange of any property directly with an owner who has a written contract granting exclusive right to another agent.

85. **c.** Net operating income divided by the investor's capitalization rate equals value.

86. **a.** Real estate includes land, structures, and appurtenants. Real estate is immobile but tangible.

87. **b.** The lender can terminate a borrower's interest in a pledged real estate property in the event that the borrower defaults on a loan. Foreclosure is a judicial process.

88. **b.** Any changes made to any offer of any kind is a new offer or a counteroffer no matter how minor the changes may be.

89. **b.** Real property is the rights, interests, and benefits that come with the ownership of real estate.

90. b. The only real requirement is that the property manager advertises using information that is accurate and truthful. The advertising can be as detailed or general as the property manager feels may attract calls as long as it is fair.

91. b. Massachusetts has its own Truth-In-Lending Law (TIL) known as MGL Ch. 140C.

92. d. All three real estate brokers that are members must have at least seven years of full-time experience as a full-time occupation in the real estate business.

93. b. The inherent rights of ownership are known as the Bundle of Legal Rights Theory. The rights include the right to use, lease, sell, enter, give it away, or any combination of these.

94. d. All advertisements of properties available must disclose that the ad is from a broker with the name of the broker, the brokerage firm name, and telephone number.

95. b. Escheat is titular power of the government that when a person dies and leaves no will or ascertainable heirs, the government can claim ownership to that person's real estate.

96. a. The Federal National Mortgage Association is also known as Fannie Mae. Other purchasers include Freddie Mac and Ginnie Mae.

97. c. The U.S. government developed the U.S. Rectangular Survey also known as U.S. public lands survey system for properties west of the Ohio River during the 1800s.

98. d. Both residential and commercial real estate with an on-site disposal system fall under Title V.

99. b. The three types of deterioration include physical, functional, and economic deterioration.

100. b. When the new owner has paid all of the contracted periodic installments, the former owner conveys title.

101. d. The first three items are grounds for a voided contract, but anyone can enter into a contract. They do not need to be an attorney to enter into a contract. Every day, people enter some type of legal contract arrangements to conduct business.

102. c. The lender had nothing to do with the buyer's decision to default and is not liable.

103. a. Death does not make a contract invalid. The seller's estate or representative would have to perform the duties of the sale.

104. c. A fully executed contract is a contract signed by buyer and seller.

105. b. The property manager needs to provide an owner with monthly statements and a final annual statement for tax and business purposes.

106. b. The annual gross income is $25,456 \times 12$ months or $305,472. The annual rent of $305,472 − annual operating expense of $211,923 = a net operating income of $93,549.

107. c. The owner is required by law to conduct a septic system assessment on or within two years of title transfer.

108. a. Each survey divides land into townships. Each township is 6 square miles or 640 acres.

109. a. These three approaches are required by the U.S. government as a basis for valuation and final methodology.

110. b. Massachusetts expanded the agency regulations as of July 1, 2005. The year prior was used to debate the new agency changes.

Scoring

Once again, in order to evaluate how you did on this last exam, find the number of questions you answered correctly. The passing score for this practice exam is 77 correct answers (70%), but just as on the real test, you should be aiming for something higher than that on these practice exams. Take a look at the following table to see what problem areas remain. Hopefully, there aren't too many!

The key to success in almost any pursuit is complete preparation. By taking the practice exams in this book, you have prepared more than many other people who may be taking the exam with you. You have diagnosed where your strengths and weaknesses lie and learned how to deal with the various kinds of questions that will appear on the test. So go into the exam with confidence, knowing that you are ready and equipped to do your best.

EXAM IV FOR REVIEW

Test IV Subject Area	Question Numbers (Questions 1–110)
Real Estate Principles and Practices	7, 11, 14, 20, 24, 25, 32, 37, 43, 47, 49, 67, 72, 75, 82, 84, 86, 89, 93, 95, 97, 99, 108, 109, 110
Property Valuation/Appraisal	4, 9, 16, 26, 39, 51, 63, 80, 85, 109
Financing	2, 23, 36, 44, 50, 59, 73, 79, 87, 91, 96, 100
Contacts/Agency Relationship	28, 34, 45, 52, 61, 70, 76, 88, 101, 102, 103 104
Law, Definition, and Nature of Agency Relationships, Type of Agencies and Agents	8, 12, 15, 21, 27, 33, 38, 42, 46, 48, 55, 60, 66 69, 74, 78, 81, 83, 92, 98, 107, 110
Settlement/Transfer of Property	6, 13, 19, 29, 41, 53, 62, 65, 77
Business Practices	5, 10, 18, 30, 40, 54, 64, 94
Property Management	3, 17, 35, 90, 105
Real Estate Math	1, 22, 31, 57, 68, 71, 106

How to Use ▶
the CD-ROM ▶

SO YOU THINK you are ready for your exam? Here's a great way to build confidence and *know* you are ready: using LearningExpress's Real Estate Licensing Tester AutoExam CD-ROM software developed by PEARSoft Corporation of Wellesley, Massachusetts. The disk, included inside the back cover of this book, can be used with any PC running Windows 95/98/ME/NT/2000/XP. (Sorry, it doesn't work with Macintosh.) The following description represents a typical "walk through" of the software.

To install the program:

1. Insert the CD-ROM into your CD-ROM drive. The CD should run automatically. If it does not, proceed to Step 2.
2. From Windows, select **Start**, then choose **Run**.
3. Type D:\Setup
4. Click **OK**.

The screens that follow will walk you through the installation procedure.

From the Main Menu, select **Take Exams**. (After you have taken at least one exam, use **Review Exam Results** to see your scores.)

Now enter your initials. This allows you to record your progress and review your performance for as many simulated exams as you would like. Notice that you can also change the drive and/or folder where your exam results are stored. If you want to save to a floppy drive, for instance, click on the "Browse" button and then choose the letter of your floppy drive.

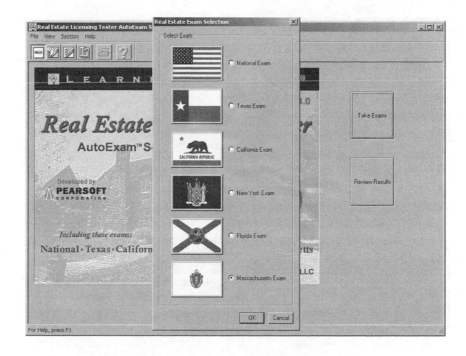

Now, since this CD-ROM supports six different real estate exams, you need to select your exam of interest. Let's try Massachusetts, as shown above.

Now you are into the **Take Exams** section, as shown above. You can choose **Start Exam** to start taking your test, or **Exam Options**. The next screenshot shows you what your **Exam Options** are.

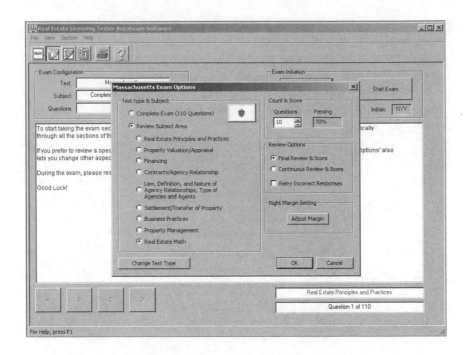

Choosing **Exam Options** gives you plenty of options to help you fine-tune your rough spots. How about a little math to warm up? Click **Review Subject Area**, and then the **Mathematics** option. Choose the number of questions you want to review right now. On the right, you can choose whether to wait until you have finished to see how you did (**Final Review & Score**) or have the computer tell you after each questions whether your answer is right (**Continuous Review and Score**). Choose **Retry Incorrect Responses** to get a second chance at questions you answer wrong. (This option works best with **Review Subject Area** rather than **Complete Test**.) If you have chosen the wrong exam, you can click **Change Test Type** to go back and choose your exam. When you finish choosing your options, click **OK**. Then click the **Start Exam** button on the main exam screen. Your screen will look like the one shown next.

Questions come up one at a time, just as they will on the real exam, and you click on A, B, C, or D to answer.

When you have finished your exam or subject area, you will have the option of switching to **Review Exams.** (If you don't want to review your results now, you can always do it later by clicking on the **Review Exams Section** button on the toolbar.) When you use **Review Results,** you will see your score and whether you passed. The questions come up one at a time. Under **Review Options,** you can choose whether to look at all the questions or just the ones you missed. You can also choose whether you want an explanation of the correct answer displayed automatically under the question.

When you are in the **Review Results** section, click on the **Find** button to look at all the exams you have taken.

By default, your exam results are listed from newest to oldest, but you can sort them by any of the headings. For instance, if you want to see your results arranged by score, you can click on the **Score %** heading. To go to a particular exam you have taken, double click on it.

In the **Review Results** section, if you click on the **Score %** button, you will get a breakdown of your score on the exam you're currently reviewing. This section shows you how you did on each of the subject areas on the exam. Once again, you can sort the subject areas by any of the column headings. For instance, if you click on the

Score % heading, the program will order the subject areas from your highest percentage score to your lowest. You can see which areas are your strong and weak points, so you will know what to review.

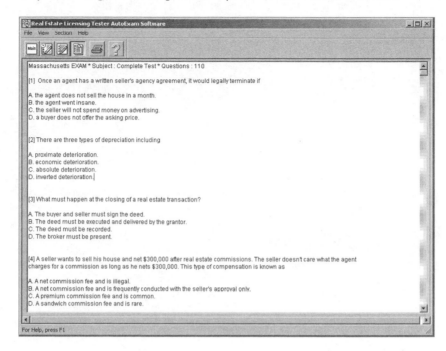

What's that? No time to work at the computer? Click the **Print Exams** menu bar button and you will have a full-screen review of an exam that you can print out, as shown above. Then take it with you.

For technical support, call 800-295-9556.